Feb 28 83

The Language Lottery

The Language Lottery:
Toward a Biology
of Grammars

David Lightfoot

The MIT Press
Cambridge, Massachusetts
London, England

This book was set in VIP Times Roman by Village Typographers, Inc.,
and printed and bound by Halliday Lithograph Corporation in the United
States of America.

Library of Congress Cataloging in Publication Data

Lightfoot, David.
  The language lottery.

  Bibliography: p.
  Includes index.
  1. Language acquisition. I. Title.
P118.L47 1982   401'.9   82–13082
ISBN 0–262–12096–8

This book is dedicated to anybody whoever met a couple of linguists in a bar and asked them what they did for a living.

Contents

Preface

It often takes only a greeting or a short sentence for us to recognize the voice of somebody we know, even through the distortion of a telephone. In fact, people's speech may be as individual and particular as their thumbprints. The voice may be high pitched, lilting, with certain consonants pronounced intensely, perhaps some vowels softened. A person's speech may be described in impressionistic terms, but it contains many cues to indicate where the speaker comes from, what his or her class origins are, and even whether it is Aunt Agatha, Uncle Sam, or the neighborhood butcher. This kind of telltale variation arises as a matter of chance and individual circumstance; a person speaks like a high-pitched New Yorker if he happens to have a high-pitched voice, to have been brought up in New York, and to have retained the essential features of the relevant accent. If things had been different, the same person might have grown up speaking some version or dialect of British English or Japanese. The possibilities are endless. This is the language lottery.

Variation and individuality enable us to know who is at the other end of the telephone line, but for some purposes variation is irrelevant and is actually ignored. We each have our own speech styles, but they meet several strict and invariant requirements. Those requirements enable us to circumvent the variation, to understand each other, and as young children to master our mother tongue when exposed to a bewildering range of expressions and styles. After all, even thumbprints and lotteries conform to certain rules.

The basic specifications for language, which enable us to learn to speak, are genetically given; they are part of human biology, part of what it means to be a human being. Therefore, we speak the way we do not entirely because we happen, say, to have a high-pitched voice and to have been brought up in New York but also because we are human beings with the usual kind of human genetic equipment. This genetic equipment entails that our speech must fit a certain pattern or template. This is a central tenet of generative grammar, the research program I shall describe in this book. The goal is to find out in some detail what these genetic specifications are.

The central question addressed by this program is: how do children master their native language in the way that they do? Eventually they come to be able to speak and understand speech effortlessly, instantaneously, and subconsciously. How does this happen? Children are exposed to linguistic experiences that involve many styles, moods, variable pronunciations, interruptions, incomplete expressions, and the like. Yet the fact is that language develops in them easily, naturally, and spontaneously, as is obvious to any parent. The problem is that nobody knows quite how this happens.

Be warned: this book is not an introduction to linguistics, nor a survey of a discipline. Many linguists take quite a different tack when they study language. They may be interested in how language may be used by poets, how it is used as a social weapon, how a language can be taught to a foreigner. Linguistics encompasses these interests and many more. This book is much narrower in scope and pursues only the question, what is the genetic, internally prescribed basis of language structure?

I have aimed at giving a taste of one particular research program, showing how it can profit from several kinds of data. The bulk of the data has to do with the description of normal language capacities, but I shall also draw on data about the way that languages change from generation to generation, how children develop language as they grow older, how language may be distorted in the event of brain damage, how sentences are analyzed and processed, how language might have evolved in the species. So one central question, but many kinds of data. I have not pursued analyses in as much depth as one finds in monographs but I have explored a few principles from several points of view; the same principles help to provide explanations even where different kinds of data are involved. By showing how a few principles are interrelated and have a wide range of explanatory power, I hope to have conveyed something of the breadth and coherence of the program.

Throughout the book I lay much stress on the relation between my central goal, to explain how children master their native language, and the kinds of technical analyses linguists offer, the kinds of strategies they adopt, and the way in which linguists try to revise and improve hypotheses. The relation between the central goal and the analyses offered is often obscured and forgotten in the professional journals, with the result that there is much confusion and misunderstanding. By never letting the reader forget the central goal of this program and by relating it to the specific analyses, I hope that this little book may be helpful to some linguists, whether or not they pursue the particular goal of generative grammar.

The subtitle "Toward a biology of grammars" should put the book on the biology and linguistics shelves in libraries and bookstores. Linguists, biologists, and people in related fields like ethology, psychology, anthropology, and philosophy make up the audience that I have had in mind. By *linguists* I mean people who think about language, regardless of where they happen to be employed and regardless of which goal they pursue when they spin up their own theories (if they do that kind of thing). I have tried to presuppose only minimal thinking about language, of the kind that most people do at school when learning how to parse sentences, but I have introduced some technical flourishes in order to avoid debasing the ideas I am describing and in order to lend a hand to the reader who wishes to go beyond general concerns and into areas of current debate. Since my intended audience is so heterogeneous, different people will skim over different sections, finding some chapters more accessible and interesting than others. Some may be more interested in specific analytical techniques, others in the treatment of meaning, others in more broadly philosophical questions, others in getting a general impression of how to make sense of language from some scientific point of view.

While I am trying to reach a heterogeneous group of people, a much smaller group has been looking over my shoulder. These are the linguists actively engaged in the work that I describe here. I have tried to describe their work accurately and faithfully, because its importance goes beyond passing fashion. But their natural habitat is the professional journal, and I have revamped some of their ideas in the interests, as I see them, of the nonspecialist audience that I want to reach. I have stolen from my colleagues shamelessly and I have not peppered the book with references and descriptions of subtle differences between alternative proposals; I leave that to the textbooks and monographs.

Foremost of the people looking over my shoulder has been Noam Chomsky. He did much of the pioneering work in orienting linguistic research toward the issue of language acquisition by the child and in construing it in a biological context. He has also dominated its development over the last thirty years, advancing countless technical analyses, debating alternative approaches at many different levels, addressing wider philosophical issues. His work has occupied center stage, and he has helped to shape the work of many others by discussing manuscripts tirelessly and writing innumerable letters. Without his work this program would look very different. My debt to Chomsky is enormous and, if he saw ideas as pieces of personal property, he above all could complain about being robbed in this book. Instead, he read an early draft and gave me much help in making it into a better book.

Sari Hornstein has devoted many hours to protecting the interests of readers with no linguistic training, filtering out pieces of jargon and catching assumptions that might not be entirely evident to nondevotees. Harry Bracken, Peter Coopmans, Hans Gilijamse, Norbert Hornstein, Alex Kacelnik, and John Marshall also read an early draft and gave me useful advice from their different perspectives.

Now let's get our bearings and first ask something nice and easy: what do we know about the nature of life?

The Language Lottery

Chapter 1
The Biological View

The Genetic Program

Life differs from other natural phenomena in that it has an internal genetic program that guides its development and behavior. Other, nonliving elements of nature are subject more or less entirely to external forces or occur at random. Consider the waves on the sea, the clouds racing across a November sky, a stone falling to the ground, a melting ice cube—these things respond almost wholly to external influences. Water has an internal structure that determines that it cannot burn, but this internal structure is mostly irrelevant to whether the ocean-waves are big or small, from the north or west. When physical phenomena do show behavioral regularities independent of external forces, they are chaotic and usually increase the total disorder of the system, in accordance with the law of entropy. Where order seems to increase, as in crystallization, the order is entirely predictable, repetitive, and uniform.

Biological phenomena have a different kind of individuality; they have a program. Organisms function and develop in a way determined largely by the genetic endowment, although some aspects of the way in which the genetic plan is realized depend on external factors. A rosebud swells and blossoms in a genetically determined process, but the appearance and strength of the blossom will be affected by factors like soil quality and access to light. A program encoded in the substance of the genes guides the growth of an organism and its functioning, exploiting various aspects of the external surroundings. There is a creative interplay between the internal structure of a particular living organism and its outside world.

In outward appearances biological and nonbiological matter are often difficult to tell apart. Readers may recall Jacques Monod's intriguing discussion of the problems in programming a Martian computer to distinguish artificial from natural objects, nonliving from living. Monod's machine had to recognize that the structure of a living being "owes almost nothing to the action of outside forces, but everything, from its overall shape down to its tiniest detail, to 'morphogenetic' interactions within the object itself. . . . External agents or conditions . . . are capable, to be sure, of impeding this development, but not of directing it, nor of prescribing its organizational scheme to the living object" (Monod 1972:21). So the rosebush is by no means a product of its environment: it owes its basic properties of shape, structure and coloring to its internal structure; it develops according to an internal, genetic clock by exploiting certain aspects of its environment, which may be available in varying degrees. For Monod, living matter has a genetic program, and nonliving matter does not; that is the difference between an amoeba and a crystal.

Modern biology has focused largely on this genetic program—its chemical basis, its effects, the kinds of things it can control, its methods of ensuring stability while allowing an enormous range of individual patterns, its ability to copy with accuracy and to change, its ability to explain why certain species flourish in certain surroundings, and so on.

This has not always been so. Molecular biology is less than thirty years old and modern biochemistry is not much older. But even in earlier times there was a similar perspective. A theory held sway for many centuries that the sperm contained a perfect miniature creature, a "Russian doll" or "homunculus," which simply grew bigger as time went on. This was Preformationism, and Stephen Jay Gould shows that it was quite a reasonable theory to hold in the eighteenth century (1978: 202–6). This theory of embryological development is now regarded as wrong, but it does suggest that the question of how to account for the way in which living things develop has long been a basis for theorizing and that scientists have long held that the development is internally directed in some way.

The modern study of heredity began with the work of Gregor Mendel (1822–1884), an Augustinian monk from what is now Czechoslovakia. Mendel grew pea plants, cross-pollinated them, and counted the number with certain characteristics in each generation. He compared the position of the flowers on the stem: they might be distributed along the main stem (axial) or bunched at the top of the stem (terminal). Cross-pollination of axial and terminal flowers always yielded axial flowers in the first generation. Of 858 plants in the second generation, all of pure axial parentage, 651 had axial flowers (he called this the *dominant* characteristic) and 207 terminals (the *recessive* characteristic), a ratio of roughly 3:1. Mendel then compared factors like the shape of the seeds, the color of the albumen, and the shape and color of the pods. He found that under parallel breeding conditions, the second generation yielded about a 3:1 ratio of dominant characteristics (round seeds, yellow albumen, green pods) and recessive characteristics (wrinkled seeds, green albumen, yellow pods). The segregation of factors in this 3:1 ratio constituted Mendel's law of segregation. The various factors segregated independently of one another, so that all possible combinations arose: axial flowers with wrinkled seeds, terminal with round seeds, round seeds with green pods, and so on—the law of independent assortment.

These two laws describe a kind of regularity that does not normally occur in nonliving material; the properties are not regulated by external forces like the ocean waves, nor do they occur at random like molecules in Brownian motion. The laws are abstract, mathematical statements about pea plants. They tell us that certain surface properties occur because a principle of dominance affects the combinations of underlying factors. Mendel assumed that these factors and principles were physically encoded, but he did not know how. He postulated them as purely theoretical units, and, apparently because of that, his work was ignored until the turn of the century.

In the course of the last eighty years a theory of heredity has emerged that is one of the more impressive bodies of scientific knowledge. Mendel's main claims have been upheld by subsequent work, even if some of his results were not entirely justified by his experiments. It is known now that Mendel's "factors" can be reduced to material units, now called *genes,* and that the genes are arranged along chromosomes and contain DNA with instructions in the genetic code. The 3:1 ratio is known to follow from the fact that most plants and animals have two and only two copies of each gene and pass one or the other to the next generation. Since the gene copies can be on separate chromosomes, they can assort separately because of the method of cell division called meiosis: for each gene, each daughter cell receives only one copy from the father and one from the mother. That is what sexual reproduction is all about, or so they tell us.

Progress in this area has been rapid and a good deal is known about the chemistry of the genetic program. Biologists have broken down heredity into its basic combinatorial elements, the genes. The cells of a given organism have different functions and structures but the same genes. The genes of all organisms consist of the same substances, deoxyribonucleic acid (or DNA to its friends) and ribonucleic acid (RNA). After discovering the structure of DNA, Watson and Crick's famous double helix, geneticists have often worked at a chemical level and have related particular genes to particular portions of nucleic acid molecules. They have cracked much of the chemical code that conveys instructions for the functions of the genes, the devices that permit genes to be copied as new cells are made, and the mechanism for translating the chemical script of the genes into the chemical structure of proteins, the essential product of the genes. At this level the biochemistry of life turns out to be rather similar for all organisms. "What accounts for the difference between a butterfly and a lion, a chicken and a fly, or a worm and a whale is not their chemical components but varying distributions of these components . . . specialization and diversification called only for different utilization of the same structural information. . . . It is thanks to complex regulatory circuits, which either unleash or restrain the various biochemical activities of the organism, that the genetic program is implemented." (Jacob 1978)

The chemistry of heredity, molecular genetics, has been at the center of modern biology. Although much is known about the mechanisms that transmit various properties, much less is known about how those properties, say the blueness of the eyes or the roundness of peas, emerge from a certain genetic structure, whether they are specified directly in the genes or follow less directly (epigenetically) as a result of the mechanicochemical or maturational properties of a developing embryo. For many questions, therefore, the complexities of this chemistry can safely be disregarded, to the relief of most readers of this book, perhaps, not to mention the author. Thomas Hunt Morgan, who ran so many of the early genetic experiments with fruit flies, stressed this point in his Nobel Prize address in 1933:

What is the nature of the elements of heredity that Mendel postulated as purely theoretical units? What are genes? Now that we can locate them in the chromosomes are we justified in regarding them as material units; as chemical bodies of a higher order than molecules? Frankly, these are questions with which the working geneticist has not much concern himself, except now and then to speculate as to the nature of the postulated elements. There is no consensus of opinion among geneticists as to what the genes are—whether they are real or purely fictitious—because at the level at which the genetic experiments lie, it does not make the slightest difference whether the gene is a hypothetical unit, or whether the gene is a material particle. (Morgan 1935)

So Mendel and Morgan could formulate important biological laws without doing nucleic acid chemistry. I stress this point because it will be important in later chapters when I present claims about the genetic basis of language; there we shall engage in the abstract biology of Mendel and make no special biochemical claim. The subsequent success of molecular genetics confirms the fundamental approach taken by Mendel; his laws suggested other questions and hypotheses and can now be incorporated into a wider body of work of enormous explanatory power in domains far beyond wrinkled versus round peas. In the words of Salvador Luria:

Today man looks upon the specific materials of heredity, including his own, from the vantage point of a comprehensive, intellectually satisfying framework of knowledge. Future research will undoubtedly add new findings, but the basic structure of biology, resting on the twin foundations of evolution theory and molecular genetics, is here to stay. (1973:26–7)

The success of this research program now shapes the kinds of questions that biologists ask even when they are not doing molecular chemistry.

Alongside work on molecular genetics and also escalating in the second half of the nineteenth century, evolutionary concerns provided the second major thrust of modern biology. Under this rubric biologists have studied the interaction between the range of biological options and the environment such that certain organisms have emerged as the most successful. An individual organism inherits a set of genes, a *genotype*. The genotype determines the organism's potential for adapting to its environment; it sets the boundaries of an organism's performance by determining what its cells can do. In organisms with sexual reproduction, an offspring derives its genotype partly from one parent, partly from the other, according to the principles of genetics. Since parents differ in the structure of certain genes, new combinations may arise in the embryos of each generation. The range of genetic variability within a species is multiplied by this method of reproduction, therefore.

A species can be defined in terms of a range of genetic programs that occur in particular embryos, but another kind of variation occurs through *mutation*. Genes are extremely stable entities, and replicate themselves accurately through countless cell divisions. But sometimes the vulnerability of the chemical structure of the genetic material or an error in copying this material results in a changed or mutant gene, always a matter of chance. These mutations do not necessarily change the chemical structure of an organism but, rather, the regulatory processes. A minor modification, redistributing the structures in time and space, is usually enough to change profoundly the shape, performance, and behavior of the final product. Mutations occur all the time but at a low frequency, so that a given gene may undergo a mutation only once in several thousand generations. Such mutant genes provide the diversity essential for evolutionary adaptations. Some of these mutant programs may flourish in one set of surroundings or perhaps die out altogether.

A mutant program will survive and prosper if it yields a phenotype with some *adaptive* feature. This means that evolution is often fairly discontinuous. If some feature emerged in certain species that was highly adaptive, permitting longer survival and greater reproductive possibilities, it might be propagated rather rapidly. A lively debate has developed in recent years on this issue: Stephen Jay Gould, among others, argues that evolution does not occur as a gradual process of innumerable small changes, as Darwin had imagined. Instead, the fossil record suggests long periods of stability punctuated by short periods of rapid change, when new forms suddenly appear and spread.

Hugo de Vries discovered the proper role of mutations at the beginning of this century. He rediscovered the long-ignored work of Mendel and filled a gap in Darwin's view of the production of hereditary variety, which lies at the basis of natural selection. Identifying the role of mutations opened the way for investigating the biochemical basis of evolutionary theory. Monod observes that Darwin had no "idea of the chemical mechanisms of reproductive invariance, nor of the perturbations which affect these mechanisms. But it is no disparagement of [his] genius to note that the selective theory of evolution could not take on its full significance, precision, and certainty until less than twenty years ago" (1972:32–3). Again we see that it may be reasonable to make biological claims without necessarily providing the biochemical specifications.

Selection does not operate directly on genes but on *phenotypes*. An individual's phenotype is the set of acquired characteristics, like having axial flowers or being tall, dark, and handsome; it is the mature expression of the genotype within a given environmental setting. So the selection of reproductively successful phenotypes entails an increase of the genes that lead to those phenotypes. This view can be contrasted with that of Lamarck (1744–1829), who thought that acquired characteristics can be inherited. So swimming birds were thought to have webbed feet because their ancestors had stretched their toes and the skin between them during their swimming activities. Today this hypothesis is not accepted. Instead natural selection leads to exactly the result that Lamarck wanted to explain: the close interconnection of anatomical adaptations and specific performances. If a new feature serves the organism well, it is adaptive; genes yielding a more adaptive phenotype have a better chance of survival in the reproductive process. Under the modern view evolution makes the best of whatever genetic material is available at some time, tinkering with what is already there and not following the canons of optimal design.

Most aspects of modern biology depend on developments in the areas of molecular genetics and evolution theory. The idea of the gene is at the center of biology. The essence of the modern biological view of any organism is very simple: the genotype and phenotype are described, distinguishing the relevant chemical properties and functions. There will be a close, highly deterministic relation such that a particular genotype, exposed to a certain environmental setting, will develop into a particular phenotype. The scope for accidental variation in biological organisms is very, very small. Any two rosebushes share many properties of shape, color, internal structure, chemistry and development. The similarities arise by virtue of identical aspects of their genotypes interacting with identical aspects of the environment. The differences depend on differences in the genotypes or in the environments. Within a given species genotypical differences are small, but environmental differences may be substantial: access to soil types, light, and water vary, as do proximity to industrial pollutants, attention by an experienced gardener, and other factors. The biological view is that an organism develops along one of a number of possible paths made available by inherited, genotypical properties; this development takes place if certain environmental conditions are met. External, nongenetic factors may determine whether a person's arms are particularly muscular, fat, shaven or tattooed, but it is clear that human arms do not emerge as a result of people's upbringing as children; rather, human beings are designed to grow arms of a certain shape, size, and structure. This view has been elaborated since Mendel cross-pollinated his peas, and some aspects, notably the molecular chemistry involved, are now quite well understood.

The regularities noticed by Mendel are of a kind not found in the physical, nonbiological world. They have given rise to what may seem to be a highly mechanistic, deterministic view of organisms, but mutations and variations in the genetic programs of individual embryos afford enormous scope for variety, as is clear when one surveys the range of species that occur at this moment and the range of information that one gene can specify. There is also scope for enormous creativity, as we shall see when we consider human beings and their ability to know things.

Man and Mind

Genetic mutation, interacting with the demands of natural selection, gave rise at a certain stage to a new species of organism, one that could think and speak: *homo sapiens.* By virtue of their analytical and communicative skills human beings were able to change their relationship to their environment to some extent, pooling resources, migrating, protecting themselves against nature's elements, and even molding the environment to their own conscious wishes, thereby altering the demands of natural selection. From the first hominids the species developed slowly to the point that its members devised agricultural systems, apparently only within the last 10,000 years. More recently they invented the wheel and primitive machines, began to smelt and shape metals, and finally devised the whole apparatus of modern, industrial society. In the development from the earliest hominid forms, some genetic changes have occurred, brought about by chance mutations and perpetuated by natural selection. The changes in available skills and machines arose not so much through processes of mutation and natural selection, however, as through analytical advances propagated through cultural development and communicated traditions. Cultural evolution does not negate biological evolution but superimposes itself on it. Cultural traditions complementing the slower biological processes have led to some highly refined achievements, as manifested in the plays of Sophocles and Shakespeare, Beethoven's string quartets, the paintings of Vermeer, the ingenuity of Watson and Crick, Truffaut's movies, and even more everyday things like chess matches, crossword puzzles, and soccer games. The cultural traditions that give rise to such achievements depend on a rich communicative system.

The key to cultural evolution is the human mind, particularly that aspect of it which is responsible for the linguistic capacity. This is what enables people to develop machines, to exploit native ingenuity for conceptual novelties, to engage in complex cooperative enterprises, to think abstractly, to recall past experiences and categorize them as a basis for generalizations and predictions for the future, and even to express individual emotions in a form that can be interpreted collectively in a theater or a concert hall. Not all of these properties are unique to human beings, but human language differs fundamentally from the communication systems of other animals. Bird songs, for example, convey only a very limited range of messages, whether they are fully inherited, as with the European cuckoo, or learned in the nest, as with the male bullfinch or the nightingale.[1] Even chimpanzees, with brains physically similar in some ways to man's and perhaps also with an ability to represent things with symbols, can use "words" and sign language—features of human language—only in a highly restricted way, even after elaborate training (although popular literature sometimes depicts them curiously as having the same capacity as human beings but simply failing to exercise that capacity by some remarkable accident). Chimpanzees may be able to communicate with each other in ways that we do not understand, but those ways, whatever they are, differ from the ways in which human beings use language. Human language is unique in its flexibility and creativity, in ways that will be shown in later chapters. It provides a means of expressing ideas, of knowing the world symbolically and of communicating this knowledge. A human being does not have to live through an experience personally in order to know it, and novel experiences, generalizations, thoughts, and predictions can be communicated in elaborate detail. The capacity for symbolic language provides the basic means for our cultural evolution.

The biological basis for these special human developments was the brain, presumably emerging through the normal interaction of mutation and selection and now constituting the most distinctive anatomical feature of *homo sapiens*. Although the functions of the brain are not proportional to its weight, the brain's weight does impose limits to intelligence. This is how Luria sees these things:

In weight, but above all in complexity, the brain of man is unique. A few million years ago, more than a hundred thousand generations, and after a much longer period of relative stability, the hominoid brain started to grow to the enormous proportions that it has today, about one fortieth the weight of the body. [Recent work suggests that this growth took place explosively.] This growth has involved mainly those parts of the brain concerned with the higher functions of cognition and co-ordination—the cortex. The idea that some sort of directional process must have taken place seems inescapable. Biologically speaking, this means that once certain mutations started to produce a more powerful brain system, this system proved so valuable for differential reproduction that any new gene combinations that perfected it further were powerfully favored. One might also say that in the recent evolution of man practically everything else was neglected in favor of increased brain power. Man lost the protective fur of the apes, their early sexual maturity, and many other adaptations useful to lower mammals. In exchange he won the brain and with it the faculty of language, speech, thought, and consciousness.

The central role of speech and language in the development of thought-power and in the success of man as a species suggests that a major part of the evolution of the human brain from that of man's apelike ancestors must have been a continuous perfecting of the speech centers, which are located on the left side of the brain. (1973:138–9)

On the evolution of language, Monod argues that

It is evident that, once having made its appearance, language, however primitive, could not fail greatly to increase the survival value of intelligence, and so to create a formidable and oriented selective pressure in favour of the development of the brain, pressure which could never be experienced by a dumb species. As soon as a system of symbolic communication came into being, the individuals, or rather the groups best able to use it, acquired an advantage over others incomparably greater than any that a similar superiority of intelligence would have conferred on a species without language. . . . The selective pressure engendered by speech was bound to steer the evolution of the central nervous system in the direction of a special kind of intelligence: the kind most able to exploit this particular, specific performance with its immense possibilities. (1972:126–7)

There are other examples of evolution prizing one specialized faculty and producing an enormous development of the corresponding part of the brain. So electric fishes, which interpret their world via electrical fields, have a spectacular enlargement of those parts of their brains concerned with emitting, receiving, and analyzing electrical impulses. Similarly the bat's brain has tremendous enlargement of areas connected with hearing. Seven-eighths of the bat's brain is devoted to hearing, the means for the bat to interpret signals reflected off objects in its path, perhaps an obstacle or a nutritious insect. The workings of evolution are channeled in a certain direction because some new fea-

ture arising by chance mutation makes available a higher level of performance and adaptation.

If the capacity for symbolic language is so central to an understanding of humanness, if it is essentially the biological basis for human
culture, the question arises: what does biology contribute to human
language? Without human companionship a child does not develop a
language, as is clear from so-called wolf children, who have lacked
normal human interaction in their formative years. Under normal circumstances, however, a child may develop any one of the many natural
languages, whether English, Hindi, Japanese, or Javanese. So it is clear
that particular languages are not genetically encoded and that the environment has some kind of shaping effect; people speak different languages which reflect differences in the verbal environment to which
they are exposed as children. In which case, why do "biologists believe
that the structure of language is not fully learned by experience but is in
part at least embedded in the network of connections of the human
brain" (Luria 1973:140)? We shall answer this question in some detail in
the next chapter, and the book as a whole will address the issue of how
we can discover the biological and environmental contributions to the
linguistic capacity that people attain in maturity.

Figuring out the proper balance between the contributions of heredity and environment, between nature and nurture, has become a standard activity for biologists. Consider the liver and the kidney, which
have no mechanical functions, only biochemical tasks, for which their
shape and surface are not important. On first principles a physicist
might expect these organs to be spheres, the solid form of minimum
energy. But they are not. The liver is shaped like a French beret, the
kidney like a bean. There is no known functional or environmental reason for them to have these shapes, but the shapes result from our genetic endowment. Biologists do not know *how* the shapes of the liver
and the kidney are controlled by the genes, but they design experiments to determine what the genetic contribution must be or at what
stage elements of it are shut off (much of the genetic system is devoted
to turning genes on and off, rather than to determining specific traits).
The contribution may be complex, as with human body height, which
is determined by many genes acting at different times to control the
growth of an individual's bones.

It is uncontroversial to hold that human beings are designed to grow
a liver and that an individual's liver does not grow as a response to
purely environmental forces. It is uncontroversial because environ-

mental conditions for the growth of the embryo are not such that one can claim that the liver is in any sense just a product of the external environment. In general whenever biologists see an intricate system emerging in a more or less uniform way and not simply determined by external forces, they assume a specific genetic structure that guides and directs the growth of that system if certain environmental needs are satisfied. The reasoning is based on arguments from the deficiency of the stimulus, showing that the stimulus, the shaping effect of the environment, is not rich enough to determine the intricacies of the mature system. So the shape of the liver is not determined by the demands of external factors, but is due to internal properties. Those internal properties may stem directly from some genetic specification or may follow less directly, being epigenetic, due to the mechanicochemical constraints that arise in the genesis of the embryo but are not actually encoded in the genes. They may also vary slightly from one embryo to another. For precisely the same kind of reason, arguing from the deficiency of the stimulus, biologists like Luria and Monod assume that cognitive and linguistic abilities "grow" along a predetermined, genetically directed course under the triggering effect of the environment.

This reasoning is pursued not only for linguistic abilities, as in this book, but also more generally for other aspects of our cognitive development. In fact, investigating the genetic and environmental contributions to linguistic capacities should be seen as one step toward understanding the human mind from this point of view.

From thinking of language as a dual entity consisting of a genetically determined component inscribed in the structure of the brain and a learned component derived from experience it is an easy step to a more general conception of the human mind. . . . To the biologist it makes eminent sense to think that, as for language structures, so also for logical structures there exist in the brain network some patterns of connection that are genetically determined and have been selected by evolution as effective instruments for dealing with the events of life. . . . Perfecting of these cerebral structures must have depended on their becoming progressively more useful in terms of reproductive success. For language this must have meant becoming a better instrument in formulation and communication of meaning through a usable grammar and syntax. (Luria 1973:140–1)

This is not a new view: in his notebooks Darwin applied his materialistic theory of evolution to all living phenomena, including what he called "the citadel itself," the human mind.[2]

Life has evolved to its current state and will continue to evolve by the creative interplay of genetic variations and mutations and the natural selection that promotes any biochemical innovation offering increased fitness. The human brain and mind are among the most remarkable biochemical inventions, and biologists seek to unravel the nature of the mechanisms responsible for these complex phenomena. Monod, noting the shock of many philosophers at the idea that the basic shape of language is genetically determined, regards it "as a most natural conclusion . . . provided its implicit biological content be accepted I see nothing whatever wrong with it" (1972:129). He identifies two major domains of research for the immediate future: "The present challenge, as I see it, is in the areas at the two extremes of evolution: the origin of the first living systems, on the one hand; on the other, the inner workings of the most intensely teleonomic system ever to have emerged, to wit, the central nervous system of man" (p. 132). The second of these domains is the concern of this book.

Notes

1. We know this because cuckoos reared in isolation, deafened, or exposed only to noncuckoo songs still come to sing the typical song of their species. On the other hand, a young bullfinch raised with a canary will sing the canary's song and pass the canary's song on to its own offspring (even where the offspring is exposed not only to their father's "canary" song but also to the normal bullfinch song). See Tinbergen 1969 for many intriguing examples of this kind of thing. The work of ethologists like Tinbergen is designed to distinguish the contribution of genetic and environmental factors to animal behavior and takes a perspective similar to ours in many ways.

2. This is one respect in which Darwin differed from Wallace. Although also arriving independently at the idea of evolution by natural selection, Wallace held that the development of the human mind required some different kind of explanation.

Suggested Reading

For an introductory account of these biological considerations and the genetic underpinnings, Luria 1973 is excellent. For a more detailed account of the genetics involved, see Dobzhansky 1970.

Loren Eiseley's *Darwin's Century* (Garden City, N.Y.: Doubleday, 1958) gives a full and fascinating account of the emergence in the nineteenth century of the concept of evolution and of the biological perspective just described. Eiseley examines successful and unsuccessful lines of thinking, empirical foundations for various ideas, philosophical and religious influences, the effects on contemporary intellectual life. Darwin's materialist attitude to the evolution of psychological properties of man can be seen most clearly in his notebooks on psychology and metaphysics, published in H. E. Gruber and P. H. Barrett *Darwin on Man* (Chicago: University of Chicago Press, 1974). Horace Judson's *The Eighth Day of Creation: Makers of the Evolution in Biology* (New York: Simon and Schuster, 1979) gives a comprehensive but eminently readable account of the major discoveries in molecular biology "that drove the abstraction of the gene down to the physical reality" of the structure of DNA.

Gould 1978 and Gould's more recent *The Panda's Thumb: More Reflections in Natural History* (New York: Norton, 1980) are delightful collections of essays, most of which first appeared in *Natural History Magazine*. They cover many different aspects of evolution theory, and the later book has essays on the current debate about whether the evolutionary process is essentially gradual or discontinuous.

Chapter 2
The Central Problem

Acquiring a Language

Since our perspective is a biological one, we shall tease out hereditary and environmental contributions to people's use of language. Properties of the phenotype will be identified which cannot arise through the shaping effect of the environment but which are due to genetic inheritance. As is usual amongst biologists, arguments from the deficiency of the stimulus will be relevant as a means to pin down the genetic contribution to somebody's eventual language capacity. The arguments are fairly complex at times and we shall need to keep an eye open for the many alternative hypotheses which will be available at various points. But the basic line of reasoning is quite straightforward and the rewards are likely to be great: it is, after all, a traditional view that language may provide a particularly good probe into the essential nature of the human mind. We shall see in a moment that there are some good reasons for that view.

The central problem is to characterize how children can master their native languages. The problem is one of the deficiency of the stimulus: people come to have a very rich, complex and varied capacity that goes far beyond what they can derive only from their childhood experience, i.e., from the experience that stimulates the growth of their languages.

Consider some primitive facts about the emergence of language in a child. The child eventually comes to be able to utter and understand an indefinite number of sentences and expressions, in each case relating its sound to its meaning, to make jokes, to engage in word play, to make up new words and expressions that can be understood by other speakers of the language, and so on. This is the capacity of all mature human beings, regardless of "intelligence" levels (except in the case of pathological impedence), and the final state attained may be that of a speaker of French, Vietnamese or Mandarin Chinese. Requiring explanation is the fact that no matter what linguistic community children are brought up in—after all, the lottery concept entails that children of Vietnamese parents may chance to be brought up in a French-speaking home—they develop the ability to utter and comprehend an infinite set of sentences of that particular language, they do this despite a deficiency of the stimulus, an inadequacy of experience on three levels.

1. The speech the child hears from adults, peers, and older children, does not consist uniformly of complete, well-formed sentences but also includes sentences not properly formed, slips of the tongue, incomplete thoughts, and even sentences that are artificially simplified supposedly for the benefit of children. If only 5 percent of the expressions the child hears are of this type, there will be a significant problem in generalizing to the set of grammatical sentences of the language because the pseudo-sentences do not come labeled as defective.

As an analogy, imagine how difficult it would be to deduce the rules of chess if one were not given explicit lessons but allowed to watch and then to participate in a number of fabricated games, knowing in advance that 5 percent of the moves observed were illegal but not which particular ones. It would be extremely difficult to learn the rules of chess and quite impossible to deduce the validity of the castling move, which may take on one of two forms, may not occur at all, cannot occur more than once per game, and is subject to various legal and strategic conditions.

2. A child encounters only a finite range of expressions but comes to be able to deal with an infinite range of novel sentences, going far beyond the sentences actually heard in childhood. To understand that there is an infinite number of English sentences, one has only to realize that any given sentence may be of indefinite length; three iterative devices permit this and they may occur in various combinations:

a. Relativization
This is the dog that chased the cat that killed the rat that caught the mouse that nibbled the cheese that . . .

b. Subordination
I think that Tom asked me to tell Fred that Susan thought that I said that . . .

c. Co-ordination
Joe went to the movies and to the concert, and Tom and Susan went out for dinner, and Harry stayed at home, and . . .

You have never encountered exactly these sentences, but like any competent speaker of English you immediately understand them. Each day people use and understand sentences they have never heard or read before; this is part of the creativity of human language.

Imperfection and finiteness of the stimuli are not overwhelming kinds of data deficiency. They do not deny that relevant experience for language learning is available; they simply assert that the experience is "degenerate," hard to sort out. The crucial deficiency is the third one, which says not that relevant experience is degenerate but that in certain areas it does not exist at all.

3. People come to know things subconsciously about their language for which no direct evidence is available in the data to which they are exposed as children learning to speak: they eventually understand and utter complex and ambiguous sentences, identify paraphrases, and distinguish sentences that can occur in their language from ones that cannot. Such judgments are based on language properties known to linguists but they lie outside the primary linguistic data available to the infant. Children are not systematically informed that some hypothetical sentences do not in fact occur, that a given sentence is ambiguous, or that certain sets of sentences are paraphrases of each other, and many legitimate and acceptable sentence types may never occur in a child's linguistic experience. Such data are not available to preschool children and are not part of their verbal experience. The distinction between the range of data known to the linguist and the much more limited data available to the child beginning to speak is of vital importance for the biological view of language development.

In the following example, questions like (1a) and (1b) can be formed in English, but (1c) is impossible (indicated by the *). If you had seen the woman who met somebody in town and if I did not know whom she had met, I could not put to you (1c) as a question: the interrogative word would need to be construed as a member of a relative clause, *the woman that met in town.*

(1)
a. Who did the woman meet in town?
b. Who did you believe that the woman met in town?
c. *Who did you see the woman that met in town?

Most languages have questions analogous to (1a); some languages have forms like (1b); but very few languages have a question like (1c). Notice that there would be nothing odd about the *meaning* of (1c) if it were to occur; it would mean, in logicians' parlance, "Who is the person such that you saw the woman who met that person in town?" What is odd about (1c) is its *form;* it needs to be rephrased. Presumably some structural principle prevents forms like (1c) from occurring in the speech of English speakers; children are not exposed to pseudosentences like (1c) and informed systematically that they are not said. Speakers come to know subconsciously that (1c) cannot be said, this knowledge somehow emerging although it is not part of the input to the child's development. Furthermore it is hard to imagine how the inventory of sentences and sentence fragments that constitute the child's linguistic environment could provide even indirect evidence that (1c) cannot occur. It is not enough to say that people do not utter (1c) because they would never hear it. This argument is insufficient because people say many things that they have not heard; language is not learned simply by imitating or repeating what has been heard, as noted in the context of the second data deficiency.

This third data deficiency is of particular importance in defining our central problem. A good deal of evidence exists that the contrast between the child's experience and the range of data available to the linguist is quite substantial. Over the last twenty years, much of the linguistic literature has focused on areas where the best description cannot be derived directly from the data to which the child has access, or is underdetermined by those data as in the questions of (1). If the child's linguistic experience does not provide the basis for establishing some particular aspect of linguistic knowledge, some other source for that knowledge must exist. That aspect must be known a priori in the sense that it is available independently of linguistic experience. It may be available genetically or arise as a consequence of some other nonlinguistic experience; I shall gloss over this distinction and speak only of genetic determination, not considering until later the possibility of some properties of language being determined by nonlinguistic experience.

It is important to note that language usually develops in a child spontaneously and without systematic instruction. In certain communities there are haphazard attempts at instruction. Schoolchildren might be taught the "proper" use of *shall* and *will,* the distinction between *who* and the archaic *whom,* or when to use *that* in a relative clause (*the bridge that you crossed*). This kind of correction comes very late and children are notoriously impervious to it, which is why teachers repeat these drills in every generation, and why Fowler's *Modern English*

Usage has been reprinted so often. Nervous parents may correct the occasional *goed* or *taked,* but children are not instructed not to say sentences like (1c), nor do they make noticeable errors of this type. They are not informed that while *John kept the car in the garage* may mean either "What John kept was the car which is parked in the garage" or "The garage was where John kept the car," the analogous question *What did John keep in the garage?* has only the second, locational reading. Parents do not teach children that while *Who do you want to succeed?* may mean either "Who is the person such that you want to succeed him?" or "Who is the person such that you want him to succeed?", *Who do you wanna succeed?* (with a contracted form) has only the former meaning. Such distinctions emerge in the mature speaker without instruction; indeed,most adult speakers, who have not had a linguistic training, are not conscious of such distinctions, which are well beyond the range of data to which children are exposed.

Even when instruction is given in the early years, children usually resist it. McNeill (1966:69) reported the following exchange:

Child: Nobody don't like me.
Mother: No, say "nobody likes me."
Child: Nobody don't like me.
(eight repetitions of this dialogue)
Mother: No, now listen carefully; say "Nobody likes me."
Child: "Oh, nobody don't likes me."

It seems clear that children can and usually do develop linguistic capacity without the aid of instruction or correction. It is probably inappropriate, therefore, to speak of language "learning," as linguists often do, but rather we should think in terms of language emergence, development, or growth, analogously to the growth of a physical organ.

If children do not receive significant instruction, it is also clear that they do not acquire a mature linguistic capacity simply by imitating their parents and older playmates. This is not to say that imitation plays no role, just that it does not provide a sufficient explanation, given the third data deficiency. Parents and other people often adopt a simple and sometimes artificial style of speech when addressing children, but (contrary to the view of Roger Brown in his introduction to Snow and Ferguson 1977) it is scarcely plausible that this "motherese" provides sufficient structure for language acquisition to take place on an inductive basis, that is, so that children simply generalize patterns without the aid of genetically determined principles.

There are at least four reasons why this kind of pattern generalization is not the answer to how children acquire speech. First, although children no doubt register only part of their linguistic environment, there is no way of knowing quite what any individual child registers. Therefore factual basis is lacking for the claim that children register only what is filtered for them through parents' deliberately simplified speech. Children have access to more than this, including defective utterances. Second, even supposing that they register only perfectly well-formed expressions (and hence that the first data deficiency does not hold), that would not be enough to show that the child has a sufficient inductive base for language acquisition. The third data deficiency still holds and the child would need to know that the pattern of (1a) and (1b) could not be extended to yield (1c). One wants to know why quite ordinary inductive generalizations like this are in fact not made; the so-called motherese does not show where inductive generalizations must stop. Third, if the child registered only the simplified and well-formed sentences of motherese, the problem of language learning would be *more* difficult because the child's information would be more limited. Fourth, careful studies of parents' speech to children (like Newport, Gleitman, and Gleitman 1977), show that an unusually high proportion consists of questions and imperatives; simple declarative sentences are much rarer than in ordinary speech. This suggests that there is very little correlation between the way the child's language emerges and what parents do in their speech directed at children. Thus, the existence of motherese in no way eliminates the need for a genetic basis to language acquisition. The child is primarily responsible for the acquisition process, not parents or older playmates. (For a good discussion of this topic, see Wexler and Culicover 1980: 66–78.)

The problem demanding explanation is compounded by other factors: despite variation in background and intelligence, people's mature linguistic capacity emerges in a fairly uniform fashion, in just a few years, without much apparent effort, conscious thought, or difficulty; and it develops with only a narrow range of the logically possible "errors." Children do not test random hypotheses, gradually discarding those leading to "incorrect" results and provoking parental correction; in each language community the ill-formed sentences produced by very young children seem to be few in number and quite uniform from one child to another, which falls short of random hypotheses. Normal children attain a fairly rich system of linguistic knowledge by five or six years of age and a mature system by puberty; this is impressive when compared with the laborious efforts of squads of adult linguists who, educated and trained up to the eyeballs, try with only moderate success to characterize explicitly what people know when they know Dutch, Hopi, or whatever.

These, then, are the salient facts about language acquisition, or more properly, language growth. The child masters a rich system of knowledge without significant instruction and despite a triple deficiency of experiential data; the process involves only a narrow range of "errors" or false hypotheses and takes place rapidly, even explosively between two and three years of age. The main question is how children acquire so much more than they experience.

Given these facts, especially the third data deficiency, certain properties must be available to the organism independently of linguistic experience, which permit language growth to circumvent the environmental deficiencies and thus to take place quickly and not solely by trial and error. The environmental stimulus is impoverished, unstructured, and fairly random; the child hears a haphazard selection of sentences and pseudosentences and receives no significant instruction. The environmental stimulus is thus viewed as only a trigger; much of the ability eventually attained is determined by genetically encoded principles, which are triggered or activated by environmental stimulus rather than formed by it more or less directly.

The further fact that children can master *any* human language to which they happen to be exposed in infancy imposes strong limitations on the kind of principles the scientist can attribute to the genotype. An answer to the problem of acquisition cannot rest content with a mere enunciation of the properties of the specific language a particular child acquires. This would amount to a claim that the specific properties of, say, Hindi are innately prescribed, which permits no explanation of how a language with a significantly different structure, Polish, say, is acquired. The genetically encoded principles must therefore be fairly abstract and not language specific. The principles must meet strict empirical demands: for each natural language, the principles must provide a basis for attaining it given the child's exposure only to the haphazard and unstructured experience. Even greater empirical demands can be made by researchers (see Chapters 8 and 9), but to require the genotypical principles to give an account of how a child may master any natural language under the conditions noted is to ask a lot. The tight empirical demands make language particularly useful as a probe into the intrinsic properties of the human mind.

A grammar represents what a speaker comes to know, subconsciously for the most part, about his or her native language; it represents the fully developed linguistic capacity and is therefore part of an individual's phenotype. Speakers know that certain sentences (in fact, an infinite number) can occur in their speech and that others cannot; they know what the occurring sentences mean and the various ways in which they can be pronounced and rephrased. Most of this largely subconscious knowledge is represented in a person's grammar. It may be put to use for various purposes, from everyday functions like expressing ideas, communicating, or listening to other people, to more contrived functions like writing elegant prose or lyric poetry or compiling crossword puzzles. For more contrived functions, people are more likely to vary in their ability to use their knowledge. (See Chapter 9 for the ways linguistic knowledge may be put to use for some everyday functions.)

The genotypical principles responsible for language acquisition can be viewed as a theory of grammar, sometimes called Universal Grammar. This represents the genetic equipment that makes language growth possible under the conditions assumed here (therefore part of the genotype) and delimits the linguistic knowledge that may eventually be attained, that is, the form and functioning of the grammar. Under this view, the theory of grammar is, in Chomsky's words,

a common human attribute, genetically determined, one component of the human mind. Through interaction with the environment, this faculty of mind becomes articulated and refined, emerging in the mature person as a system of knowledge of language. To discover the character of this mental faculty, we will try to isolate those properties of attained linguistic competence that hold by necessity rather than as a result of accidental experience, where by "necessity" I of course mean biological rather than logical necessity. We will therefore be particularly interested in properties of attained linguistic competence that are vastly underdetermined by available experience in general, but that nevertheless hold of the linguistic competence attained by any normal speaker of a given language, and in fact by all speakers of all languages (perhaps vacuously in some cases) on the natural assumption of uniformity across the species. The commitment to formulate a restrictive theory of U[niversal] G[rammar] is nothing other than a commitment to discover the biological endowment that makes language acquisition possible and to determine its particular manifestations. . . . we can explain some property of attained linguistic competence by showing that this property necessarily results from the interplay of the genetically-determined language faculty, specified by UG, and the person's (accidental) experience. (Chomsky 1977:164)

It need hardly be said that there is nothing necessary or God-given about this research goal, nor do I want to give the impression that all linguists adopt it. In fact, people have studied language with quite different goals in mind, ranging from the highly specific (to describe Dutch in such a way that it can be learned easily by Indonesian speakers), to more general ones, such as to determine how a language may differ from one historical stage to another (comparing, for example, Shakespearian and present-day English). One may want to study how the elements of language can be put together, the way they are used in thought, in art, or in everyday social discourse. I do not disparage these goals or claim that they lead to insignificant or unfruitful research programs; indeed, generativists often use observations made by workers pursuing other goals. However, the central empirical problem for the approach taken here will be to characterize how children can master their native language. This goal will shape the way we describe particular languages, once we make a few preliminary hypotheses. In later chapters I shall present various proposals and show that a research program pursuing this goal leads to insightful and fruitful analyses and has significance for our conception of the mind, therefore being relevant for work in psychology, philosophy, and politics. Under this view, the study of language will have a fairly general intellectual interest, going far beyond the immediate technical concerns. I shall suggest that an approach of this kind might form an appropriate basis for developing a general theory of human cognitive capacities, or, to use Noam Chomsky's recent metaphor, a system of "mental organs."

There are good reasons to suppose that Monod and Luria were right to assume that the basic shape of language is genetically determined. Their biological perspective can be used to try to establish as precisely as possible the contributions of the genes and of the environment, of nature and nurture, to the linguistic capacities eventually attained by human beings and to work out the proper balance between the theory of grammar and the trigger experiences that children have. The hypotheses will be subject to strict empirical demands since the genetic principles postulated must provide an explanation for the attainability of any natural language, given a normal trigger experience. Under this perspective, linguists will not be dazzled by curious phenomena in Czech, Mandarin Chinese, or the Quechua of Peru but will struggle to get beyond the limits of their own experience and to use these phenomena to build a platform from which they can observe the human mental organ, or cognitive capacity, rather as a biologist observes laboratory fruit flies.

In order to do this, we need to gain some distance from facts that are in some sense too familiar to notice. Just as people who live in a certain cultural setting often take it for granted as natural and unchangeable and do not see what is special or nonessential about it, so too most of us do not think about something as familiar as everyday speech. Once we see that there is something to be explained, perhaps these familiar and "obvious" facts can be honed into a tool by which we can discover something about our own mental makeup. If so, the study of language will be integrated with the general body of natural sciences, dealing with the nature, function, and origin of a particular mental capacity.

Mentalistic Grammars

In order to show how children master their native language, we shall need to characterize their mature capacity, when they can be said to know their mother tongue. This capacity develops in stages but by puberty reaches a fairly steady state, after which it changes only in minor ways. The characterization of this capacity is a *grammar*. Using this definition means commitment to psychological or mentalistic claims; it is a move away from the layman's sense of the word *grammar*.

A dictionary might define grammar as a list of the sounds, words, inflections, and syntactic constructions of a language, and their inter-relations: so, Classical Latin had five noun declensions, four major verb classes, and much more. This kind of grammar is really a piece of natural history, analogous to the claim that there are so many kinds of butterflies with so many characteristics. Indeed, such grammars are often called taxonomic grammars, echoing the taxonomies of Linnaeus. But just as Linnaeus knew that the botanical world can be divided up in many different ways, so too taxonomic grammarians face even greater problems due to the infinite number of sentences in any language, as noted in the last section, and because of difficulties in defining languages, in deciding when two dialects should be classed as different languages. The problems of the taxonomist manifest themselves in indeterminacy, for there is often no reason to prefer one classification over another unless one has a specific interest. There is enormous latitude for those who want to "describe a language in its own terms" or to treat a grammar as an uninterpreted, neutral means of listing well-formed utterances. Taxonomic grammars provide basic raw material and are indispensable for anybody working on linguistic matters from whatever viewpoint, just as Linnaean taxonomies were essential reference points for evolutionary biologists. But a molecular biologist works with different kinds of hypotheses from a Linnaeus, and our analyses will differ from those of taxonomic grammars.

A grammar is a psychological entity; it is part of the psychological state of somebody who knows some language. I shall use *grammar* to refer sometimes to the real entity and sometimes to a hypothesis about that entity. The relevant sense should be clear in each context.

Distinguishing between the contribution of intrinsic, genetically encoded properties and that of environmental factors will constrain descriptions and minimize indeterminacy problems. For any area of grammar, any aspect of linguistic knowledge, three intimately related items will be included in the account: there will be a formal and explicit characterization of what some mature speaker knows; this will be part of a *grammar,* which in turn is part of that person's phenotype. Since it is represented somehow in the mind/brain, it must be a finite system, which can relate sound and meaning for an infinite number of sentences. Also to be specified are the relevant genetic principles common to the species and characterizing the initial state of the organism; these principles make up the *theory of grammar* or *Universal Grammar,* and they are part of the genotype. The third item is the *trigger* experience, which varies from person to person and consists of an unorganized and fairly haphazard set of utterances in some language, of the kind that any child hears (the notion of a trigger is from ethologists' work on the emergence of behavioral patterns in young animals). The universal theory of grammar and the variable trigger together form the basis for attaining some grammar; any grammar must be attainable on the basis of a certain trigger and the genotype. One may think of the theory of grammar as making available a set of choices; the choices are taken in the light of the trigger experience, and a grammar emerges when the relevant options are resolved.

Each of the items in the triplet must meet various demands: the trigger must consist only of the kinds of things that children routinely experience; the mature grammar must define an infinite number of expressions as well-formed, and for each of these it must specify at least the sound and the meaning; the theory of grammar must hold universally such that any person's grammar can be attained on the basis of naturally available trigger experiences. A description will always involve these three items; and changing a claim about one of these closely related items usually involves changing claims about the other two. This tight and ambitious system of description must meet many empirical demands; it is therefore hard to imagine problems of indeterminacy of the kind that plague the natural historian or the taxonomist who does not take a psychological view of grammars.[1]

A grammar, then, is a representation of the linguistic capacity eventually attained by a native speaker, or at least a fundamental part of that capacity, and therefore is a claim about part of a person's mental makeup. If the correct grammar is defined as the one that the native speaker has actually acquired, the one that represents his or her linguistic competence, then it follows definitionally that the correct grammar is the one triggered by the primary linguistic data available to the child and the best, most explanatory theory. Some people call this grammar the *descriptively adequate grammar,* as opposed to other kinds of grammars, which are useful, accurate, and maybe even in principle exhaustive but not subject to a psychological interpretation; these they call *observationally adequate.* I shall be a little more cavalier and usurp the term *grammar* for a representation of a psychological state; the correct grammar is the correct representation of that state. Under this view, I shall discuss grammars only in terms of whether they characterize people's linguistic capacity and whether they are attainable under normal childhood experience.

So far I have been talking somewhat abstractly about what it means to know a language and what a mentalistic grammar actually looks like. I ask for your indulgence on this matter for a few more pages and promise to home in on it a little more in Chapter 3. Whatever a grammar is going to look like, it is clear that grammars, representations of mature psychological states, are of primary interest; the notion of a language is not central. Unlike much earlier work, the focus here is not on the properties of a particular language or even on general properties of many or all languages. A language under this view is an epiphenomenon, a derivative concept, the output of certain people's grammars (perhaps modified by other mental processes, as discussed in Chapter 3; this depends on how one chooses to define "language"). Relegating the notion of language in this way avoids various problems of classification: we no longer need decide whether dialects of Swedish and Norwegian are always members of different languages, or whether two dialects of Chinese would be better classified as different languages. A grammar is of clearer status: the finite system that characterizes an individual's linguistic capacity and that is somehow represented in the mind. No doubt the grammars of two individuals whom we regard as speakers of the same language will have much in common, but there is no reason to worry about defining "much in common," about specifying when the outputs of two grammars constitute one language. Just as it is unimportant for most work in molecular biology whether two creatures are members of the same species (as emphasized, for example, by Monod 1972:chap. 7 and by Dawkins 1976), so too the notion of a language is not likely to have much importance if our biological perspective is taken (I shall return to this matter in Chapter 5).

The theory of grammar is a hypothesis about the initial state of the mental organ, the innate capacity of the child, and a particular grammar conforming to this theory is a hypothesis about the final state, the grammar eventually attained. These are hypotheses about truth, about reality in the domain of psychology. This has led to much confusion in the literature and is sometimes misconstrued in terms of an independent concept of psychological reality. Some writers assume that one can discover various grammars that "work" simply and elegantly and that one can then ask which of these grammars is psychologically real. This presupposes the existence of psychological evidence, as distinct from linguistic evidence, which has some special status for establishing claims about psychological reality. There seems to be little virtue in deciding that data from, say, developmental stages in young children are inherently psychological and not linguistic, or vice versa. Rather we should seek simply "the correct grammar" for a certain person, presupposing a restrictive theory and using whatever data can resolve the questions we want to answer, data from well-formedness judgments, ambiguity, paraphrase, language acquisition, historical change, pathology, and whatever else may be useful. When we achieve a good grammar, it will be as unnecessary to ask the further question of whether the account is psychologically real, as it would be for a physicist, having constructed a good theory about the internal structure of the sun or some other object that we cannot actually get inside, and having accounted for the manner in which radiation is emitted and other data that can be observed from the earth, to ask whether the theory corresponds to physical reality, to what is actually happening inside the star. The answer in both cases is that the theory proposed purports to be the best available account. The researcher may seek to improve a theory, looking for new evidence and ideas, but cannot hope to achieve a new *type* of reality.

Let us simply seek the "correct" grammar of a language: the grammar to which the child is driven by the theory of grammar with which he or she is endowed, in order to use and understand his or her native language. This does not deny an interest in certain kinds of facts; it denies any independent psychological area of validation for grammars or theories of grammar. Evidence about ambiguity or grammaticalness is no less evidence about psychological reality than is evidence about language development in children, pathology, or historical change. It is just different evidence. *Any* claim about the correctness of grammatical hypotheses must have a psychological interpretation (given the nature of the goal) and therefore be a claim about truth in the domain of psychology, hence a contribution to a general theory of mind; thus there is no valid notion of psychological reality independent of a claim of simple correctness. The accessibility and usefulness of data from any given domain will vary according to the development of the various theories. Certain data may be uninterpretable—beyond the range of explanation—at one stage but may come to form a part of the basis for justifying and revising hypotheses as the theories are developed further. For now at least the overwhelming mass of crucial evidence bearing on the correctness of grammar (its psychological reality, its truth in the domain of psychology) comes from what is misleadingly called "linguistic evidence," data about well-formedness and the meaning of utterances.

In the same vein it is sometimes claimed that all explanation must be "reductionist" and no explanation exists until grammatical claims correlate with what is known at a level involving less abstraction, about neurology and the workings of the brain. But this misses the point that chemists do not stop doing chemistry because they believe that everything can be explained in terms of quantum mechanics; interesting properties may hold at higher levels of abstraction. Perhaps one day linguistic descriptions will be related to neurological networks (then to chemistry, and then to quantum mechanics), but it does not follow that all future work must be conducted in those terms. After all, it is possible to formulate a theory of vision without having to ask whether, in the simplest case of viewing a white square on a black background, there is a one-to-one relation between the neurological activity involved in defining the right-hand vertical side and some component of the theory. Similarly, it is an unrealistic and unnecessary requirement to impose on a theory of grammar that any hypothesis about its various individual components should demonstrably correspond in some strict way to the neurological processes involved in uttering or comprehending some sentence. This requirement also suggests that understanding of neurological workings is now advanced enough to form a productive basis for the study of grammars, but too many gaps remain for this suggestion to have any merit. The investigator attains the level of abstraction that can be reached and that is appropriate to the task at hand. At this stage it seems a reasonable strategy to work at a fairly high level of abstraction, at a level that can be thought about and grasped. It should always be borne in mind that the principles arrived at may hold more generally over more domains and at a different level of abstraction; one may be interested in how a grammar can be realized in the workings of the brain (see Chapter 9).

There is no reason to work only at the lowest levels of abstraction or to write grammars only in terms of what is known of physical, neurological processes. I assume that grammars must be represented somehow in the brain but that representation may turn out to be a complex matter. It seems more productive to try to figure out as precisely as possible what properties a grammar must have before asking how it is represented in the brain. Only when a good deal is known about neurology and a good deal about grammars will it make sense to ask about the relation between the two. This kind of view reflects the usual procedure in other sciences. Consider the following passage from Koyré, discussing Newton's *mathematical* laws:

Fortunately, as Newton knew full well, we need not have a clear conception of the way in which certain effects are produced in order to be able to study the phenomena and to treat them mathematically. Galileo was not obliged to develop a theory of gravity—he even claimed his right to ignore completely its nature—in order to establish a mathematical dynamics and to determine the laws of fall. Thus nothing prevented Newton from studying the *laws* of "attraction" or "gravitation" without being obliged to give an account of the real forces that produced the centripetal motion of the bodies. It was perfectly sufficient to assume only that these forces—whether physical or metaphysical—were acting according to strict mathematical laws (an assumption fully confirmed by the observation of astronomical phenomena and also by well-interpreted experiments) and to treat these "forces" as *mathematical* forces, and not as real ones. Although only a part of the task, it is a very necessary part; only when this preliminary stage is accomplished can we proceed to the investigation of the real causes of the phenomena.
This is precisely what Newton does in the book so significantly called not *Principia Philosophiae*, . . . but *Philosophiae naturalis principia mathematica,* that is, Mathematical Principles of Natural Philosophy. (Koyré 1957:176–7)

Some Alternatives

Under the mentalistic definition of grammars, the grammar consists of a finite set of statements that characterize an individual's linguistic capacity, and it develops on exposure to some triggering experience. Its basic character is determined by genetically encoded principles. Endowed with these principles, a person exposed to adequate experience will develop a grammar. Certain genetic structures make this development possible.

Even with this basic approach, quite different research programs might still be developed. I shall briefly mention three other programs, to give some sense of the range of alternatives and so to locate our own perspective somewhat.

First, many linguists in the 1930s and 1940s sought organizing techniques for the analysis of languages, sometimes called "discovery procedures." They postulated procedures of segmentation and classification whereby an analyst could gradually discover the basic elements of a language: first the sound units, then the meaning units, inflectional markers, then words, and so on. If these procedures could be refined sufficiently, a linguist need only apply them rigorously to discover the correct grammar. The procedures would be sufficient to determine the grammar of particular languages and so to express the nature of language in general. Most linguists developing these procedures saw them as convenient techniques for organizing perplexing material so as to arrive at a taxonomic grammar; they did not see their work as a branch of psychology. But some, notably Charles Hockett, Roman Jakobson, and Edward Sapir, explicitly took a realist stance and interpreted the procedures as represented in the mind in some way. In fact, it has sometimes been argued that implicitly all these linguists were taking the realist stance, since they debated the appropriateness of certain procedures in terms of the plausibility of the resulting taxonomies, claiming that some taxonomies were psychologically more realistic than others; Hockett and some others were unusual in being so explicit about this.

Whatever the intent of these linguists, if their kind of analysis is interpreted as a claim about human psychological processes, then the analytical procedures actually proposed could not correspond to the processes of language development in a child. Even from the little known about developmental stages, it is clear that children do not first establish the phonetics of their language, then the phonemes, then

larger elements like meaning units, then larger ones like words and
sentences, as those procedures would imply. Also, the procedures involved could not enable a child to derive an adequate grammar from
the kinds of linguistic experience available, circumventing the deficiencies of the stimulus identified earlier in this book. Some technical issues
are involved, discussed most clearly in Chomsky 1964.

Many variants of the search for general analytical procedures have
been tried. The early linguists mentioned sought procedures of segmentation and classification; other researchers seek "generalized learning
strategies" with procedures of induction, analogy, and generalization.
Although they differ somewhat from theory to theory, it is usually assumed that these strategies constitute the whole of the innate cognitive
faculty and that they are quite general: there is nothing specific for
language or any other particular subject matter, nor are they limited to
any particular species. Rather than being a complex system of interacting faculties, the mind is viewed as consisting of more uniform, homogeneous principles of general intelligence. In this approach scientists
may seek one general learning theory that characterizes how rats come
to run mazes, how children acquire a language, and how adults learn to
play chess. Alternatively, they may hold with Piaget that language
growth is parasitic on growth in other domains. What is common is that
they think that the language faculty consists only of a few principles, all
of which also apply to domains other than language. It is certainly too
dogmatic to require *in advance* that these various abilities be treated
identically and that there can be no principles specific to the language
faculty. In fact, it seems most unlikely that there will be significant
analogies between such activities. This kind of approach is not followed in physiology; nobody suggests that scientists must study the
eye, the liver, and even the lobster's antenna only with a view to establishing analogies in function or structure. It would be more appropriate
to follow the example of biology and to assume that the mind is made
up of "mental organs" just as specialized and distinct as physical organs. Analogies may emerge, but they should not be required a priori.

A second approach holds that the basic form of language is determined not by genetic principles but by its communicative function;
therefore there is no need to attribute a highly structured language faculty to the organism. Proponents of this view do not say how the communicative function allows children to circumvent the problem of a
deficient stimulus or how it prevents them from making the ordinary
inductive generalizations illustrated earlier, specifying for example

why *want to* cannot be pronounced *wanna* in *Who do you want to go?* An analogous view of a physical organ makes little sense: the heart serves the function of pumping blood and one might say that its structure is determined by that function. But a heart does not just happen to develop in each individual because it would be useful to pump blood; a group of cells do not "decide" to become a heart. A heart develops because the genetic program determines that it will develop as it does. Functional explanations do not account for how organs develop in an individual embryo; they do not hold at the ontogenetic level, although they may cast some light on evolutionary change at the phylogenetic level. Similarly with cognitive capacities: if it were proposed that some aspect of a grammar is determined by communicative needs, the proposal would hold of the evolutionary development of the species, not of an individual child attaining a particular language. Functional considerations may complement claims about genetic structure, but they do not usually offer an alternative to genetically prescribed principles. This becomes clear if genetic principles are viewed as the means to attain rich structures on the basis of a deficient stimulus.

In this context we should resist thinking of the "essential" purpose of language as "communication," as is often claimed. Language is used in many ways: for transmitting information, expressing thought, for lying, for play, for establishing personal relations, for creative activities like poetry, to arouse emotions, to indicate class backgrounds, and more. There is no reason to regard one particular mode as essential. Nor is there any reason to salvage *communication,* to redefine it to include all modes of language use, so that expression of thought becomes "communication with oneself"; under that view the notion of communication loses all content.

As a third possible approach, a theory might have sufficient latitude to allow a wider range of possible grammars than actually occur, perhaps even an infinite number of grammars consistent with a particular child's trigger experience. The theory would specify a system, a so-called evaluation metric, which enables the child to choose the best of the various grammars consistent with that child's linguistic experience. Within this program, the burden of work will lie in the development of an evaluation metric, permitting the child to choose one grammar over the other possible ones. Such evaluation metrics are usually based on notions of simplicity, and simplicity criteria may be able to distinguish the simplest of three or four grammars, but it is difficult to imagine them choosing among billions. It cannot be shown that this is impossible in principle, but as a matter of historical fact very little work has been done in this area by proponents of grammatical theories permitting a wide range of grammars; there seem to be scant grounds for optimism. Again as a matter of historical fact, such simplicity criteria have played a significant role only in resolving more general questions, such as the choice between a grammar with only phrase structure rules and a grammar with phrase structure rules and transformational rules (Chomsky 1955; see Chapter 3); on finer questions such as have arisen in the subsequent development of transformational grammar, competing theories usually turn out to be empirically nonequivalent in such a way that it is unnecessary to appeal to an explicit and carefully defined simplicity metric, even if a general notion of simplicity is tacitly assumed.

Although a notion of simplicity is important to keep our grammatical hypotheses in order and to prevent proliferating alternatives, one needs to be wary of the idea that the mind entertains a range of grammars and then "chooses" one or another as the best of those compatible with the experience that it has encountered. Certainly there is no conscious choice, any more than a person consciously chooses a particular body height. A person involuntarily and without choice attains a certain height and a certain grammar as a result of his genotype and his particular experience, nutritional and linguistic. It is unlikely that trial and error plays much role in the emergence of language in a child, in the way that it does when we play chess or voluntarily develop a set of political views, a scientific theory, or decide to take the bus instead of the train. Children do use trial and error to some extent, trying out forms that are not correct and later discarding them in favor of better ones. They do use induction to make some generalizations, but they can only succeed by virtue of the genetic constraints, which severely limit the hypothesis space and therefore the range of their inductions. It is probably better to think of the child as being driven inexorably to a particular grammar or body height, given a certain genotype and certain experience.

I have just outlined three alternative ways of pursuing the basic goal that we have set ourselves. What is novel about the perspective taken here is the importance ascribed to the salient facts of acquisition: the triple inadequacy of the stimulus, the rapidity of the development, and the narrow range of errors. The deficiency of the stimulus highlighted by these facts has shifted attention to the psychological theories postulating substantial innate properties. These innate mechanisms make acquisition possible under the impoverished input conditions discussed earlier. So languages are assumed to have a partially determined structure as a matter of biological necessity, just as the general character of the heart or liver is fixed for the species.

There are limits on how this study may proceed, sometimes of an ethical nature. Suppose that somebody claims that grammars must have some property P and that P is determined by genetic structure rather than by experience, although relevant experience may be needed to "trigger" proper growth and functioning of a system with P. Such a claim might in principle be tested in various ways: by some intrusive experimentation debarred by ethical considerations; by designing an environment neutral with regard to P, and by determining whether grammars invariably have P (where presence and absence of P are equally compatible with the triggering experience); by designing an artificial language violating P and showing that it is not learned with normal facility. This kind of testing is not often available, but that does not make language study necessarily unempirical. Rather, the investigator must often devise intricate and ingenious arguments and experiments to test a claim that grammars must have P as a matter of biological necessity. This is part of the intellectual fascination of the study of natural language, which demands even more ingenuity than has been used in the studies of vision and ethology because of the ethical limits to experiments and the fact that there are no other species with language that we feel free to mutilate.

Given the limits, it seems most productive to focus attention primarily on properties for which the linguistic environment (which researchers cannot control) is neutral, which are not determined by the experience normally available to the child. I shall postulate that P is a function of biological necessity if (a) P holds for some grammar (that is, speakers' judgments and other behavior conform to P, structures violating P do not occur, and so on), and (b) P cannot plausibly arise by instruction or induction because it is too abstract and crucial evidence for it is too sparse and contrived. So properties like the nonambiguity of *Who do you wanna succeed?* and *What did John keep in the garage?*, discussed earlier, are phenomena requiring such an explanation.

In such examples P is postulated as a property of genetic encoding after investigating only a single language. As an investigator one is entitled to do this because knowledge is apparently attained without relevant experience and therefore must be derived in part from the innate language faculty. Of course, such a hypothesis is open to revision by subsequent inquiry into the same language or other languages and it must be sufficiently abstract to hold for all languages, but deep analysis of a single language may reveal interesting properties of Universal Grammar, just as extremely detailed experiments on the fruit fly provided geneticists with crucial insight into general genetic properties.

This approach does not suffer from the defects of the other three approaches outlined and has recently become the basis for some fruitful work, some of which I shall sketch in later chapters. It is the productivity and fruitfulness of the research that is the hallmark of a well-conceived program. However, despite differences in research strategies, all four approaches share an essential mentalism and make claims about psychological reality.

Notes

1. There has been some interesting mathematical work recently concerning the learnability of grammars. If one makes certain assumptions about the trigger experience, then any hypothesis about the mature system, about the grammar, must have certain properties for it to be learnable on the basis of that trigger. A series of papers by Culicover, Hamburger, and Wexler have investigated this from a mathematical viewpoint; the work culminates in Wexler and Culicover 1980. They construct a mathematical model that incorporates some more or less reasonable assumptions about the language learner, and they provide a proof that this model is capable of learning transformational grammars of a certain sort. This is an impressive achievement. The model specifies the boundary conditions for a theory of language learning and therefore grammars must be no less constrained than those of their model. In fact, it is likely that grammars are more restricted than they suppose, but at this stage it is useful to have a mathematical proof that at least some kind of transformational grammar is learnable under reasonable assumptions about the language learner.

Suggested Reading

For a recent elaboration of the acquisition problem and the triple deficiency of the stimulus, see the introduction to Hornstein and Lightfoot 1981. Chomsky (1975, 1980) discusses some alleged conceptual difficulties for the psychological orientation adopted here, trying to sort out some of the confusions in some of the critical literature.

See Tinbergen 1969 and Tinbergen's *The Animal in Its World*, vol. 2 (Cambridge, Mass.: Harvard University Press, 1972) for many ethological experiments uncovering innate and learned aspects of animal behavior. This experimentation, often identifying an acquired property not determined by the young animal's experience, has encouraged the line of reasoning pursued here.

John Marshall's "On the biology of language acquisition" (in D. Caplan, ed., 1980) is a particularly clear and careful discussion of how biologists might make sense of the psychological view of grammar and has a history of some of the central ideas.

Chapter 3
The Form of a Grammar

A Generative Grammar

It is now time to be rather more specific and therefore more technical about how to characterize people's linguistic capacity, about the shape of the mature grammar. A person's ability to deal with an infinite range of sentences is reflected in the claim that he attains a finite grammar. The finite grammar must be an algebraic system that can allow for and thus "generate" all the structures of his language, explicitly specifying the sound and meaning for any particular sentence.

Such a generative grammar must fall within a narrow range of formal possibilities; the theory of grammar prescribes the genetically specified limits on human grammars that enable acquisition to proceed despite the imperfection of the input. The relevance of such an approach to acquisitional concerns is straightforward. The more restricted the options the theory makes available to children, the less surprising it is that they acquire their mother tongue in a few years on the basis of degenerate and deficient data. For the narrower the range of "options" the language acquirer must resolve, the less the structure of his acquired knowledge depends on environmental stimulus. In addition, an adequate theory of grammar will explain the structural principles which hold of grammars and for which there is no direct evidence in the trigger experience; these principles stem from our genetic endowment.

Such a generative view of grammar can be contrasted again with informal grammars, pedagogical grammars, grammars written on historical principles listing construction types and informally describing their history, or with grammars classifying elements of language according to co-occurrence and paraphrase relations (Harris 1957, 1965). Such taxonomic, nongenerative grammars essentially classify data according to some selected dimensions. A generative grammar, on the other hand, purports to describe the linguistic capacity of a mature native speaker of some language.

Since speakers can use and understand indefinitely many sentences, a generative grammar must be a finite system that can characterize an infinite number of sentences. Such a grammar contains explicit and formal statements, what linguists call descriptive *rules,* which fall into the narrow class defined by the theory of grammar and which assign to the sentences of the language correct descriptions of their structure and associate their phonological form with a representation of their meaning. The rules of the grammar relate sound to meaning for an infinite range of sentences. The correct grammar will so generate all the well-formed sentences of somebody's language and none of the deviant ones (but see the caveats in the next section and Chapter 5).[1]

Generative grammars have been formulated in various ways, with different types of rules. Chomsky (1957) discussed three kinds. A *finite state grammar* is inspired by mathematical communication models involving so-called Markov processes. Sentences are generated by a series of choices made one after the other. One picks the first word, then the second, then the third, and so on. In a first-order Markov process each choice is determined by probabilities that are a function of the immediately preceding word and only that word. An n-order Markov process looks back n words, where n must be finite. The rules define the transition from one word to the next and the definitions are stated in terms of probabilities. Chomsky (1957:21–4) argued that a grammar based on such systems cannot characterize human linguistic capacity because they cannot deal with nonadjacent dependencies, such as between *apples* and *are* in *The apples in the blue box . . . are (*is) red,* where an indefinite amount of material may intervene. Quite a different argument was used against *phrase structure grammars,* consisting only of one class of rules, which defined constituent structure; the argument was that while these grammars might succeed in distinguishing the grammatical sentences of some language, they could do so only with unnecessarily complex (hence unattainable) rules (Chomsky 1957:34–48). Therefore criteria of simplicity and elegance, as are standard in scientific theorizing, suggested the need for another model, allowing a simpler account of the phenotype or the ability eventually attained by the native speaker. Chomsky argued that a grammar incorporating *transformational* rules would meet this requirement. This is a *transformational grammar.*

It is worth noting that *generative* and *transformational* are terms of different status. To say that a grammar is transformational means that it contains a particular formal device, namely a rule moving an item elsewhere in certain prescribed ways. But to say that a grammar is generative represents a different kind of claim and is a methodological assertion, independent of any particular formal devices in the grammar. A generative grammar is an algebraic system of formal rules that can assign the correct structural descriptions to an infinite number of well-formed utterances in a person's speech. Adopting a standard mathematical definition, a function is said to generate when values are given for variables, but this can be carried out in a number of ways.

I turn now to the specific form of a transformational generative grammar that provides the basis for this book. Here I shall give only a very brief, schematic outline, reserving details for later chapters. The general model in (1) sketches the so-called Extended Standard Theory developed in the 1970s building on the early work of Chomsky (1955, 1965) and many others. Such a grammar has more equipment than just phrase structure and transformational rules, but it formally relates phonetic form to logical form for any given sentence.

(1)

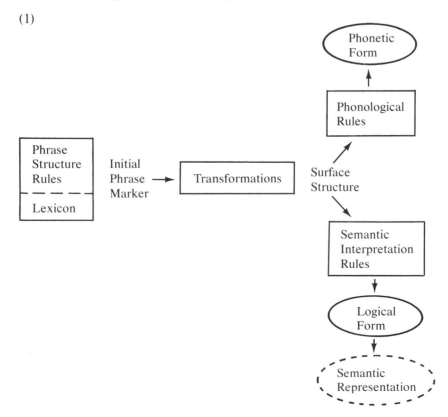

Starting at the left, the base subcomponent consists of *phrase structure* (PS) rules and a *lexicon,* which together define the *initial phrase marker* for any given structure. There is one set of PS rules for any grammar and they define basic constituent structure, the structural relations among the various units. The lexicon specifies properties of lexical items, stipulating, for example, that *eat* is a verb (V) that may occur in a structure like (2a), followed by a direct object noun phrase (here labeled N̄ instead of the more familiar NP; there are some good reasons for the change of notation, which we'll come to in a later chapter). A structure defined, or generated, by the PS rules and the lexicon, is sometimes called a *phrase marker,* in fact an initial phrase marker. A phrase marker can be represented as a tree (2a) or, equivalently, a labeled bracketing (2b). So the whole thing is a sentence (S) consisting of a subject noun phrase (N̄), an auxiliary element, and a verb phrase (V̄). Each of these three units consists of other units, as I shall discuss in Chapter 4. The items *John, present, must, eat, spinach* are particular values for the variables N̄, Tense, and so on; different items might have been chosen.

(2)

a.

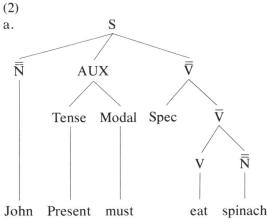

b. [[John]$_{\bar{\bar{N}}}$ [[present]$_{Tense}$ [must]$_{Modal}$]$_{AUX}$ [Spec [[eat]$_V$ [spinach]$_{\bar{\bar{N}}}$]$_{\bar{V}}$]$_{\bar{V}}$]$_S$

The initial phrase marker is the structure resulting from the application of only the PS rules and the insertion of lexical items. This is fed into the transformational subcomponent, where it may be amended by successive applications of various *transformational rules.* These rules move constituents to different places in the phrase marker. The second phrase marker results from amending the initial phrase marker by moving one item. One additional movement would yield a third phrase marker, and so on. For example, a rule (3) moves an auxiliary element to the front of anything else ("..." stands for anything else in the phrase marker); this eventually yields a sentence *Must John eat spinach?* If the rightmost $\bar{\bar{N}}$ contained *what* instead of *spinach,* a rule moving *wh* words might also apply (4), moving the *wh* word to the left of any other material and yielding *What must John eat?*

(3)
... Aux ... $\Rightarrow$ Aux ...

(4)
... [wh...] ... $\Rightarrow$ [wh...] ...

These two subcomponents, the base and the transformations, make up the syntactic component, which I shall discuss in Chapter 4. The output of this component, the last phrase marker, is a *surface structure,* which in turn is then assigned a phonetic and a semantic interpretation.

The surface structure, which is a phrase marker that has been amended by movement rules like (3) and (4), constitutes the input to the phonological component; this produces a phonetic representation. The surface structure is also the input and the sole input to the semantic interpretation rules. The interpretive rules produce a logical form, which is a description of the scope of quantifiers, which nouns refer to other nouns, the semantic functions of noun phrases, subject-predicate relations, various entailments, and more. I distinguish tentatively between logical form and a fuller representation of the meaning of an expression; I assume that logical form can be fully specified by formal rules of sentence grammar, but I leave open the possibility that there is more to semantic representation, perhaps involving beliefs, expectations, legitimate inferences, conditions of appropriate use and matters beyond what can be usefully formalized. After all, many philosophers have disputed the feasibility of a coherent notion of semantic representation. Even if we admit the possibility of semantic representation broadly conceived, it may not constitute part of our grammars; I leave this as an open question and I shall say nothing more about it until Chapter 6.

The sequential application of all these rules is often called a *derivation.* If some derivation is successful and well-formed, the grammar will have related a phonetic representation to a corresponding logical form for a particular initial phrase marker. The phonetic and logical forms are the two outputs of the grammar; they are related by the syntactic component, which provides a surface structure, which in turn is the raw material for the phonological and semantic rules.

Let us hypothesize that the grammar of English contains transformational movement rules like (3) and (4), the PS rules that generate initial trees like (2) and many others, the particular lexical items *eat, must,* and so on. This represents knowledge acquired by people who know English. But the basic organization of a grammar (1), the fact that PS rules are available, that they define trees that may be amended by movement rules, and so on, is all part of the genotype, part of what children each bring to the task of developing a native language and of analyzing what they hear. Also, the rule classes are each subject to constraints on their possible form and on the way in which they may function. For example, in phonology many different physical dimensions could in principle be exploited by the sound system of a language, but only a small range of the logically possible sound systems are actually used; the sound of grinding teeth plays no role in the sound system of any language, for example. Research will be designed to discover the most restrictive principles on the form and function of the available grammars.

These principles, when formulated, may be hypothesized to be a part of the innate equipment brought by the child to the task of acquiring a native language. Endowed with these principles, a child is free to select particular PS and transformational rules, in accordance with the particular trigger experience encountered. A particular grammar is simply a selection of particular values for the options or "parameters" defined by the theory.

A Theory of Mind: Modularity

If the theory of grammar has the general properties discussed in the last section, then the mind is a wider ranging object, encompassing a grammar as just one component. Other components include perceptual strategies and an account of knowledge of the world. Each of these components has an internal structure, but we need not concern ourselves with the subcomponents of perceptual and conceptual knowledge. One might think of this as three (perhaps more) intersecting capacities, as in diagram (5).

(5)

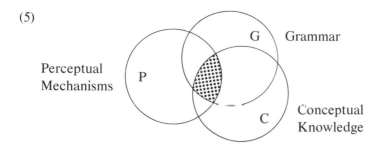

The circles specify well-formed objects in each domain: the circle P indicates objects that can be perceived by human beings (analyzed and understood), circle G specifies objects that are well-formed grammatically, and circle C sensible beliefs about the world (no doubt a rather large circle with various subdomains). The shaded area, where all three circles intersect, encompasses objects that are well-formed from all three viewpoints. These will be sentences—grammatical objects—that accord with human perceptual mechanisms and reflect a sensible view of the world. However some objects are well-formed from only two viewpoints. For example, let us assume a perceptual mechanism that makes nesting structures (one sentence contained in the middle of another) difficult for speakers to interpret. This is called *center embedding* and multiple center embedding is usually avoided in areas such as natural language, music, and arithmetic. Thus some objects may be well-formed with respect to grammatical rules and may reflect a coherent world view but violate restrictions on center embedding, thereby having a structure that cannot be perceived naturally, like (6).

(6)
[[that [that [that the moon is bright] is obvious] disturbs me] surprised Harry]

Other objects may be grammatically well-formed and perceivable but may convey only nonsense, such as the well-known *Colorless green ideas sleep furiously* or a structure like (2) with the noun phrases interchanged, *Spinach must eat John*. Another possibility might be multiple center embedded nonsense that is grammatically well-formed, although perceptually and cognitively deviant. Similarly there are perceptual mechanisms dealing with, say, properties of vision and color differentiation that do not interact at all with the domain of grammar and may or may not have anything to do with knowledge of the world.

Under this approach the mind encompasses a grammar as one sub-component, which in turn intersects with other cognitive capacities. A grammar can generate structures that may fail to meet the requirements of a set of perceptual strategies or of somebody's beliefs about the world. When it is said that a grammar generates only grammatical sentences, the word *grammatical* means 'generated by a grammar'; so (6) may be grammatical, although it is quite unacceptable as a sentence of English and nobody would ever utter it under normal circumstances outside a discussion about linguistics.

Analysts have no a priori, theory-independent basis for deciding where a given phenomenon should be located in (5). Whether (6) violates a principle of grammar or a perceptual constraint can be decided only in light of the success of the theory of mind as a whole; there are no valid discovery procedures here and what one analyst treats under a grammatical rubric another might treat perceptually, the choice being made as a function of the *overall* success of the competing theories.[2]

As an example, consider a sentence (7), where *his* may refer ambiguously to *John* or *Mike* (or to some third person, but let's ignore that possibility). If one adds a second clause of precisely the same structure (8), then if the second *his* refers to *Fred* or *Bill,* it must be interpreted in parallel fashion to the first *his*. In (8) if the first *his* refers to the subject of its clause, *John,* then the second *his* refers to its subject *Fred* and not to its object *Bill*. Conversely, if the first *his* refers to the object of its clause, *Mike,* then the second *his* will refer to *Bill* and not to *Fred*.

(7)
John persuaded Mike to fix his bicycle.

(8)
John persuaded Mike to fix his bicycle and Fred persuaded Bill to fix his car.

Thus either John's bicycle and Fred's car are being fixed, or Mike's bicycle and Bill's car; but no other combination. A grammatical rule could be formulated to make the relevant distinctions, but the rule would be extremely complex, perhaps even unstatable, and even if statable, not attainable by a child with access only to usual childhood experience; childhood experience does not include instruction about the possible and impossible meanings of sentences like (8).

A similar problem arises in simpler contexts where pronouns are not present. Sentence (9a) is ambiguous according to whether *must* expresses an order or a supposition: it may be that John is obliged to do the shopping or that, given what we know of his circumstances, it is reasonable to suppose that he does in fact do the shopping. But in a sentence like (9b) the two *musts* must be interpreted in parallel fashion. (9b) has two readings, not four: either both John and Sam are obliged to do the shopping, or it is reasonable to suppose that they both in fact do the shopping.

(9)
a. John must do the shopping.
b. John must do the shopping and Sam must too.

Rather than complicating each of the grammatical rules involved, we can propose a very simple rule allowing the pronouns in (8) to refer to any of the preceding nouns; this simple rule will "overgenerate" and characterize (8) too generously as having all four readings. Similarly each occurrence of *must* will be allowed to have one or two readings, with no special restrictions; therefore there will be four possible logical forms for (9b). The grammar is kept simple and a separate perceptual strategy is exploited, which assigns parallel interpretations to adjacent ambiguous objects, as suggested by studies of vision: a Necker cube is ambiguous in terms of which square surface is nearer to the observer, but if two are placed side by side, they will usually be interpreted in the same way unless the observer engages in some visual gymnastics.

(10)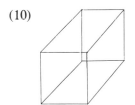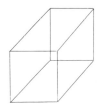

If we interpret this perceptual strategy generally so that it applies not only to visual objects like Necker cubes and the like but also in the cognitive sphere, then the grammar may have a simple rule allowing a pronoun to refer back to any noun phrase on its left. This grammar allows (8) to have four possible logical forms, but only two of them could actually be perceived by the mind. Similarly for (9b). In this way a simple and general rule of grammar intersects with a simple and general perceptual strategy, and in combination they yield the correct predictions: namely that (8) has only two relevant interpretations. This

illustrates the modular approach to the study of mind: the mind is reck-
oned to consist of distinct subsystems, which interact in specified
ways.

Like the grammar, each of the other modules is likely to develop in
time and to have distinct initial and mature states. One example of a
developing module is that the conceptual knowledge of a young child
differs substantially from that of a normal adult. Conceptual knowledge
develops in the light of experience, although always within the framework of what the genetic program prescribes. Similarly the visual system of man and other animals develops in light of early interactions
with certain features of the environment and the brain "learns" to perceive certain kinds of retinal images and not others. Monod (1972:141)
mentions the frog's system, which allows it to see a fly that is moving,
but not one at rest; the image of the motionless fly is registered on the
frog's retina but is not transmitted. An octopus can learn to distinguish
figures like a triangle, circle, or square, and Hubel and Wiesel (1962,
1968) have determined that recognition of such objects is due to the
structure of the circuits that filter and recompose the retinal image. So
certain nerve cells respond only to a straight line sloping downward
from left to right, other nerve cells to lines sloped in different directions. The range of angles that an individual neuron can register is set
by the genetic program, but experience is needed to fix the precise
orientation specificity.

The idea is that when the nervous system learns, "new or better
paths [are established] for the exchange of messages among the cells of
the brain. Experience translates itself in an increased complexity,
structural or functional, of the patterns of connection between nerve
cells" (Luria 1973:108). This view of learning is not a new one: Gesell
(1947) and McGraw (1947) argued that locomotion in man is governed
by an innate co-ordination pattern. The pattern is innate and most of
the improvement shown in the first years of life is due to growth of
nervous connections. Hubel and Wiesel's work brings a new richness
to this view. In the mid-sixties they and their colleagues devised an
ingenious technique to identify how individual neurons in an animal's
visual system react to specific patterns in the visual field (including
horizontal and vertical lines, moving spots, and sharp angles). They
found that particular nerve cells were set within a few hours of birth to
react only to certain visual stimuli, and furthermore that if a nerve cell
is not stimulated within a few hours it becomes totally inert in later life.
In several experiments on kittens it was shown that if a kitten spent its

first few days in a deprived optical environment (a tall cylinder painted only with vertical stripes), only the neurons stimulated by that environment remained active; all other optical neurons became inactive because the relevant synapses degenerated, and the kitten never learned to see horizontal lines or moving spots in the normal way. Therefore, we can see learning as a selective process: various parameters are provided by the genetic equipment and relevant experience fixes those parameters (see Blakemore 1974 for a review of this work). Furthermore a certain mature cognitive structure will emerge at the expense of other possible structures which are lost irretrievably as the inactive synapses degenerate. The view that there is a narrowing down of possible connections out of an overabundance of initially possible ones is now receiving more attention in light of Hubel and Wiesel's success. For the moment this seems to be a more likely means to fine tune the nervous system as learning takes place, as opposed to the earlier view (see the quotation from Luria, above) that there is an *increase* in the connections among nerve cells. For more on this view of learning, see Jean-Pierre Changeux's contribution to Piattelli-Palmarini (1980), outlining his theory of "selective stabilization" of developing synapses and discussing its implications for the approach to language learning pursued in this book.

Considerable progress has been made recently in understanding how the visual system develops in various organisms, notably through the Nobel prize winning work of Hubel and Wiesel. Something has been learned of how elements are acquired through experience:

They are acquired according to a *program,* and that program is innate—that is to say, genetically determined. The program's structure initiates and guides early learning, which will follow a certain pre-established pattern defined in the species' genetic patrimony. This is, no doubt, how we should understand the process whereby the child acquires language. And there is no reason not to suppose that the same holds true for the fundamental categories of cognition in man, and perhaps also for a good many other elements of human behaviour, less basic but of great consequence in the shaping of the individual and society. (Monod 1972:143)

So human cognitive capacity is made up of identifiable properties that are genetically prescribed, each developing along one of various pre-established routes depending on the particular experience encountered. These genetic prescriptions may be extremely specialized, as Hubel and Wiesel showed for the visual system. They assign some order to our linguistic experience, which then elicits or triggers certain kinds of specific responses but does not determine the form of the response.

This view of the mind, consisting of specific subsystems interacting with each other in specified ways, differs from the ideas of most psychologists. Theorists as different as Skinner and Piaget share the notion that for the cognitive faculties the intrinsic properties of the organism are homogeneous and undifferentiated, their development uniform from one to the other. Piaget's "developmental constructivism" holds that no principles of language structure are genetically determined or even present at a very early age. Rather, the linguistic principles arise as a result of the child's early sensorimotor development.[3] This denies the kind of modularity supposed here, at least for the initial state.

Piaget might be right, but so far no suggestion has been made of how sensorimotor development might relate to grammatical principles, such as the availability of a transformational rule like (4) or the principle of Domains, to be discussed later. Piagetians suppose that early language is modeled on prior sensorimotor development, and that later capacities depend on general principles such as "assimilation" and "accommodation," which are also involved in other cognitive functions; these principles are reminiscent of the "generalized learning strategies" discussed earlier. Since these analogies are so vague and lack any empirical support, there is no reason to lay much stock in the idea that cognitive structure is undifferentiated and homogeneous; there is certainly no reason to require in advance of empirical investigation that the mind *has* to be structured in this way.

The debate in Piattelli-Palmarini (1980) offers more specific commentary on Piaget's developmental constructivism and its potential for explaining how children acquire their mother tongue. The biologists who participated in that debate were highly critical of some of Piaget's evolutionary and genetic assumptions, particularly his notion of a quasi-Lamarckian phenocopy, by which the environment can change the structure of an organism, and his historicist approach to ontogenetic development. Chomsky was concerned that Piaget and his colleagues should address themselves to problems of the deficiency of the stimulus, problems of the kind that we sketch throughout this book and which motivate our various genetic hypotheses; he wanted the Piagetians to show how their generalized learning strategies would enable the child to circumvent the deficiency of stimulus problems. There were also two very straightforward challenges which never received an adequate answer in the course of the debate: first, Monod (p. 140)

raised the issue of children with serious impairment to their sensorimotor skills, such as paraplegics. If the development of language in the
child were closely related to sensorimotor experience, one would expect paraplegics to have a distorted language development; there is no
evidence that this is so. Second, Mehler (p. 350) pointed out that generally the Piagetian approach offered a series of static models describing the stages of a child's cognitive development, but the theory never
accounts for what makes a child pass from one stage to the next.

The idea that cognitive structure is undifferentiated and homogeneous does not seem very promising; in physical domains, nobody
would suggest that the visual system and the system governing the cir-
culation of the blood are determined by the same genetic regulatory
mechanisms. The possibility should not be excluded that the linguistic
principles postulated here may turn out to be special instances of principles holding over domains other than language, but before that can be
established more must be known about what kinds of principles are
needed for language acquisition to take place under normal conditions
and what kinds of principles are needed for other kinds of cognitive
development. Only then can meaningful analogies be detected. Meanwhile Hubel's view seems to be more plausible and that is what I adopt
here:

We are led to expect that each region of the central nervous system has
its own special problems that require different solutions. In vision we
are concerned with contours and directions and depth. With the auditory system, on the other hand, we can anticipate a galaxy of problems
relating to temporal interactions of sounds of different frequencies, and
it is difficult to imagine that the same neural apparatus deals with all of
these phenomena . . . for the major aspects of the brain's operation no
master solution is likely. (Hubel 1978:28)

Notes

1. Notice that the grammar does not specify what sentences will be uttered by
which speakers under which circumstances. This is a function of free will and
appropriateness and is not part of our linguistic capacity. (See Chapters 3, 6,
and 10.)

2. Such choices have little importance at this stage of research. As noted, one
works at the level of abstraction one can grasp, always bearing in mind that the
generalizations that one arrives at may hold at another level of abstraction,
over more domains. As a heuristic, one will assign to the theory of grammar
principles that seem to hold only of linguistic objects; linguists might invoke a

nongrammatical, perceptual mechanism if their generalization has an apparent analogue in, say, properties of vision.

3. See several papers, including Piaget's contributions, in Piattelli-Palmarini 1980. Also Piaget 1970 and Inhelder, Sinclair, and Bovet 1974.

Suggested Reading

For the idea of a generative grammar, the basic references are Chomsky 1955, 1957, 1965. F. J. Newmeyer's *Linguistic Theory in America: The First Quarter Century of Transformational Generative Grammar* (New York: Academic Press, 1980) gives an interesting account of the early development of generative grammar. For the view of mind adopted here, see Chomsky's review of B. F. Skinner's *Verbal Behavior*, which appeared in *Language* 35 (1958):26–58 and was reprinted in J. A. Fodor and J. J. Katz, eds. *The Structure of Language: Readings in the Philosophy of Language* (Englewood Cliffs, N.J.: Prentice-Hall, 1964). See also the debate reported in Piattelli-Palmarini 1980.

Chapter 4
Syntax

An Illustration of the Logic

If we are going to explain how a child masters a native language, we shall use working methods quite different from those usually followed in the linguistic literature. The methods must distinguish properties of the genotype from those of the phenotype in such a way that the following claim can be made: given the hypothesized genotype, exposure to the kind of linguistic experience that children have suffices to trigger the correct phenotype. This logic can be illustrated by reworking some observations of Baker (1978) concerning the pronominal *one* in English, as used in simple sentences like (1).

(1)
You bought an old box and I bought a new one.

Some technical material is needed in order to form precise descriptions and therefore a fuller and more accurate account of the logic we are pursuing.

Let us compare two grammars, two claims about the phenotype, about the knowledge eventually attained by a mature English speaker. One of these grammars will turn out to be plausible, the other not. Grammar A contains phrase structure (PS) rules like (2a), which define constituent structures, or trees, as in (3a); Grammar B contains the PS rules of (2b), yielding trees like (3b). The rules of (2a) say that a noun phrase, $\overline{\overline{N}}$, consists of a specifier (which might be an article) and a smaller noun phrase, $\overline{N}$; the $\overline{N}$ may consist of an adjective followed by either a noun or another small noun phrase, and then either a clause ($\overline{\overline{S}}$) or a prepositional phrase ($\overline{\overline{P}}$). The rules of (2b) do not use the notion of a "small noun phrase," $\overline{N}$. The grammars make different claims about the basic units: so Grammar A, but not Grammar B, entails that in an expression *the old man, old* and *man* constitute a unit in a way that *the* and *old* do not. To say that something is a unit means simply that it is something to which a rule of grammar, e.g. a transformation or a semantic rule, can apply.

(2)

a. $\bar{\bar{\text{N}}} \rightarrow \text{Spec } \bar{\text{N}}$

   $\bar{\text{N}} \rightarrow \text{Adj } \begin{Bmatrix} \bar{\text{N}} \\ \text{N} \end{Bmatrix} \begin{Bmatrix} \bar{\bar{\text{P}}} \\ \bar{\text{S}} \end{Bmatrix}$

b. $\bar{\bar{\text{N}}} \rightarrow \bar{\text{N}} \begin{Bmatrix} \bar{\bar{\text{P}}} \\ \bar{\text{S}} \end{Bmatrix}$

   $\bar{\text{N}} \rightarrow \text{Spec Adj N}$

(3)

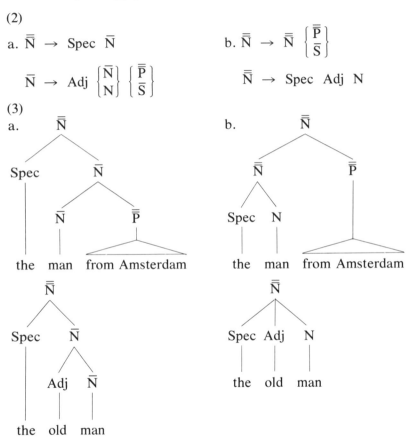

a.

b.

Assuming Grammar A, it can be stipulated that *one* may be generated under any N and that it will be interpreted as referring back to any $\bar{\text{N}}$ containing a countable noun (any noun that can occur in the plural, like *box* but not like *sincerity*). This can be formulated with a semantic interpretation rule (4).

(4)

One Interpretation

one refers to a preceding $\bar{\text{N}}$ that contains a countable noun.

Given Grammar B, *one* would also occur under any N and the interpretation rule would be identical except that *one* would refer back to a N, not to a N̄, because Grammar B does not use N̄s.

Both grammars work equally well for the generation of simple sentences like (1). Under Grammar A the sentence contains the structures of (5a) and *one* refers back to the circled N̄; under Grammar B, the structures are as in (5b) and *one* refers to the circled N. Notice that under Grammar A, rule (4) also allows *one* to refer to the larger N̄, *old box*. This would entail that the second half of (1) could mean not only the correct 'I bought a new box,' but also 'I bought a new old box,' which is senseless (except where it is taken to mean an additional old box). Again, the grammar may overgenerate, and another component of the mind, the conceptual knowledge that new old boxes do not exist, may prevent the structure from occurring.

(5)

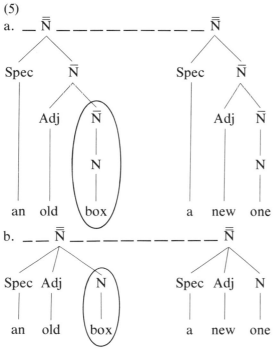

Grammar A becomes more plausible than Grammar B, however, when certain facts are considered about paraphrase and nonoccurrence, known subconsciously by every mature native speaker. Sentence (6a) may be paraphrased by (6b) or, more naturally, by (6c); and (7a) does not occur in normal English speech, unlike (7b).

(6)

a. You want a big box, but you've got the only one I have.

b. You want a big box, but you've got the only box I have.

c. You want a big box, but you've got the only big box I have.

(7)

a. *The student of chemistry was older than the one of physics.

b. The student with short hair was older than the one with long hair.

Grammar A captures these facts accurately, but Grammar B does not. Under A, *a big box* may have a structure like (8a) and *one* refers ambiguously to either $\overline{N}$; if it refers to the higher $\overline{N}$, it will correspond to (6c), and to (6b) if it refers to the lower $\overline{N}$ (it is usually easier to take the largest possible $\overline{N}$ and here to interpret (6a) like (6c), but this preference can be overridden if there is a contrastive stress on *box* or if taking the larger $\overline{N}$ gives an inconceivable logical form, as in (5a)). Under Grammar B, however, the relevant structure is (8b) and *One* Interpretation applies unambiguously to the only N, indicating that the sentence can have the meaning of (6b), but not the more natural (6c).

(8)

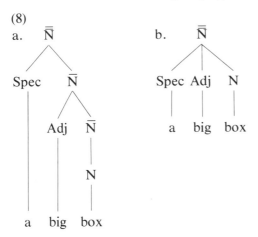

Grammar B also fails to account for the nonoccurrence of (7a), because *student of chemistry* would have to have a structure precisely parallel to *student with short hair*, there being no alternative. Therefore, if *one* can refer back to the lowest N in (9bii), it will also do so in (9bi). The PS rules of Grammar A, however, allow two different structures (9ai,ii); while *one* may refer back to *student* in (9aii), it cannot refer back to *student* in (9ai) because there is no $\overline{N}$ containing only *student*.[1]

(9)
a.

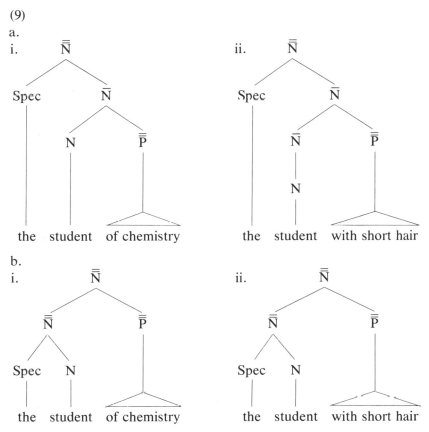

b.

Here is the problem: Grammar A and not Grammar B seems to represent part of the linguistic knowledge eventually attained by adults, because it accounts well for the facts that seem to be relevant; how, then, is it arrived at? I have claimed that both grammars work equally well for simple sentences like (1) and (7b), and these are the kind of data available to children. Data about paraphrase and nonoccurrence are crucial for choosing A over B, but these data are not available systematically to children developing their language: children are not informed that (7a) does not occur and that (6a) can mean the same as (6b) or (6c), although they eventually come to know this automatically, without instruction. Therefore one cannot say that children select Grammar A on the basis of the facts we have just discussed, and so the choice is not determined by the facts to which they have access. Children would need evidence that *one* refers back to a N̄, more than just a

N, and therefore that (4) is the correct version of the rule; this evidence does not seem to exist in normal childhood experience.

One can imagine evidence that *would* force the child to the correct choice. Sentence (10a) would not suffice because, regardless of whether Heidi actually has a big or a small cup, the sentence could always be interpreted as specifying only that Heidi has some cup regardless of size (with *one* referring only to the N *cup*).

(10)
a. Kirsten has a big cup, and Heidi has one too.
b. Kirsten has a blue cup, but Heidi doesn't have one.

Sentence (10b), however, would suffice if uttered in a situation where Heidi has a cup that is some color other than blue; only the interpretation with *one* representing *blue cup* would be consistent with the facts. Such events might occur but they would be rare in the child's early experience and are too contrived to constitute part of the primary data that trigger the eventual grammar for every English-speaking child.

This suggests that something makes Grammar B unavailable and drives the child to Grammar A, when exposed to just a few simple sentences of the kind that any child certainly encounters. The desired effect will be obtained if one hypothesizes the constraints of (11), where (11a) and (11b) limit the available PS rules and (11c) limits the form of semantic rules, barring an interpretation rule that refers to a nonphrasal category like N. These will be statements in the theory of grammar, restricting the options for grammars of particular languages.

(11)
a. $\bar{\text{N}}$ consists of a Specifier and $\bar{\text{N}}$, with the order to be specified for each particular grammar.
b. $\bar{\text{N}}$ consists obligatorily of N or $\bar{\text{N}}$ and an optional Adj, $\bar{\bar{\text{P}}}$, or $\bar{\text{S}}$ with the order to be specified for each particular grammar.
c. Rules dealing with reference apply only to major categories (categories that may contain a phrase, that is, more than a single word).

Postulating the constraints of (11) as part of the child's genetic endowment yields an explanation of how the child can arrive at the correct structures through exposure to only minimal primary data. Under this view the child has to learn through experience that in English *one* is a pronominal element, that specifiers precede the $\bar{\text{N}}$, and that a noun is optionally preceded by an adjective or followed by a preposition phrase or a clause; the rest is given. The child can learn that *one* is a pronoun in English by hearing a sentence like (1) and realizing that I bought a box. Similarly, exposure to phrases like *the man from Amsterdam* and *the man who lives in Amsterdam* will suffice for the child to learn that English specifiers precede the noun and "satellites" like preposition phrases and relative clauses follow it. This experience will allow the child to fix the parameters of (11a) and (11b).

Of course, there is more to acquiring English than this: the child must identify sounds, words, and categories like noun; but the syntactic structures are part of the problem. With such a theory Grammar A is selected without further experience and Grammar B is not even entertained as a possibility; that is, it is not an available option. The child must analyze sentence (1) in accordance with (11), which is a genetically given template. With such restrictions, the correct grammar is triggered by a small environmental stimulus. Therefore children need not be thrown off course by any ill-formed or incomplete sentences they may encounter; they attain the ability to deal with an infinite range of noun phrases on the basis of exposure to just a few sentences; they are already equipped with knowledge of structural principles for which there is no evidence in the primary data they encounter and therefore they do not deduce those principles from data; they make only a narrow range of decisions and therefore only a narrow range of errors. To get the correct structures, the children have to decide whether in their language the specifiers are at the front or at the back of the noun phrase and whether the optional satellites precede or follow the nucleus noun; these parameters need to be fixed and the rest is given. A child can thus acquire the correct grammar in a short time without training, and the salient facts of acquisition are explained.

But how deep is this explanation? The constraints of (11) impose restrictions on available grammars, but my reasoning is based so far on a relatively small circle: it is limited to one set of facts concerning one phenomenon in English and I have set up some constraints that enable me to provide an explanation of the desired kind for those particular facts. In postulating such constraints, analysts must meet two immediate requirements that tie their hands rather tightly: the constraints must be specific enough to provide an explanation for the relevant facts of the language under investigation, facts of grammaticality, ambiguity, paraphrase, coreference and a host of other things, and also general enough to hold of everybody's grammar, regardless of language. The *one* facts could have been explained by claiming that the PS rules of (2a) were part of the genetic equipment, but that would have been too specific and would have been refuted on finding a grammar, like those of French speakers, that requires adjectives to be generated in post-nominal position. Given these requirements, the problem lies not in choosing between various accounts that work, but in finding just one theory of grammar that meets the empirical demands.

A productive research program will yield hypotheses like (11), which turn out to participate in explanations for a wide range of facts in a wide range of languages and to require grammars that provide insightful accounts of facts from language pathology, historical change, and so on. In that way the circle of reasoning will be enlarged. Analysts should always be ready to reformulate constraints in order to achieve deeper levels of explanation and to pursue those reformulations wherever necessary, abandoning a particular formulation only in the face of clear evidence and never on the basis of "gut feeling" that "genetic encoding couldn't look like that," since what the genes encode is exactly what we are trying to find out.

Phrase Structure Rules

Constraints (11a) and (b) hold of the available phrase structure rules. As indicated in the general model on page 39, these rules yield an initial phrase marker,[2] which specifies the basic units of analysis: it provides a constituent structure with category labels, and then lexical entries (very roughly, words) are inserted by rules which I shall discuss in a later section. The trees of (3a) are examples of parts of initial phrase markers. The PS rules, like all other rules of grammar, cannot be postulated in arbitrary fashion for each new language analyzed; they must meet certain requirements, of which (11a) and (b) are special cases. I shall now pursue these constraints a little further and show how we can reach some deductive depth in our theorizing.

Before considering what kinds of PS rules are available for human grammars, a note on the evidence for a particular set of rules is in order. The rules define units, or constituents, and these are the material that later rules (transformational, semantic, and phonological) need so as to work properly. Therefore the vast majority of the evidence for a particular set of rules is grammar-internal. Another kind of evidence has to do with how people perceive sentences, however. In so-called click experiments, which achieved a certain amount of notoriety, Fodor, Bever, and Garrett (1974) presented subjects wearing headphones with a tape-recorded sentence in one ear and a click noise in the other ear. The click occurred at some point in the sentence and subjects were asked to indicate where in the sentence they heard it. The subjects tended to hear the clicks at major constituent breaks, as defined by the usual kind of PS rules. They perceived the clicks in these positions even where in fact the click occurred at a nonmajor constituent break or in the middle of a word. These experiments have been taken as support for the kinds of PS rules that I shall invoke here, but it must be said that this kind of evidence is rather controversial. For some discussion of the controversies, see Fodor, Bever and Garrett (1974) and Clark and Clark (1977).

According to the logic outlined earlier, the theory of grammar prescribes the most restrictive possible template for PS rules in order to account for how such rules might arise in the course of a child's development. A general schema like (12) is a restrictive and plausible hypothesis, where X represents any lexical category: noun, verb, preposition, adjective, or adverb. The bars indicate the dominance relations, $\bar{\bar{X}}$ containing $\bar{X}$, and $\bar{X}$ in turn containing X. This template allows an English speaker's grammar to have the PS rules of (13) and (14). So an English noun phrase (13) has three levels of structure: the whole noun phrase $\bar{\bar{N}}$ consists of a specifier followed by a smaller noun phrase $\bar{N}$; $\bar{N}$ consists of a nucleus N or another $\bar{N}$, and then (optionally) a satellite. Similarly for an English verb phrase. Schema (12) claims that one particular satellite structure is always available for all phrases in all grammars: any nucleus—that is, any noun, verb, preposition, adjective, or adverb—can have a satellite, which can be any major category or a clause (the curly brackets indicate the option). Like the specifier, this satellite structure may precede the nucleus in some grammars or follow it in others, depending on the data that the child encounters. That ordering option is indicated by the angled brackets.

(12)

$$\bar{\bar{X}} \rightarrow \langle \text{Spec } \bar{X} \rangle$$

$$\bar{X} \rightarrow \langle \begin{Bmatrix} \bar{X} \\ X \end{Bmatrix} \begin{Bmatrix} \bar{\bar{X}} \\ \bar{\bar{S}} \end{Bmatrix} \rangle$$

Schema (12) would allow a particular grammar to have the PS rules of (13) and (14), which provide the initial structure of noun phrases and verb phrases. Similar expansions would be available for prepositional, adjectival, and adverbial phrases. Grammars also have a rule expanding S (sentence) as $\bar{\bar{N}}$ AUX $\bar{\bar{V}}$, where AUX specifies the tense and modality. These PS rules allow an initial phrase marker like (15), on the assumption that a specifier in a noun phrase may contain an article, demonstrative, or a genitive noun phrase (*the mayor's desk*) and that a specifier in a verb phrase may contain perfective (*have*) or progressive (*be*) markers (or both: *John has been reading*). I use Det (Determiner) to indicate an article or demonstrative.

(13)

$$\bar{\bar{N}} \rightarrow \text{Spec } \bar{N}$$

$$\bar{N} \rightarrow \text{Adj} \begin{Bmatrix} \bar{N} \\ N \end{Bmatrix} \begin{Bmatrix} \bar{\bar{X}} \\ S \end{Bmatrix}$$

$$\text{Spec} \rightarrow \begin{Bmatrix} \text{Det} \\ \bar{\bar{N}} \end{Bmatrix}$$

(14)

$$\bar{\bar{V}} \rightarrow \text{Spec } \bar{V}$$

$$\bar{V} \rightarrow \begin{Bmatrix} \bar{V} \\ V \end{Bmatrix} \begin{Bmatrix} \bar{\bar{X}} \\ S \end{Bmatrix}$$

$$\text{Spec} \rightarrow \text{Perfective Progressive}$$

Tree (15) is an *abstract* structure in the sense that it conveys a lot of information that is not immediately available, least of all available through the mere sound of a sentence. To some extent speakers have intuitive ideas about the proper constituent structure, some of which are taught in schools under the rubric of "parsing" or "sentence diagramming." So, for a famous example, a phrase like *old men and women* is ambiguous in that *old* may refer just to *men* or to *men and women*. This ambiguity can be expressed structurally through constituent structure: in one reading *old* and *men* are a unit, a constituent; in the other reading *men and women* make up a unit and *old* refers to that whole constituent. Likewise most schoolchildren are taught about subjects and predicates. But here we are not talking only about the constituent structure of sentences but about abstract structures like (15), which is not a sentence. Certain changes must be made to it before it can be made into an ordinary sentence: an *of* needs to be inserted between [picture]$_N$ and the following $\bar{\bar{N}}$, and an apostrophe *s* needs to be added to [the mayor]$_{\bar{\bar{N}}}$. If those changes are made, we shall derive the sentence *Those clerks have put the picture of Reagan right on the mayor's desk*. But other changes could be made: [the picture Reagan]$_{\bar{\bar{N}}}$ could be made into *Reagan's picture*, for example. These changes are effected by transformational and morphological rules, and (15) is the initial phrase marker for several different sentences.

The rules (13) and (14) are both recursive in that they characterize an infinite number of noun and verb phrases. So in (13) $\bar{N}$ can always be rewritten with another $\bar{N}$, indefinitely. If we make this move three times, we can derive a complex noun phrase *the man from Amsterdam with long hair whom I met*. This is one large noun phrase with the internal structure of (16).

(15)

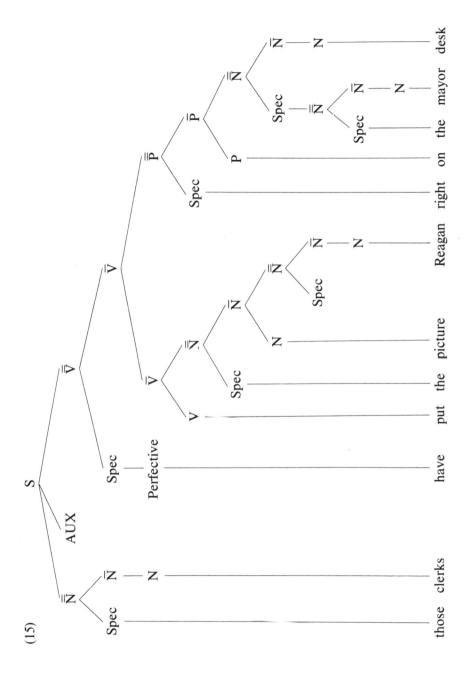

(16)

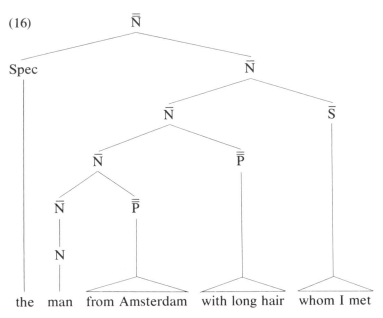

This is a complex noun phrase and the rules of (13) allow speakers to produce much bigger ones, even an indefinitely big one. In fact no one does this because of limitations of time and memory capacity, but limitations of this kind are not a function especially of linguistic capacity; they affect many other areas of life. They are therefore not part of our grammars, since grammars express our full *linguistic* capacity disregarding limitations that may be imposed by other aspects of human makeup.

The conventions of (12) provide a template for the available PS rules, restricting their form in grammars of particular individuals and disallowing the rules of (2b) and many others that one might imagine. The constraints of (11) are special instances of (12), where I have stated things more generally and more accurately. These templates are part of the theory of grammar and not part of particular grammars; rather, they allow a certain range of particular grammars by stipulating the available options. The conventions do not fully determine the shape of PS rules, but they provide the parameters, which have to be fixed by each child. For example, the angled brackets indicate that the order of the specifier and the nucleus has to be fixed and this is a way in which grammars may vary, some grammars having $\overline{\overline{N}} \rightarrow$ Spec $\overline{N}$ like English, others having $\overline{\overline{N}} \rightarrow \overline{N}$ Spec, where articles follow the noun (Kikuyu, a Bantu language of East Africa, seems to have this order but it is not common). Moreover the inventory of categories may vary from grammar to grammar, although within narrow limits. So some grammars seem not to have a distinct class of prepositions; in languages like Yoruba, for example, one often translates an English preposition with some kind of verbal expression: *He visited Rome with Mary* might come out along the lines of 'He visited Rome accompanied Mary.' There are other possible variations in the shape of PS rules as well.

The PS rules of (13) allow an adjective to occur before a N or $\bar{\text{N}}$, but the conventions of (12) say nothing about possible adjective positions. This is appropriate because PS templates stipulate the basic geometry of categorial structures; this basic geometry can be supplemented in response to experience. The position of adjectives is fully determined by a normal child's experience; exposure to phrases like *the tall student* will suffice to show that English $\bar{\text{N}}$'s can have adjectives at their front. As far as I can see, there is no deficiency of stimulus problem for such adjectives, which would require a richer system of PS templates in the theory of grammar. This analysis stems from viewing the theory of grammar, including PS templates, not as a means of capturing regularities but as part of a solution to the problem of language acquisition, as we have defined it. Languages may have many regularities having nothing to do with the genotype; all languages have a word for 'arm' but this has to do with the structure of our bodies and the way in which we view them and presumably nothing to do with genetically determined properties of grammars.

Talking of accidental regularities, grammars of English happen to be symmetrical in that for all categories they have the specifier preceding the nucleus (17) and all satellites following it (18).

(17)	(18)
[*the* dog]$_{\bar{\bar{\text{N}}}}$	[the picture *of Reagan*]$_{\bar{\bar{\text{N}}}}$
[*has* gone]$_{\bar{\bar{\text{V}}}}$	[lies *on the table*]$_{\bar{\bar{\text{V}}}}$
[*right* to his kennel]$_{\bar{\bar{\text{P}}}}$	[on *the table*]$_{\bar{\bar{\text{P}}}}$
[*completely* red]$_{\overline{\overline{\text{Adj}}}}$	[obvious *to Mary*]$_{\overline{\overline{\text{Adj}}}}$
[*fully* naturally]$_{\overline{\overline{\text{Adv}}}}$	[happily *for John*]$_{\overline{\overline{\text{Adv}}}}$

There is no necessary reason for there to be such harmonies between the categories. In the language lottery are languages, like some of the Dravidian group, that do not have this symmetry; thus verbal specifiers follow the verb, while nominal specifiers such as articles precede the nucleus noun (that is, one finds sentences of the form *John gone has* but noun phrases like *the house*). People interested in language types and particularly in harmonies between categories describe languages without the English kind of symmetry as unusual and transitional, assuming them to be in the process of changing from one type to another. Some people have suggested that the templates of (12) should be supplemented to express the idea that grammars must have the same kind of cross-category symmetry as English unless there is specific evidence to the contrary. That is, a child can postulate two asymmetrical rules $\bar{\bar{N}} \rightarrow$ Spec $\bar{N}$ and $\bar{\bar{V}} \rightarrow \bar{V}$ Spec only if there is a special kind of evidence in the trigger experience that demands these rules. However, it is hard to see how supplementing (12) in this way (assuming that one can find some precise and successful formulation along those lines) would contribute anything to explaining the acquisition of some particular language. Suppose it is the case that, say, 75 percent of the world's languages have the symmetry of English and 25 percent do not have it, or at least do not have it across the board for all categories. The theory of grammar must allow for both classes of grammars since both occur. Weighting the theory of grammar in favor of the symmetrical grammars may help to account for the typologist's percentages, but it must still allow for the asymmetrical grammars to occur; presumably people "learn" those minority grammars naturally and successfully and do not suffer from it for the rest of their lives. At this stage it seems a better strategy to focus attention on invariant properties of grammars that allow the child to circumvent the problems of deficiency of the stimulus. If it is the case that there are more grammars with cross-category symmetry than without, it is hard to see what consequences that has for the hypotheses about the grammatical genotype. This is not to say that there are no consequences but simply to urge caution in interpreting cross-language statistical surveys.

A similar caution is needed in physical biology when interpreting cross-species surveys. Just as there may be more symmetrical than asymmetrical grammars, so in the physical world there may be more species with antennae than with retinal receivers, perhaps in a 3:1 ratio. This may turn out to be fully or partially explicable through genetic considerations (like Mendel's ratios for axial and terminal pea plants), but a theorist would not be content to build in a simple weighting factor to a theory of genetics in order to "predict" the relevant percentages. This is a complex issue that deserves a fuller treatment than can be given here.

With regard to cross-language surveys, it is important to realize one moral of the discussion of the English pronoun *one:* to determine the correct PS rules requires careful analysis carried out from a particular point of view. Languages do not wear their PS rules on their sleeves, nor can a linguist take a quick look at a couple of traditional grammars to find out what the correct rules are. Although many linguists have analyzed many languages from many different points of view and with different goals in mind, relatively few languages have been subjected to anything like the intensity of analysis that has been directed at English, French, Dutch, and Italian. An increasing amount of cross-language research is now conducted from the biological perspective. Perhaps this work will help to shed light on the parameters of (12) that have to be fixed for each particular language. Whether or not (12) is the correct convention depends on whether it is compatible with the optimal, or most readily attainable, grammar for each language. That in turn will require a great deal of work and analysis, refining and improving hypotheses constantly.

Before we leave PS templates, note that PS rules overgenerate in the sense that they provide the *total* set of positions for lexical categories. Individual lexical items will also be subcategorized for the particular frame in which they may occur. So a PS rule like (14) specifies that a verb may occur to the left of $\bar{\bar{N}}$, $\bar{V}$, $\bar{\bar{P}}$, $\overline{\overline{Adj}}$, $\overline{\overline{Adv}}$, $\bar{S}$, or zero. Any particular verb may have a more limited distribution and its lexical entry contains a subcategorization, specifying its co-occurrence possibilities. *Believe* may occur before a $\bar{\bar{N}}$ (*believe the story*), a $\bar{\bar{P}}$ (*believe in marriage*), a $\bar{S}$ (*believe that the marriage will work*), or before zero (*the Pope believes*), but *go* is more limited and occurs only before a $\bar{\bar{P}}$ or zero. *The, both, each,* may occur in a Spec that occurs in front of a $\bar{N}$; *have* occurs in a Spec in front of a $\bar{V}$.

Unlike verbs, English nouns can never be followed by $\bar{\bar{N}}$ in surface structure. However, the PS rules do not generate surface structures directly; they generate initial structures which can be amended by transformational rules. [[Picture]$_N$ [Reagan]$_{\bar{\bar{N}}}$]$_{\bar{\bar{N}}}$ is a perfectly well-formed initial structure that underlies the phrase *picture of Reagan* or *Reagan's picture,* depending on what changes are made in the initial tree before it reaches its phonetic form. The nonoccurrence of *the picture Reagan* as a phonetic form follows from other principles, which have to do with the general requirement that all nouns must have "case" and the language-particular fact that English nouns do not assign case to their objects (see Chomsky 1981b, Lightfoot 1981a, who develop an idea of Jean-Roger Vergnaud's). This is another example of various aspects of the system interacting in specified ways, or of modularity.

We are now some distance from (11). I attributed the constraints of (11) to the genetic endowment in order to explain how children might attain what seems to be the right description of English *one* by exposure to only limited data. The purpose has been to show how to go about devising a system with a rich internal structure, providing a highly restrictive template for PS rules and subsuming the PS constraints of (11) in a wider ranging framework. Hypothesis (11) was based on a detailed examination of some facts from one language, carefully distinguishing the subset of facts to which children have access; we aim toward general constraints like (12), which, it is hoped, will entail the most readily attainable grammar for every language. This is the empirical base for the present investigation.

Of course, the acquisition of noun phrases involves more than fixing the parameters of (12). Children have to be able to distinguish certain categories, figuring out that *old* is an adjective and *the* an article, say. Indeed they have to be able to distinguish words and basic units of sound. PS templates say nothing about these aspects of the problem and solve only part of the acquisition problem. It is a reasonable strategy to divide the overall problem into small, solvable problems, and it is to be hoped that a similar approach, focusing intensely on the deficiency of the stimulus, will cast light on how children come to distinguish words and how they assign category membership. In Chapter 9 we shall look at some work that complements these hypotheses on PS templates by illuminating what is involved in our ability to distinguish categories.

Transformational Rules

The PS rules and the rules that insert lexical material together generate an initial phrase marker, which may then be transformed in certain ways. A transformational rule operates on the basic units provided by the PS rules and changes an abstract phrase marker into another phrase marker, moving a unit, or constituent, to another position. It does *not,* as is sometimes said, change a sentence into another sentence. It has a *structural description* specifying the class of phrase markers to which it applies and a statement of the effect on an arbitrary member of this class. The structural description may specify what is to move and where it may move.

Transformations, like PS rules, share certain properties that are by no means logically necessary and for which there is no systematic evidence in the experience of a child acquiring a first language. An often cited example concerns a rule relating a statement *The book on the shelf is dull* to a corresponding question *Is the book on the shelf dull?* Such a rule has the effect of moving *is* to the front in this particular example. The issue is: how is this rule to be stated? The rule might be stated in *structure-dependent* fashion, moving *is* over the subject noun phrase, here *the book on the shelf;* a structure-dependent rule uses units provided by the PS rules—units in the phrase marker. Alternatively the rule might be *structure-independent,* making no reference to structural notions like *noun phrase* but being sensitive only to the sequence of words; such a rule might simply identify the first *is* and move it to the front.

Although both proposals are adequate for the simple cases, a slightly more complex case necessitates the first option and therefore demonstrates the need for the kind of analysis that PS rules provide. In (19) the structure-independent rule would move the first *is* to the front and yield the nonoccurring (20); the structure-dependent rule would identify *the book which is on the shelf* as a noun phrase and would move *is* from the position immediately to its right, yielding correctly (21).

(19)
The book which is on the shelf is dull.

(20)
*Is the book which _____ on the shelf is dull?

(21)
Is [the book which is on the shelf]$_{\bar{N}}$ _____ dull?

The structure-dependent formulation is not logically necessary, nor is it simpler or communicatively more effective. In fact, if we were designing a language for use by a computer, we might prefer structure-independent operations; they would be simpler for the machine, which would merely scan the words of the sentence and ignore abstract structures not manifested in the acoustic signal. Also, in a child's normal experience there is no real evidence for the structure-dependent formulation: children are not systematically told that (20) does not occur, least of all that it is "ungrammatical." Nonetheless, despite lack of an environmental stimulus for structure dependence and despite the simplicity of the structure-independent formulation, children invariably use the structure-dependent operation when first uttering questions of this kind; questions like (20) simply do not occur and are not among the "errors" made by children. Example (20) represents another instance of an ordinary-looking inductive generalization that is not in fact made. Moreover, wherever grammars have movement rules they are structure dependent, suggesting that this is an invariant property. If this is invariant and not deducible directly from childhood experience, it is reasonable to suppose that structure dependence is part of what the mind brings to the analysis of experience, not something hypothesized on the basis of evidence; structure-independent rules are simply not available.

Structure dependence is a restriction on the possible form of a transformational rule, a requirement that structural descriptions be stated in terms of phrasal categories of the type provided by the PS rules. A transformation may be said to specify a category to be moved and a position where it will end up. An analyst states this as straightforwardly as possible, bearing in mind that introducing complexities into a rule requires showing how those complexities can be triggered by the kind of data to which any child has access. Some of the so-called transformations in the linguistic literature, even in introductory textbooks, are enormously complex and unattainable under normal childhood conditions, but they are postulated by people who do not subscribe to the goals outlined here or do not take them seriously.

A restriction on the way that transformations function (as opposed to their form) lies in the structure-preservation principle, formulated by Emonds (1976). This stipulates that transformations fall into three classes, being root, local, or structure preserving. *Root transformations* effect drastic changes but they apply only in root sentences, that is, to a topmost S or to a S immediately dominated by a topmost S, broadly speaking main clauses. A *local transformation* affects only a sequence C′-C or C-C′, where C is a non-phrase-node and C′ is an immediately adjacent constituent; the rule permutes the two items, is insensitive to any condition exterior to this sequence, and can apply in main and subordinate clauses. An example is a rule that moves a quantifier like *all* to the right of an AUX, relating *We all can speak Russian* to *We can all speak Russian*. A *structure-preserving* transformation moves a constituent into a position in a phrase marker dominated by the same category node. Such a transformation may move a $\bar{\bar{N}}$ to an empty $\bar{\bar{N}}$

position, a $\bar{P}$ into a $\bar{\bar{P}}$, but not a $\bar{\bar{N}}$ into a $\bar{P}$ or vice versa; such a rule may apply in any clause type. So a rule applying to a subordinate clause will be either local (a small class of rules) or structure preserving. If English has the PS rules of the preceding section, an inversion rule moving AUX to the front of a clause (see (3) of Chapter 3) would be a root transformation; the rule would derive *must John leave* from an initial *John must leave*. It would be a root transformation because neither is the rule local nor does it move AUX into a position where the PS rules allow AUX to be generated; the PS rules do not generate AUX in clause-initial position but only between $\bar{\bar{N}}$ and $\bar{\bar{V}}$. This inversion rule therefore does not apply in subordinate clauses: *I asked whether John must leave* and not **I asked whether must John leave*. Compare this to a rule that moves a $\bar{\bar{N}}$ to a position where the PS rules do allow a $\bar{\bar{N}}$ to occur. For example (15) contains a noun phrase consisting of Spec[[picture]$_\text{N}$ [Reagan]$_{\bar{\bar{N}}}$]$_{\bar{N}}$. Here [Reagan]$_{\bar{\bar{N}}}$ could move to the Specifier position because the PS rules (13) allow a $\bar{\bar{N}}$ to occur in a Specifier to a $\bar{N}$. If *Reagan* moves to the Specifier position, the result (with insertion of *'s*) is *Reagan's picture*. The rule effecting this movement is structure preserving and therefore it can occur in any clause type. If this definition of rule types follows from human genetic structure, then the child can attain PS rules and know automatically that an AUX movement rule cannot apply in subordinate clauses and therefore that **I asked whether must John leave* does not occur.

To illustrate another way to restrict the way that transformations function consider the sentence *John kept the car in the garage,* mentioned earlier. This ambiguous sentence can have one of two constituent structures: (22a) correlates with the locational meaning that the garage was where John kept the car, but (22b) has the adjectival meaning that John kept the car that was in the garage, where *in the garage* is a satellite modifying *car*. The corresponding question *What did John keep in the garage?* and the passive *the car was kept in the garage* are unambiguous and have only the locational and not the adjectival reading. Examples (23a) and (24a) are interpretable surface structures, where *what* and *the car* have moved from the positions indicated; they have a locational meaning. On the other hand, in (23b) and (24b) *what* and *the car* have moved from a position inside the bigger $\bar{\bar{N}}$; such surface structures are not well-formed, cannot be interpreted, and have no meaning.

(22)
a. John [kept [the car]$_{\bar{N}}$ [in the garage]$_{\bar{P}}$]$_{\bar{V}}$
b. John kept [the car in the garage]$_{\bar{\bar{N}}}$

(23)
a. what did John [keep _____ [in the garage]$_{\bar{P}}$]$_{\bar{V}}$
b. what did John keep [_____ in the garage]$_{\bar{\bar{N}}}$

(24)
a. the car [was kept _____ [in the garage]$_{\bar{P}}$]$_{\bar{V}}$
b. the car was kept [_____ in the garage]$_{\bar{\bar{N}}}$

Presumably children attain a movement rule that yields (23a) and (24a), but it is unlikely that they have sufficient evidence in their linguistic experience for formulating a rule that does not also yield (23b) and (24b). Children hear sentences like *What did John keep in the garage?*, but it is hard to imagine what systematically available evidence would indicate that this could mean only (23a) and not (23b). Therefore it would not be appropriate to analyze an individual's acquired grammar as having a rule rich enough to distinguish between the (a) and (b) structures. Rather, it seems that children attain a simple movement rule and that some other principle blocks the derivation of (23b) and (24b). That principle might say that a $\bar{\bar{N}}$ cannot be extracted from within a larger $\bar{N}$. As linguists we can see that a principle along these lines is plausible, but there is no evidence for such a principle in the restricted data base that makes up a child's linguistic experience. Again, the correct analysis does not follow only from the data normally available to the child.

In such situations the analyst always seeks to hypothesize independent principles that would enable the child to obtain the correct analysis when exposed to some simple sentences and without further instruction or exposure to exotic experience. For these examples a principle might be postulated forbidding extraction of a $\bar{\bar{N}}$ from within another $\bar{\bar{N}}$. Call this the Maximalization Principle. If a transformation applies to any category, it must apply to the maximal phrase of that type.

If such a principle were part of the child's genetic equipment, no further evidence would be needed to know that the derivations of (23b) and (24b) do not exist in English. It would also follow that none of (25) would occur, where the italicized $\bar{\bar{N}}$ has been moved from within another $\bar{\bar{N}}$. The structures of (25) do not occur in adult speech nor in the "errors" made by young children.

(25)
John stole [pictures of _____]$_{\bar{\bar{N}}}$
John was bought [_____ house]$_{\bar{\bar{N}}}$
John was believed [the claim that Fred saw _____]$_{\bar{\bar{N}}}$
John was met [the woman who invited _____]$_{\bar{\bar{N}}}$
whose did you buy [_____ house]$_{\bar{\bar{N}}}$
who do you believe [the claim that John saw _____]$_{\bar{\bar{N}}}$
who did you meet [the woman who invited _____]$_{\bar{\bar{N}}}$

Sentences like (26) are apparent counterexamples to the Maximalization Principle, seeming to manifest structures like those of (25). There are reasons to suppose that the initial phrase markers underlying (26) include nesting structures like those of (25) (where a $\bar{\bar{N}}$ is contained within another $\bar{\bar{N}}$) but that a reanalysis rule transforms these to (27), wherein *who* is no longer contained in a larger $\bar{\bar{N}}$. Now *who* can be moved to the front without violating the Maximalization Principle. Indeed, if something like the Maximalization Principle is correct, the child would need some sort of reanalysis process in order to analyze and to make sense of sentences like (26). The reanalysis rule changes the constituent membership in a phrase marker and would need to be formulated in such a way that it could apply to the structures of (26) but not to (22b) or (25).

(26)
who did you see [pictures of _____]$_{\bar{\bar{N}}}$
who did you write [a book about _____]$_{\bar{\bar{N}}}$
who did you make [the claim that Fred saw _____]$_{\bar{\bar{N}}}$

(27)
you saw [pictures]$_{\bar{\bar{N}}}$ [of who]$_{\bar{\bar{P}}}$
you wrote [a book]$_{\bar{\bar{N}}}$ [about who]$_{\bar{\bar{P}}}$
you [made the claim]$_{V}$ [that Fred saw who]$_{\bar{S}}$

Noting these examples as potential problems, let us proceed to seek better explanations judged by the usual criteria, seeking perhaps greater coverage of data or deeper principles that will subsume the existing principles as special and less accurate cases. A reanalysis rule has much to recommend it, but there are some residual problems dealt with in the technical literature. On the other hand, it would be wasteful simply to abandon such explanations as we have on the spurious grounds that there are some facts that they do not account for.

So far I have assumed that a transformation can designate an item to be moved and the target position. One might speculate that the form of transformational rules is even more restricted than I have suggested so far. Suppose, for example, that a child can hypothesize nothing richer than (28) as a transformational rule, where categories are defined in the PS rules.

(28)
Move category.

If we focus on the movement of $\bar{\bar{N}}$, we can see that it follows from the structure-preservation principle that in nonroot clauses a $\bar{\bar{N}}$ may move only into another $\bar{\bar{N}}$ position as provided by the PS rules (which, recall, are themselves heavily constrained in their possible form). The movements of (23b), (24b), and (25) are precluded by the Maximalization Principle, which is a condition on how rules may function.

Consider now sentences where a $\bar{\bar{N}}$ is extracted from a lower clause. The extractions of (29a,b) are precluded by the Maximalization Principle because the $\bar{\bar{N}}$ *Susan* has been moved from within a larger $\bar{\bar{N}}$. But if a general rule like (28) is postulated, there are no means so far for distinguishing the grammatical (29c) from the ungrammatical (29d,e). The Maximalization Principle says nothing about these examples because here *Susan* has not been moved out of a bigger $\bar{\bar{N}}$.[3]

(29)
a. *Susan* was transmitted [the message [for _____ to leave]$_S$]$_{\bar{\bar{N}}}$
b. *Susan* is expected [[pictures of _____]$_{\bar{N}}$ to be on sale]$_S$
c. *Susan* is expected [_____ to win]$_S$
d. *Susan* is expected [_____ will win]$_S$
e. *Susan* is expected [Mary to see _____]$_S$

The structural description of (28) might be enriched so that the rule will apply in (29c) but not in (29d,e), but this would be a bad first move (although this *was* the kind of move taken in much of the early work on transformational grammar). The enriched structural description would hold of a rule in the particular grammar of English and would therefore constitute part of what emerges in children on exposure to experience, part of what they "learn." But the evidence that analysts can use for this enrichment is not available to young children because it consists partly of judgments about nonoccurring sentences. If we, as analysts, take our fundamental goal seriously, we should pursue another course, as is now familiar.

Suppose that (28) is part of the mature native speaker's knowledge of English and that the nonoccurrence of (29d,e) was not part of the linguistic experience that triggered the development of the grammar. Therefore the nonexistence of (29d,e) will result either from the universal principles that constitute part of the human genetic endowment or from properties of the particular grammar that *are* triggered by available linguistic experience.

As a first guess, a universal principle might be postulated saying no rule may move anything from a lower clause that is either finite ((29d); compare the nonfinite (29c)) or contains a subject (29e)—that is, a subject other than what is being moved. A more formal and more accurate statement of the principle is (30).

(30)
In a configuration ...X... [...Y...]$_S$, no rule may involve X and Y, where
    (i) S is a finite clause
or (ii) S contains a subject other than Y.

With this universal principle, the simple rule (28) will yield (29c), where the movement violates neither (i) nor (ii) of (30). It will yield neither (29d), precluded by (30i), nor (29e), precluded by (30ii). This is a perfectly adequate explanation for the facts so far discussed. However, the circle of reasoning is very small and it remains to be seen whether (30) can be sustained as a universal principle.

In fact, there are problems for (30) as soon as we consider questions where a *wh* word occurs at the front of the sentence. The questions of (31) are analogous to (29c-e) and the grammaticality judgments are parallel, suggesting that (30) may be right. But compare (32), where *who* originates in a finite clause (b) and in a clause containing a subject (c), but where the resulting structures nonetheless correspond to acceptable sentences. In (32) *who* moves not to a subject position, but to the front of the clause, to the position called COMP (read as "complementizer"). This position occurs at the front of every clause and is dominated by $\bar{\bar{S}}$. The PS rules thus include $\bar{\bar{S}} \rightarrow$ COMP S in addition to the now familiar S $\rightarrow \bar{\bar{N}}$ AUX $\bar{\bar{V}}$. So the structure of (32a) would be [[who]$_{COMP}$ [you expect ...]$_S$]$_{\bar{\bar{S}}}$.

(31)
a. who is expected [_____ to win]
b. *who is expected [_____ will win]
c. *who is expected [Mary to see _____]

(32)

a. who do you expect [_____ to win]
b. who do you expect [_____ will win]
c. who do you expect [Mary to see _____]

It seems that we must distinguish between movement to the subject of a higher passive verb ((29c–e), (31)), and movement to the front of a higher active clause. Movement of *Susan* or *who* to the subject position of a passive verb like *is expected* is impossible from out of a finite clause or over an intervening subject. This is not so if *who* is moved to the higher COMP position in the front of the clause, as in (32). Somehow this distinction must be made, and presumably it must be made on principled—universal—grounds, because the relevant data include the fact that certain sentences do not occur and such data are ex hypothesi not available to the child.

Given the PS rules postulated earlier, the initial structures of (29e) or (31c) and (32c) will be as in (33) and (34), and the successful movements of (34) would be as indicated. Let us suppose that when an element moves to COMP, first, it leaves behind something that is a *variable* in logical form (35), and second, on any subsequent movement it can only move to another COMP (that is, COMP is a kind of quantifier position). This permits the successive movements of (34), which violate no principles. But in (33) movement of *who* to the lower COMP, then into the higher $\bar{\bar{N}}$ and then into the higher COMP is now impossible; movement of either *who* or *Susan* direct to the subject $\bar{\bar{N}}$ would violate (30ii).

(33)

COMP $\bar{\bar{N}}$ is expected [COMP [Mary to see $\begin{Bmatrix} \text{who} \\ \text{Susan} \end{Bmatrix}$]$_S$]$_{\bar{S}}$

(34)

COMP you expect [COMP [Mary to see who]$_S$]$_{\bar{S}}$

(35)

for which person x, you expect Mary to see x

We are now in a position to draw the relevant distinctions. We can build into (30) the notion that COMP is an escape route for the purposes of the two conditions. That is, if an element is contained in a tensed clause (32b) or is to the right of a subject (32c), it can be extracted from that clause if it moves first to the COMP, but not if it moves to a higher $\overline{\overline{N}}$. This means that (30) is revised to (36), which can be referred to as an *Island Condition*.

(36)

In a configuration ...X...[...Y...]$_{\overline{S}}$, a rule may involve X and Y if and only if (i) Y is the subject of a nonfinite S
   or (ii) Y is in COMP and moves to a higher COMP.

Condition (36) essentially defines subordinate clauses as *islands* from which nothing can be moved except via one of the two escape routes, the COMP position or the subject of an infinitive. It is formulated as a constraint on the application of rules but one might keep in mind an alternative possibility, that it holds as a constraint on the possible logical forms, distinguishing a logical variable (the residue of a *wh* word moving to COMP) and a nonvariable (the residue of movement to another $\overline{\overline{N}}$). For the moment, let us note simply that (36) attains a greater depth of explanation than (30) because it covers a greater range of facts.

If the Island Condition of (36), the Maximalization Principle, and structure-preservation principles are postulated as part of Universal Grammar, part of what children bring to the development of their language, then it is reasonable to think that particular grammars of English contain the very simple transformational rule Move Category stated as (28). Exposure to some simple sentences like *John seems to be happy/It seems that John is happy,* or *Susan has seen John/Who has Susan seen?* will suffice to trigger the growth of (28). Because these three principles are available independently of linguistic experience, the rule will not overgeneralize and yield the various unacceptable sentences discussed in this section; hence children will need no instruction or correction but will simply not utter such sentences.[4]

Now, it is unlikely that the child is endowed with this knowledge in the specific form given here. Condition (36) has a certain perceptual naturalness to it since, at the risk of oversimplification, it essentially forces a rule to move the most prominent $\overline{\overline{N}}$ in the embedded structure, the $\overline{\overline{N}}$ closest to the target position; if such an account could be made precise, it might emerge that (36) is just a special case of a more general perceptual strategy affecting cognitive domains other than language. At this stage, this is mere speculation and the perceptual account would still need to distinguish finite and nonfinite clauses.

Condition (36) will be revised in the light of further investigation. The version here is probably too specific to be regarded as a general defining property. Some rules of Korean seem to be subject to a similar condition: Korean has no formal distinction between finite and nonfinite clauses, but the complements to certain kinds of verbs are islands in the same way as English finite clauses. Therefore a variant of (36i) must be formulated for Korean, which suggests the need for a more abstract formulation, of which the English and Korean versions are special cases. Perhaps work on other languages will suggest a more abstract form of the constraint, on which particular grammars may draw, adapting it for their own purposes within fixed limits. Similarly the definition of *subject* may vary from grammar to grammar, but within universally prescribed parameters. Therefore, the conditions cited here should be regarded as instances of condition schemata.

Condition (36) might be refined along other dimensions. For example, it might be fruitful to collapse the Island and Maximalization principles into one condition. This could be done by rewriting the relevant configuration as $...X...[...Y...]_{\bar{S} \text{ or } \bar{N}}$. The revised condition would now prevent a rule from moving anything out of a larger $\bar{\bar{N}}$ or clause that contains it (except for (i) and (ii) of (36)); this would subsume some of the effects of the Maximalization Principle. Making this revision would certainly have empirical consequences but I shall not examine them here. Analysts making hypotheses must always bear in mind alternatives: maybe one's pet principle should be stated more generally or more narrowly; maybe it should be subsumed as a special instance of a more comprehensive principle; maybe just some of its effects should be covered by another principle. Whatever the analytical move, there will usually be many consequences to be checked; if theories have some deductive depth there will be no shortage of empirical consequences for most revisions contemplated. In the biological perspective on language the goal is continually to try to define grammars attainable under normal childhood conditions, distinguishing the contributions of experience and of intrinsic human nature.

Recall that the rationale for such research is that of the detailed work by geneticists like Thomas Hunt Morgan on the fruit fly and the subsequent generalization to other species (Dobzhansky 1970). Let us now pursue our particular fruit fly, the grammar of English, from a different angle, examining lexical rules. We shall then take a break from all this technical discussion. But don't forget about the Island Condition (36). It will re-appear in Chapter 6, then in greater glory.

The Lexicon

The base component contains not only the PS rules but also a dictionary or "lexicon" listing the words of the language. For each word the
lexicon contains at least three things: a phonological specification, an
indication of its meaning, and the syntactic frame in which it can be
inserted in a phrase marker. The lexical entry for the transitive and
intransitive senses of *break,* omitting phonological specification, is
given in (37). The upper line of each entry specifies the syntactic frame
in which it may occur, stating in (b) that the item is a verb and occurs
between two noun phrases; the lower line gives a semantic representation, which indicates (in (37b)) that the transitive *break* has a causative
sense, that the subject is the causer and the object is what breaks.

(37)
a. $\begin{bmatrix} +V, N_1 \underline{\hspace{1cm}} \\ N_1 \ \text{BREAK} \end{bmatrix}$

b. $\begin{bmatrix} +V, N_1 \underline{\hspace{1cm}} N_2 \\ N_1 \ \text{CAUSE} \ (N_2 \ \text{BREAK}) \end{bmatrix}$

If the categorial rules generate an initial structure with subject and
object positions like (38), then the transitive *break* can be inserted and
the meaning will be that Susan caused the pot to break. Notice inciden-
tally that the transitive *break* could equally well be inserted into (39),
which would mean that sincerity caused the milk to break. Now, most
of us believe that sincerity cannot break milk, except in the wildest
poetic fancies or after a lot of scotch or marijuana. But that belief is not
part of our *linguistic* capacity and, in any case, a grammar should not
preclude poetic fancies or scotch—we can leave that to the philistines
and prohibitionists, respectively.

(38)

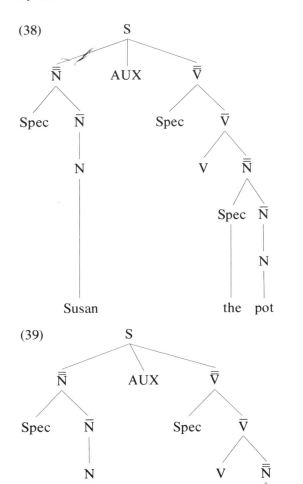

(39)

The lexicon also contains rules that express the relation between morphologically similar words like the verb *decide* and its corresponding noun *decision,* and the relation between various syntactic constructions in which a given word may occur. So the lexical rule (40) expresses a relation between clauses with "inchoative" verbs and those with corresponding causatives. For example, it expresses the fact that in the transitive and intransitive examples of (41) the semantic relations between *pot* and *break* are identical; thus the semantic strangeness of somebody breaking milk is precisely the same as the strangeness of milk breaking. So *break* can occur in either of the two frames of (37) and these two frames are related by the general rule of (40). Here W covers the meaning of whatever intransitive verb happens to undergo the rule, e.g. *break, melt, drop, show.*

(40)

$$\begin{bmatrix} +V, N_i \underline{\hspace{1cm}} \\ N_i \; W \end{bmatrix} \leftrightarrow \begin{bmatrix} +V, N_j \underline{\hspace{1cm}} N_i \\ N_j \; \text{CAUSE} \; (N_i \; W) \end{bmatrix}$$

(41)
a. The pot broke.
b. Susan broke the pot.

Under this view (41a,b) have quite different syntactic structures at all levels of analysis and are not related by a transformational rule deriving one from the structure underlying the other; that kind of derivation was suggested in very early versions of generative grammar in the fifties and early sixties.

It might appear that this is an unwarranted introduction of a new kind of rule to express relations that could be expressed by syntactic transformations. In fact it is another good illustration of the general logic of modularity: enriching the theory of grammar, in this case by distinguishing two classes of rules, lexical and transformational, restricts the class of available grammars—always a desirable consequence. Lexical rules have various properties distinguishing them from transformations, and transformations can consequently be defined in more restrictive fashion than would otherwise be possible. Wasow (1977) deals with this matter in some detail, but the point can be illustrated by focusing on just two differences:

(42)

a. Transformations move items regardless of their grammatical relations; lexical rules refer only to those elements in a word's subcategorization frame. So, if a lexical rule mentions a verb, it may refer
only to nouns bearing a grammatical relation to that verb: its subject, object, or indirect object.

b. Transformations move categories regardless of what particular lexical material happens to be present; in two given structural configura-
tions, a lexical rule may apply only if certain lexical items are
present.

Given this definition, the causative:inchoative relation must be han-
dled by a lexical rule and not by a transformation mapping $\overline{\overline{N}}$ *broke the*
pot into *The pot broke*. Consider criterion (42a). If a lexical rule is involved, it would relate only direct objects to subjects. Crucial evidence
emerges from sentences involving the verb *show* (43), where under a
transformational analysis (43b) could be derived from an underlying
(43c).

(43)

a. The champion showed his experience.
b. His experience showed.
c. $\overline{\overline{N}}$ showed his experience.

A transformational analysis of (43) would also permit a parallel derivation of (44a) from (44b), where *his experience* is not the direct object but
the subject of the lower clause, as in (44c). This is incorrect. If, however, the rule is lexical, it will not operate on (44b) because *his*
experience bears no grammatical relation to the verb *show* and therefore criterion (42a) would prevent the subject of the intransitive form
from being related to anything contained within the complement of the
transitive form.

(44)

a. *His experience showed to be a big advantage.
b. $\overline{\overline{N}}$ showed [his experience to be a big advantage]$_S$
c. The champion showed [his experience to be a big advantage]$_S$

Second, the causative:inchoative relation shows a lot of lexical irregu-
larity, which by criterion (42b) is consistent only with a lexical and not
a transformational treatment.

(45)

a. John $\left\{\begin{array}{l}\text{dropped}\\\text{lowered}\end{array}\right\}$ the rope   the rope $\left\{\begin{array}{l}\text{dropped}\\\text{*lowered}\end{array}\right\}$

b. John $\left\{\begin{array}{l}\text{shattered}\\\text{demolished}\end{array}\right\}$ the pot   the pot $\left\{\begin{array}{l}\text{shattered}\\\text{*demolished}\end{array}\right\}$

c. John $\left\{\begin{array}{l}\text{darkened}\\\text{tinted}\end{array}\right\}$ his hair   his hair $\left\{\begin{array}{l}\text{darkened}\\\text{*tinted}\end{array}\right\}$

d. John $\left\{\begin{array}{l}\text{moved}\\\text{transported}\end{array}\right\}$ the boxes   the boxes $\left\{\begin{array}{l}\text{moved}\\\text{*transported}\end{array}\right\}$

If transformations can be defined in such a way that they do not have the capacity to derive (43b) from (43c), then the two *show* structures (43a,b) will both be base-generated, no movement rule will operate, and the child will be able to relate the two structures only by a lexical rule. If so, then it follows automatically that (44a) will not occur, and that the inchoative:causative relation will hold only for certain verbs, as indicated by the pairs of (45). That is what we would want from a good theory. In a theory of grammar allowing only one class of rules this kind of clustering of properties would presumably have to be stipulated explicitly and therefore be attributed to the ingeniousness of the maturing child.

Recall that the PS rules provide the total range of possibilities in which nouns, verbs, and other words occur in initial structure. Subcategorization frames specify the more limited possibilities of a particular item. As noted earlier, there may be discrepancies between initial and surface possibilities because of other aspects of the grammar: so English grammar allows transitive nouns in initial structure, but these are always transformed into something else because of requirements of case assignment (which I shall not discuss). Hence [picture]$_N$ [Reagan]$_{\bar{N}}$ in (15) is transformed into either *picture of Reagan* or *Reagan's picture*. It is also true that some frames are more common than others. So the English PS rules allow transitive verbs, nouns, and adjectives; transitive verbs are very common and transitive adjectives much less so. Such statistical differences may be purely accidental or due to nongrammatical factors. As a third alternative, perhaps the theory of grammar should predict these differences. Perhaps intrinsic properties make it very easy for a child to postulate a transitive verb without any direct experience, say, always allowing a transitive counterpart for certain kinds of intransitive verbs heard. There is some work along these lines by van Riemsdijk (1979), but that work would demand a long excursus here about the background proposals of Kean (1975).

This chapter has presented enough technicalities. Time for a breather and to stand back a bit and see what we've been up to.

Notes

1. Under Grammar A the syntactic structures must be as in (9a) for semantic reasons, as I shall discuss in Chapter 6; so, for semantic reasons *student with short hair* could not be generated under a structure like (9ai). To put it differently, if *student with short hair* did occur in a structure like (9ai), it could not mean what in fact it means. For the moment, what is important is that the grammar must make available two syntactic analyses for a noun followed by a prepositional phrase; Grammar A does this, but Grammar B does not.

For ease of exposition I assume that *of chemistry* is a $\overline{\overline{P}}$ in initial structure. In fact, the correct analysis would have an initial [student]$_N$ [chemistry]$_{\overline{\overline{N}}}$, with *of* being inserted by a transformational rule. Nothing hinges on this here; what is crucial here is that there is no $\overline{N}$ containing only *student* in (9ai).

2. This initial structure used to be called a *deep structure,* but this terminology has now been dropped by many people because it has been misleading. Some people took the deep structure (the initial phrase marker) to be where the deep and profound properties were stated, but there are equally deep and profound properties holding of other levels, such as surface structure, the phonetic level, and logical form.

3. Compare the grammatical sentences (i)–(v), where the main verb is in the active voice and we can see that the gaps in (29) are positions in which a $\overline{\overline{N}}$ can occur.

i. Sam transmitted the message for Susan to leave.
ii. Sam expected pictures of Susan to be on sale.
iii. Sam expected Susan to win.
iv. Sam expects Susan will win.
v. Sam expects Mary to see Susan.

4. Although I have discussed only a small number of facts here, the facts can be duplicated indefinitely. This is so because there is an indefinite number of, say, *wh* questions (see Chapter 2). Also, there are other construction types that share the relevant properties of *wh* questions, for example relative clauses (i) and topicalized sentences (ii).

(i)
the woman who I expect [_____ to win] wore pink
the woman who I expect [_____ will win] wore pink
the woman who I expect [Mary to see _____] wore pink

(ii)
Kirsten, I expect [_____ to win]
Kirsten, I expect [_____ will win]
Kirsten, I expect [Mary to see _____]

Suggested Reading

C. L. Baker's "Syntactic theory and the projection principle," *Linguistic Inquiry* 10 (no. 4, 1979) approaches syntactic descriptions from the viewpoint of this chapter. He discusses several grammatical claims in the generative literature and shows that the grammars postulated could not be attained under usual assumptions about childhood experience. He presents a number of puzzles, where children attain more than they experience in ways hitherto unexplained.

Similarly, Howard Lasnik's "Restricting the theory of transformations: A case study," in Hornstein and Lightfoot 1981 examines earlier analyses of English auxiliary verbs and shows them to be unattainable by a child under normal assumptions. He offers something that seeks to meet the requirements sketched in this chapter.

My "Trace theory and explanation" (Lightfoot 1980) examines some developments in syntactic theory during the 1970s and shows how the developments sought greater explanatory success. Chomsky 1981a reviews other developments from the viewpoint of how they contributed greater insight to the central problem of language acquisition. This paper also sketches some aspects of the "Pisa theory" (see Chapter 6).

Chapter 5
Interlude: Reflections on Methods

Imaginative Reasoning

Professional linguists are great ones for anecdotes about exotic phenomena they have discovered. At the bus-stop they tell you about Hixkaryana, a Carib language spoken by about 350 people living on the Nhamundá and Mapuera rivers in northern Brazil, whose basic word order is object–verb–subject, which they say is not known to occur in any other language, dead or alive. At parties they talk about Quileute and two other Salishan languages, unparalleled in having no nasal consonants, like *m* and *n*. Or what about a Bushman dialect of Wishram, called Kung and spoken by a few thousand natives of the Kalahari; this dialect has a set of clicking and breathing sounds which seem to occur nowhere else. The American Indian language Hopi has no words or affixes referring specifically to dimensions of time. One could compile a mighty tome of exotica, taking a *National Geographic* approach to language description; and this is done in certain quarters. Linguists' notebooks grew fatter and more numerous as the Bible was translated into more and more languages, and as the old British empire and its more recent American counterpart extended their ranges; for Bible translation and government-sponsored language-teaching programs provided the impetus for certain approaches to the study of language. Clearly there is no shortage of recorded facts and phenomena, and human languages appear to be very diverse.

Although linguistic anecdotes may be amusing, intriguing, or challenges for one's descriptive talents, the example of the more mature sciences suggests that as analysts of language we should restrict attention initially to familiar and everyday data, which provide enough puzzles. Instead of listing and describing more phenomena, we should try first to give some account for readily available data. As we improve our accounts, we shall need to seek out certain kinds of less readily available facts relevant to the refinements.

Science, after all, is not natural history and it does not consist simply in amassing more and more facts, or in pursuing supposed objective information, even if the popular imagination often conceives it so. Scientists are selective in their fact-gathering, considering facts that are relevant for refining and revising their theories: modern physicists do not weigh the pebbles on the beach, but they do nowadays weigh subatomic particles, because the weight of the particles and not of the pebbles is relevant for evaluating and refining current theories that concern physicists. Nor does the scientist first collect facts in the hope that they will automatically lead to the appropriate description and theory provided only that certain well-defined procedures of "objective" data organization are followed, although this is another common conception of science. Science is a more complex intellectual undertaking, aimed at understanding aspects of the world and seeking explanations. It progresses not just through the accumulation of more facts, but by a kind of leap-frogging process, achieving from time to time greater insight by a world view which is changed to some extent. It is a creative activity and the great scientific geniuses act more like artists than information processors.

A scientific explanation does not simply describe phenomena and identify links; it presents an idea of how and why the links arise. One does not explain thunder by pointing to the flash of light that usually precedes it and saying "If there's a flash, there'll be a bang." A good explanation should say why and how the lightning is associated with the thunder and should involve an account of the nature of electrical discharge, the consequent air disturbance, and so on. Theoretical explanations are deep or shallow according to the number of primitives and principles they offer, the range of data covered, and how much they contribute to the fundamental problem they are to solve.

Scientific work differs from other imaginative activities, like choreography or playwriting, in that the ideas are subject to the discipline of the experimental method. Besides being selective in collecting data and performing experiments, scientists must be cautious in interpreting experimental results, which often have been derived through complex and abstract chains of deduction. Nonetheless, theories do have consequences, and if a theory predicts phenomena that are not observed experimentally, it must be modified, either radically or peripherally, or some defect must be demonstrated in the experiment or the reasoning behind it. Two aspects of science are therefore essential: the imagination of the theoretician and the discipline of the experimental method.

The *inductive* method of reasoning is distinct from the *hypothetico-deductive*. The inductive method is often associated with Francis Bacon, William of Ockham, and John Stuart Mill; it starts from observational data and proceeds to a generalization or law. An example is provided by Mendel's account of how he discovered his laws. Mendel did a lot of counting, listing the numbers of pea plants with various characteristics in various generations. He found that under parallel breeding conditions, the second generation of plants yielded about a 3:1 ratio of dominant:recessive characteristics. The 3:1 overall ratio was arrived at inductively, and that ratio formed the basis for his laws of segregation and independent assortment (although there is now some evidence that some of Mendel's counting was "idealized," not to say fudged; see Brannigan 1981).

Compare this with the hypothetico-deductive reasoning of Kepler in figuring out the orbit of Mars. He used the existing observations of the positions of Mars relative to the background of the fixed stars and tried to work out the precise shape of its orbit. It seemed that it must be a circle but changing its shape and diameter according to some theory of oscillation. This conclusion was unsatisfactory. Later, working on another problem, Kepler hit on the hypothesis that the orbit was elliptical; he proceeded to show that from this notion one could deduce the positions in which Mars had been observed. So Kepler tells his success story in *Astronomia Nova* (1609), which details a mode of reasoning different from induction. The law of elliptical motion is the starting point for the reasoning; the conclusions deduced are judged by their correspondence with facts. The scientist then reasons (inductively, in a sense) from the adequacy of the tests to the adequacy of the hypothesis. The public aspect of science usually deals exclusively with comparing and testing hypotheses. Scientists do not often discuss publicly why and how the hypotheses were formulated, how, for example, Kepler came upon the idea of an elliptical orbit or, for that matter, why Mendel wanted to cross-pollinate peas. This is regarded as a private matter, often involving aesthetic concerns or perhaps religious ideas, and hypotheses are judged not by their motivations but only by their results.

So, although scientists reason inductively, particularly in the early stages of a science, Mill's canons (the classical formulation of the inductive method) do not constitute an exhaustive theory of science. Books by the historian of science Gerald Holton (1973, 1978) cast interesting light on the balance between inductive and hypothetico-deductive reasoning in physics. Holton quotes this passage from Einstein, who argues that induction is not enough.

The simplest conception [model] one might make oneself of the origin of a natural science is that according to the inductive method. Separate facts are so chosen and grouped that the lawful connection between them asserts itself clearly. . . . But a quick look at the actual development teaches us that the great steps forward in scientific knowledge originated only to a small degree in this manner. For if the researcher went about his work without any preconceived opinion, how should he be able at all to select out those facts from the immense abundance of the most complex experience, and just those which are simple enough to permit lawful connections to become evident? (Einstein 1919)

Induction itself is an unreliable form of thought for several reasons discussed extensively by philosophers. It does not allow one to get far beyond one's observations and is not concerned with explanatory force. Observed facts can usually be described in more than one way. The ambiguity of the description can often be resolved by taking more into account than the observed facts, but that involves some preconceived notion, a particular goal for one's description and an imaginative hypothesis, as allowed by a hypothetico-deductive logic. Take the trivial example of describing a bottle of wine; the description depends on the speaker's (and listener's) interest in the wine, on whether it is a question of deciding what wine to serve with cheese or haddock, or comparing the wine with that of another vineyard or another year, or using the bottle ornamentally. As in intellectual and scientific matters, the goal shapes the description. The last chapter pointed out how seeking to explain language acquisition limits what can count as a plausible description for some range of phenomena.

Scientists are free to formulate their goals of inquiry in various ways and should not be dogmatic about them. The appropriateness of the goals can be gauged by the fruitfulness of the research program that they support and the consequences for other domains of inquiry; to this extent the choice of goals is a matter for rational discussion. Research goals ought to be broad enough to have interesting consequences for other domains of inquiry, narrow enough to permit useful work, not so ambitious as to be unattainable. Biologists do not formulate research in terms of something as broad as a theory of life, nor do physicists seek a theory of matter; such goals are too general, too ambitious for viable research. Rather, scientists formulate basic questions in terms of a theory of genetically determined hereditability, a theory of electromagnetism, or of more limited concepts. So, although the formulation of goals is partly a matter of taste, the success of a research program and its consequences for other areas of inquiry will depend largely on the skill with which the goals are adumbrated.

In the later chapters of *Astronomia Nova,* having figured out the elliptical orbit of Mars, Kepler went on to postulate distinct forces for the propulsion of planets along their orbits and for the radial component of motion. He then sought one universal force law to explain the motions of the planets (particularly Mars), gravity, and the tides. To achieve this greater depth of explanation, he entertained the notion of combined magnetic forces and animal forces in the planetary system. The attempt failed, for it was too ambitious. Of course, solvable questions vary according to the development of the theory: physicists from Kepler to Einstein wanted an account of the nature of gravity, which therefore constituted an overarching theme, but the questions they could pose as the basis for empirical research varied considerably from one century to the next. At all stages theories are open to two kinds of criticism: internal criticism relating inadequate analyses or false predictions to the stated goals and basic hypotheses, and external criticism dealing with the fruitfulness, significance, or perhaps the coherence of the research program. The internal and external evaluation are usually distinct.

Unfortunately, one often encounters in the linguistic literature debates about the correct form of a grammar of some language or even of a theory of grammar, in which the participants do not first agree or even discuss the goals of linguistic research in general or of a theory of grammar in particular. This is probably quite normal in young sciences, where available theories do not have much internal deductive structure and inductive reasoning plays a disproportionately large role. The disregard for goals leads people to try to describe language with no particular explanatory aim in mind. Such description seems characteristic of much of the social sciences today, as if, given enough reliable observations, the correct theory will emerge naturally and imaginative leaps beyond the available data will somehow not be necessary. The major issues concern how one can devise techniques to ensure that the data are objective, complete, and so forth. In much of recent psychology the effect has been to center the whole field around a few techniques, such as mazes, problem boxes, multiple choice apparatus, and the like. Given the richness of the theories reached in physics, a young science might follow the example of Copernicus, Kepler, Galileo, and Newton, who prized insight and depth of explanation above objectivity, unbiased collection of data, and other such shibboleths of the younger, psychological sciences. For the early physicists the problem was the primary concern, and this dictated what kinds of observational and experimental techniques might be used. The question was What method can I use to solve this problem? and not What can I do with this method?

Perhaps one reason for the pervasive descriptivism in linguistics and the lack of concern for explanatory goals has been a tendency to think in terms of a "theory of language" and to assert that a theory of language must deal with metaphor, the interrelationship of language and culture, how a language changes historically, and other large topics. This seems to me to be now not a useful concept and is analogous to the overambitious biologist's theory of life or perhaps to Kepler's universal force law of 1609. Such a theory of language is equivalent to "linguistics"—a group of related areas of study, perhaps a useful notion for organizing university departments but, as theory, too broad to sustain a coherent research program in the foreseeable future. It will be impossible to formulate interesting and testable hypotheses until more is known about individual components, subtheories of grammar, metaphor, and so on. In any case, such a broadly conceived theory of language bears no relation to the psychological goals of generative grammar, which is what we are concerned with here.

Some Idealizations

It is usual in the natural sciences to idealize and to ignore many things that are tentatively regarded as irrelevant at some stage of inquiry. Any particular idealization may turn out to be unfruitful or misleading, but to refuse to idealize, to refuse to emphasize certain things, is to limit oneself to natural history and data collection. Weinberg (1976) recommends a radical idealization he calls "the Galilean style," wherein "abstract mathematical models [have] a higher degree of reality than . . . the ordinary world of sensations." Remember the similar view of Koyré cited in Chapter 2. So here I have viewed a grammar, which is an abstract, mathematical model, as being a real object with clearer properties than the more everyday notion of a "language."

(Recall the earlier caveat: the term *grammar* is used to refer either to the linguistic knowledge in somebody's mind or to the linguist's representation of this. The latter is a scientific theory, correct insofar as it corresponds to the real entity, the internally represented grammar.)

The notion "language" is not well defined and itself involves a certain idealization. People distinguish the Dutch and German languages, but some dialects of German are more similar to some Dutch dialects than to other, more remote dialects of German. Danish, Norwegian, and Swedish have the status of different languages, whereas Chinese is considered one language with many dialects; but the so-called dialects of Chinese may be mutually incomprehensible and are at least as dissimilar as the Scandinavian languages. Political factors play a large role in these definitions, and the best that linguists can do is to define a language as a "dialect with an army and a navy." Even individual speakers often use different modes of speech depending on the social conditions, using highfalutin or colloquial styles and many gradations in between. A "language" disappears in a flux of styles and dialectal variations.

Since dialects and styles can vary so much, very little is known about the precise trigger experiences of individual children, about which expressions a certain child heard and registered and with what frequencies at what ages. Linguists are therefore not in a position to explain all variations between adult grammars and must build theories on the basis of what seem to be plausible triggers for a class of people. It can be assumed, for example, that all children raised in an English-speaking environment hear phrases like *the man from Amsterdam, John seems to be happy, Who has Heidi seen?* Something can then be learned about the properties of mature grammars by looking at what is known by every speaker of English, for example. Something can also be learned about the properties of grammars from what one individual speaker knows. Speaking of the grammar of English or even of human grammars in general is a little like speaking of "the human lung" or perhaps "the French liver"; the linguistic analyst tentatively ignores certain properties that vary from speaker to speaker. In fact, speakers may vary in mature systems, childhood linguistic experience, and even individual genetic specifications as embryos; after all, if the embryo of a red-headed person is slightly different from that of a blond, embryos may also vary somewhat in their mental organs. Some genetic specifications are no doubt essential and invariant for all normal persons, whereas others may vary to some extent—another aspect of the lottery. As long as we understand the idealization, and are sensitive to it, there is every reason to try to establish what properties the grammar of any mature English speaker must have. Likewise, we know things about the linguistic environment of any English-speaking child, and therefore we can hope to find out something about the genetic specification of any person. If we can identify some properties that the grammar of any English speaker has, it is also reasonable to ask how those properties could be attained given what is known about childhood experience and the deficiency of data, disregarding dialect differences and possible variations in individual embryos. Difficulties in defining what an English speaker is exactly are irrelevant, as is the impossibility of knowing the details of an individual's particular trigger experience.

Quite similar reasoning applies to properties of a physical organ or even, at a higher level, to the human genotype. Monod (1972:117) estimates that in each new generation of human beings some 100 billion to 1 trillion genetic mutations occur. A fair bit is known about the human genotype but scarcely an inkling about this generation's mutations and about which individual has which mutations.[1]

Variation-free language does not exist in the world of sensations, hence must be called "ideal." It represents an attempt to abstract away from data tentatively regarded as irrelevant. Our idealizations are justified if and only if they support productive research, allowing us to discover deep explanatory principles underlying the generation of sentences by grammars; such discoveries suggest that an important aspect of the real, internalized system has been captured.

Therefore, saying (Chapter 3) that a grammar must generate all the well-formed sentences of a language and no ill-formed ones means engaging in a far-reaching idealization and some qualification is in order. There is no reason to suppose that all the sentences of the English language constitute a recursive set, that is, that they can be distinguished mathematically by a mechanical algorithm from nonsentences. Nor is it even the case that all the sentences of an individual's speech must be mathematically definable.[2] Individuals each attain a grammar, some productive system of linguistic knowledge, but they also typically use certain idiosyncratic, idiomatic expressions and nonproductive formulae (like greetings). These expressions may not be a function of their productive grammar but may be acquired as so many accretions, independently of the natural growth of a grammar, and sometimes quite late in life. Such factors make individual speech unique, as presupposed by the language lottery. I shall discuss why this may happen and its possible effects when we look at how languages change from generation to generation in Chapter 8.

I have been concerned here so far with knowledge of language (rather than its use), turning to some considerations of language use in Chapter 9. It is claimed that in principle speakers can utter and understand sentences of arbitrary length and complexity; in characterizing that ability we ignore irrelevant limitations of time, memory capacity, and patience. So some complex sentences may be incomprehensible when spoken, becoming understandable when repeated or written down, like multiply center-embedded sentences. Also to be ignored are sentences with incomplete thoughts, slips of the tongue, and other "errors" made when speakers actually use their language. In the same way a theory of arithmetic characterizes what people know when they can add, subtract, multiply, and divide. If I "know" these processes I can carry them out or check any computation involving them. Occasional mistakes I make would not be represented in a characterization of my knowledge of arithmetic; nor would a theory of arithmetic seek to predict the fact that complex computations may require more time and perhaps paper and pencil. People do not have to learn anything new when they use paper and pencil to extend their memory capacity.

Linguistic knowledge differs from knowledge of arithmetic, however, in that it is almost wholly subconscious. Furthermore, a speaker's reports about his linguistic behavior and competence are often false. So a generative grammar tries to specify actual rather than reported knowledge, just as a theory of visual perception seeks to describe what is actually seen, not what is perceived (Gregory 1970).

Because linguistic knowledge is intimately connected with other cognitive capacities, a theory of grammatical competence plays a role in a theory of language use and actual performance, which also deals with memory capacity, perceptual modes, and so on. Actual inquiry about language necessarily deals with how people behave in various circumstances, with their performance, though linguistic researchers try to pose questions unaffected as far as possible by extraneous factors. Performance data are examined that seem likely to reveal speakers' competence more or less directly. Sometimes, just as in visual studies, where discrepancies between what strikes the retina and what is perceived may provide crucial evidence for a theory of visual perception, discrepancies between performance data and properties of the grammar can be used as crucial evidence about some aspect of human cognitive makeup. Chomsky has written,

Study of performance relies essentially on advances in understanding of competence. But since a competence theory must be incorporated in a performance model, evidence about the actual organization of behavior may prove crucial to advancing the theory of underlying competence. Study of performance and study of competence are mutually supportive. We must simply try to be clear about what we are doing in attempting to investigate something as complex and hidden as the human faculty of language and its exercise. (1980:226)

Improving the Hypotheses

Any object may be studied by investigating abstractly the principles by which it operates and by examining the physical realization of the elements and processes postulated in the abstract investigation. A student of visual perception might hypothesize abstract elements (say, a feature detector, which identifies a moving spot) and then investigate the physical, neurological processes matching the abstract constructs. So too in physics, Newton was free to study the laws of gravitation without giving an account of how the effects were produced, although such an account might be pursued at later stages. In linguistic research, direct experiments on physical, neurological processes do not now offer a fruitful line of inquiry and imaginable experiments are often impossible to carry out; very little is known about the relation between grammatical hypotheses and the physical mechanisms of the brain. Although the study of language is ultimately part of human biology, therefore, the abstract level must now carry much of the weight of inquiry. Limitations on available experiments do not make research necessarily unempirical, however. This is important to recognize, because it is sometimes said that generative research is unempirical or even a form of metaphysics. People who make that claim are repeating errors made in the reception of Mendel's laws at the end of the last century.

Mendel formulated abstract, mathematical laws that can be represented with tree diagrams or other models. He did not point to a particular gene and say it embodied the law of segregation. The relation between his formal theory and physical mechanisms turned out to be more indirect. In 1903 the cytologist W. S. Sutton showed that Mendel's laws were a function of factors (genes) being on separate chromosomes that separate pairwise during sexual reproduction. If genes can be on separate chromosomes, they can also assort separately. Forty years earlier Mendel had known nothing of the method of cell division and, of course, nothing of the structure of DNA. And for forty years

Mendel's work was ignored. There was allegedly no evidence for his hypotheses; he had simply made computations. His using algebra in botany was wildly unconventional and made it hard for his audience to realize that his computations *were* the evidence.

Even after Sutton had subsumed Mendel's laws into a theory of greater explanatory depth, skepticism lingered. Lyle Jenkins (1979), who has tracked down some of this history, notes that even in 1916 the well-known geneticist William Bateson, who popularized Mendel after his rediscovery, could not imagine the physical existence of Mendel's factors, as shown by the following remarks:

It is inconceivable that particles of chromatin or of any other substance, however complex, can possess those powers which must be assigned in our factors or gens [sic]. The supposition that particles of chromatin, indistinguishable from each other and almost homogeneous under any known test, can by their material nature confer all the properties of life surpasses the range of even the most convinced materialism. (Bateson 1916)

Some forty years after Bateson expressed his skepticism, the structure of DNA was unraveled and then the genetic code was cracked. Now we have some fairly firm and elaborate knowledge about what Bateson could not imagine. Jenkins points to the work of Bentley and Hoy (1974) on the song of *Teleogryllus oceanicus* and other species of crickets. Jenkins (1979:111) reports the story:

First they worked out the "grammar" of the cricket's song—its pitch, amplitude, and timing were investigated in order to determine the features of the signal significant to the cricket. They furthermore discovered the genetic component of the song by seeing if the cricket could learn its song when raised in isolation or when exposed only to the song of other species. They then traced the physical mechanism of the song to certain thoracic neurons (nerve cells) that control the muscle contraction which causes the wings to scrape during singing. In addition, they were able to perform an analysis at the level of the chromosomes by conducting hybrid breeding experiments to locate the song genes on the cricket's chromosomes that transmit the song behavior from generation to generation. They found, e.g., that the interval between trills was controlled by genes on the cricket's X chromosome. Finally they were able to follow the song through the cricket's instars (developmental stages).

Despite such real progress, many questions remain unanswered and very little is yet known about *how* various characteristics emerge from the biochemistry of the genes. The earlier citation from Thomas Hunt Morgan suggests that biologists have gradually been cured of their original antipathy to abstract, mathematical theories, and such theories have provided the basis for some extremely productive research during recent decades. So today although some problems in genetics are not amenable to biochemical analysis, biologists do not hesitate to deal with them at the abstract level of Mendel's laws, if that is what seems most appropriate. In younger disciplines, like linguistics, the moral has not yet been learned and it is sometimes argued that so-called empirical work on underlying physical mechanisms, which is supposed to be the "real" subject matter of the science, should precede formal theories. Jenkins points out that "in the case of Mendel, this was certainly not true. Cytological study of the cell and identification of the chromosome did not produce the discovery of Mendel's laws; it was the other way around. And discovery of the chromosome helped narrow the search for the genetic material to nucleic acid" (1979:114).

In one widely held view, stemming from Karl Popper (1959, 1963), scientific theories arise in a cloud of conjectures, not necessarily in accordance with any rational principles, but they must be falsifiable experimentally; no theory can ever be verified in any significant sense (except in nonempirical domains like logic and finite arithmetic). Thus progress in scientific endeavors can be viewed as the successive elimination of theories shown to be false through empirical investigation. So, R. Harré (1972) points out that in seventeenth-century anatomical investigations Malpighi's discovery of capillaries should be viewed not as confirming a hypothesis of William Harvey but as falsifying some opposing conjecture.[3]

But physics and biology do not meet Popperian standards. First, theories are replete with existential statements ("There exist capillaries") and probabilistic ones ("The chances are that this dice will show 3 on the next throw"). The first are in principle unfalsifiable because one cannot confirm a negative existential ("Capillaries do not exist") in Popper's technical sense, and the latter are unscientific because the failure of the dice to show 3 in that throw or even in the next six throws is not taken as strong enough evidence to falsify the statement. Existential statements, in particular, play an enormous role in most sciences.[4]

Physics and biology do not meet Popper's standards because at all stages of their history contrary data that refuted available theories have been disregarded in the hope that they would somehow be taken care of elsewhere. Often much fruitful science arises in the attempt to explain away apparently contrary evidence and to preserve a principle or theory. In general, the Popperian view understates the role of idealization and the way in which conflicting evidence is sometimes ignored or dealt with tentatively by some general, informal solution. So early geneticists, when they found counterexamples to Mendel's laws, sometimes assumed that some factor elsewhere was responsible; some of these ideas proved to be productive (there are factors in the cytoplasm, separate from the nucleus), and others far off course.

This approach is quite different from that of rejecting a theory whenever counterexamples are discovered. Olby (1966) shows that genetics was stymied for thirty-five years because many workers overvalued counterexamples and used them to reject Mendel's laws as fundamentally wrong. Some critics rejected altogether Mendel's principle of dominance on the assumption that it must be absolute; today Mendel's principle survives but we have intermediate and co-dominance. Karl von Nägeli presented Mendel with a big counterexample, the plant hawkweed, which absorbed much of the energy of Mendel and others. It eventually turned out that this plant reproduced not sexually but by apogamy; Mendel could have circumvented the problem by saying that his laws were confined to sexually reproducing plants. On the other hand, Mendel's followers treasured counterexamples and used them to refine and improve the theory; exceptions led them to a deeper understanding of the field. Exceptions to segregation included nondisjunction in fruit flies and alternate disjunction in de Vries' evening primrose; exceptions to independent assortment included linkage and crossing over, epistasis in mice (fur color). To find out what all that means you will have to go to Rothwell (1976). The point is that there is no principled way to deal with anomalies and counterexamples; proper solutions may vary wildly. But it would be quite unreasonable to say that genetics at a certain stage was empty because it worked only where it worked and had no principled way to exclude counterexamples.

Imre Lakatos (1970) and Gerald Holton (1973) discuss many such examples in the history of physics. Copernican and Newtonian theories were at variance with much of the available observational data and it is by no means clear that they could be seen, least of all in the early stages, to give more correct predictions than existing theories. Some of the existing data turned out to be incorrect, and other apparently contrary data came to be accommodated in various ways, perhaps by invoking additional principles or by refining existing ones. The real point is that the new theories gave deeper explanations within the narrower range in which they were not falsified by clear and impressive data.[5]

Application of Popper's demarcation criteria, narrowly conceived, would at once destroy any living science, which is why they are never invoked in practice. But if Popper's criteria are too rigorous for physics and biology, it is certainly unreasonable to apply them to less mature sciences like the study of grammars.

Given the kinds of idealizations invoked here, falsification of a particular theory will be a complex matter; discussion is necessarily somewhat abstract and bound by theory. A theory of grammar is refuted by presenting an analysis, showing that the optimal, most readily attainable grammar for some language does not accord with the theory under examination. The refutation is precisely as convincing as the analysis offered. So refutation is not a trivial matter, to be effected by simply citing an unanalyzed fact about some language.

Refutation by rigorous analysis is a recent development for linguistics, but well-established in more mature disciplines. For example, from ancient times scientists have held that an optical theory ought to be able to explain why a clear sky is blue, why light passing through empty space and then being refracted into the atmosphere should produce the familiar blueness. No theory was able to offer an explanation until the early twentieth century, when Rayleigh produced a theory of atmospheric dispersion. Only since Rayleigh's work does the inability of an optical theory to explain the color of the sky count as a major argument against it. It is not the case that in early centuries all optical theories were rejected or refuted because of their failure in this area.

Of course, principles postulated must account for some range of facts, but the need for coverage of data is sometimes misconstrued because of a widespread belief that the theorist can know in advance for which facts a theory is responsible independently of any particular theory of those facts. But there are no valid theoretical notions on what facts must follow from any given principle. For example, suppose that it is a fact that children generally acquire the use of simple, one-clause structures before compound sentences; there is no reason to assume a priori that this fact must follow from some particular principle of the theory of grammar, as opposed, say, to some property of perceptual maturation or the developing short-term memory capacity. To take another example, some linguists assume that *Himself likes John is ill-formed by virtue of a misapplied transformation; others believe that an interpretive semantic rule is involved. Since ungrammaticality judgments, like facts in general, do not come labeled as inherently syntactic or semantic, there is no a priori theory-independent way of evaluating these alternative analyses. The preferable analysis of a sentence is whichever is compatible with the overall most highly valued theory of grammar. Hence a theory cannot be refuted simply by showing that some particular fact does not follow from some particular principle. A principle is responsible only for the *relevant* facts, but since facts do not come labeled, one cannot know which facts are relevant until one has a theory. The relevance of some fact, as a function of a particular principle, lies in the overall, global success of the theory. There is a certain circularity to this, whereby we justify a theory in terms of the relevant facts it explains, and we determine the relevance of the facts by the success of the theory that entails them. The circularity is inescapable but not vicious, and theories are subject to rational debate though not refutable by the citation of a single recalcitrant or unexplained fact.

Again, this procedure is not peculiar to work on language acquisition. Larry Laudan points out that doubts about the appropriate domain for some unsolved problem have often been of decisive importance.

The vicissitudes of comets provide a neat example. During antiquity and the Middle Ages, comets were classified as sub-luminary phenomena and thus fell within the domain of meteorology. Astronomers, whose concern was exclusively with problems in the celestial regions, felt no need to offer theories about comets, nor even to plot their courses. By the sixteenth century, however, it had become customary to classify comets as celestial phenomena. This domain transition was crucial for the Copernican theory, since the motion of comets came to constitute one of the decisive anomalies for geocentric astronomy and one of the solved problems for the heliocentric theory. (1977:21)

The crucial factor in science is depth of explanation, not coverage of data. Any nontrivial theory may be incompatible with some apparently relevant data, but the theorist persists with it if it is providing explanations within some domain and affords a useful and productive research program.

With this view of science, stressing depth of explanation, the formulation of generative grammars can be shown to provide explanatory models and therefore to have empirical consequences. It is not the case that theories either have or do not have explanatory adequacy; rather, they have more or less of it. Given the central empirical problem defined here the depth of explanation offered by different theories can be compared as a function of these criteria, where (3) is of primary importance.

1. Coverage of data
2. Criteria of simplicity and elegance
3. Insight provided into the acquisition of grammars

The citing of a counterexample is to show that a theory is rated lower by criterion (1) and has lower empirical force by that single criterion. That theory, however, may yield greater insight into the nature of acquisition, that is, be more highly valued by criterion (3) and therefore be of greater empirical force elsewhere and be preferred overall. This is to adopt normal scientific practice. Scientists do not abandon theories simply on the basis of a fact that does not follow from one of their principles. All theories are inadequate in the sense that certain facts do not follow from the principles hypothesized. To be a real counterexample, the recalcitrant fact must be shown first to be relevant (not a simple matter if facts do not come so labeled) and be shown to follow from another theory equally or more highly rated along criterion (3). Refutation is not impossible. In practice theories are refuted or revised constantly by offering a theory more highly rated overall by the three weighted criteria, showing perhaps greater coverage of data or greater elegance or greater insight (see Hornstein and Lightfoot 1981: Introduction).

Having discussed some of our methods at a fairly abstract level, it is time now to pause for a beer and then to take up some more analysis, seeing again how our technical descriptions will be shaped by our basic explanatory concern, and how we can improve our theories. Remember the Island Condition?

Notes

1. Of course, some of these mutations may affect the grammatical genotype and people may vary somewhat not only in their mature capacity but also in their genetic endowment relevant for language acquisition. If we hope eventually to learn something of these mutations, we must first understand something about the normal situation. That involves the initial idealization of a theory of grammar represented uniformly in the species.

2. Putnam (1961) has argued the opposite position, that the sentences of a language are a recursive set. His arguments are refuted by Lasnik (1981) and Matthews (1979). The question does not really have any importance for the view of language acquisition adopted here, wherein children attain grammars, not sets of sentences. There is certainly no reason to say that the sentences of English *must* be a recursive set for our research program to be coherent, as is sometimes said.

Another issue that is sometimes conflated with the question of the recursiveness of English sentences has to do with the number of particular grammars compatible with a given theory of grammar. It may be the case that the best theory allows a large or even infinite class of grammars, only a small number of which are actually attainable on the basis of the kinds of trigger experiences that children actually have. So one might explain acquisition with a permissive theory of grammar, but where the nonoccurring grammars could not be learned under normal circumstances because they require a certain sort of exotic data not in the child's experience. What is important is not the number of grammars defined by the theory but the class of grammars attainable under normal childhood experience. There is no reason to require in advance that any theory of grammar that explains language acquisition must define only a finite class of grammars. See Wexler and Culicover (1980) for more discussion of this and related issues.

3. Crucial aspects of Popper's theory of science were foreshadowed in the work of C. S. Peirce, but Peirce did not minimize the role of idealization or assign data-coverage as important a role.

It is a great mistake to suppose that the mind of the active scientist is filled with propositions which, if not proved beyond all reasonable cavil, are at least extremely probable. On the contrary, he entertains hypotheses which are almost wildly incredible, and treats them with respect for the time being. Why does he do this? Simply because any scientific proposition whatever is always liable to be refuted and dropped at short notice. A hypothesis is something which looks as if it might be true, and which is capable of verification and refutation by comparison with facts. The best hypothesis, in the sense of the one most recommending itself to the inquirer, is the one which can be most readily refuted if it is false. For after all, what is a *likely* hypothesis? It is one which falls in with our preconceived ideas. But these may be wrong. Their errors are just what the scientific man is out gunning for more particularly. But if a hypothesis can quickly and easily be cleared away so as to go toward leaving the field free for the main struggle, this is an immense advantage. (Peirce 1966: vol. 1, p. 120)

4. Harré (1972:50) also points out that the Popperian view would require a radical reinterpretation of the process whereby experimental results are averaged to give the value of some natural constant: "The experimental results, all of which differ from the final assigned value, would have to be regarded as falsifying the hypothesis that the value was the average value. There can be no notion of acceptable error on this theory, so the usual move of treating divergent results as failing to falsify the hypothesis because they are within the acceptable margin of error, is not open." Popperians have discussed extensively how to interpret probabilistic statements.

5. Laudan (1977:112) makes the same point in the context of Galileo's work:

The Galilean research tradition, for instance, could not in its early years begin to stack up against its primary competitor, Aristotelianism. Aristotle's research tradition could solve a great many more important empirical problems than Galileo's. . . . But what Galilean astronomy and physics did have going for it was its impressive ability to explain successfully some well-known phenomena which constituted empirical anomalies for the cosmological tradition of Aristotle and Ptolemy. Galileo could explain, for example, why heavier bodies fell no faster than lighter ones. He could explain the irregularities on the surface of the moon, the moons of Jupiter, the phases of Venus, and the spots on the sun. . . . Galileo was taken so seriously by later scientists of the seventeenth century, not because his system as a whole could explain more than its medieval and renaissance predecessors (for it palpably could *not*), but rather because it showed promise by being able, in a short space of time, to offer solutions to problems which constituted anomalies for the other research traditions in the field.

Suggested Reading

Following the seminal work of Popper's *The Logic of Scientific Discovery,* a minor industry has developed that seeks to describe and prescribe truly scientific activity. Among others, Thomas Kuhn, Imre Lakatos, and Paul Feyerabend have engaged in lively debates, perhaps the best of which is recorded in Lakatos and A. Musgrave, eds., *Criticism and the Growth of Knowledge* (Cambridge, England: Cambridge University Press, 1970).

Harré 1972 gives a useful survey of some major lines of thought, and Laudan 1977 offers a readable and commonsensical view, stressing the importance of judging a theory in the light of what it takes as its central empirical problem, its explanatory goal.

Holton 1973, 1978 provides several case studies in the history of physics, examining general concerns and casting light on why a problem was construed and tackled in a certain way at a certain time. Richard Gregory's *Mind in Science: A History of Explanation in Psychology and Physics* (London: Weidenfeld and Nicolson, 1981) takes a similar approach to case studies in psychology and studies of vision.

Chapter 6
Meaning

The Need for Interpretive Rules

Transformational rules are structure dependent only; they do not refer to semantic or grammatical relations (Chapter 4). For example, the rule Move Category applies to a $\bar{\bar{N}}$ regardless of the meaning of the particular noun and regardless of whether it was a direct object in its original source position (1a), the subject of a lower clause (1b), the object of the lower clause (1c), the indirect object (1d), the object of a preposition (1e), or even the subject of the second clause down (1f). In (c)–(f) *the scientist* moves first from the gap indicated to the subject position of the embedded clause, and then to the subject slot for *be believed;* but always the $\bar{\bar{N}}$ can move irrespective of its semantic relations.

(1)
a. the scientist was believed _____
b. the scientist was believed [_____ to be a genius]
c. the scientist was believed [to have been arrested _____]
d. the scientist was believed [to have been given _____ the prize]
e. the scientist was believed [to have been talked about _____]
f. the scientist is believed [to be thought [_____ to be a genius]]

If transformations are this limited in their expressive power, being structure dependent and only structure dependent, then they do not have the capacity to refer to any aspect of meaning. This idea, sometimes called an *autonomy thesis,* holds that syntactic rules operate independently of elements of meaning.[1] To handle semantic phenomena, another class of rule is needed: a class of interpretive rules, which for any given surface structure derives a representation indicating the scope of quantifiers like *all, many,* the items that refer back to some-

thing else in the sentence, and other aspects of meaning. This representation is called *logical form*.

Some writers reckon that there is no good reason to distinguish yet
another class of rules, and that interpretive rules are really just no-
tational variants of transformations, or transformations "working
backward." They point to the apparent equivalence of (i) a pronominalization transformation, which changes a fully specified $\overline{\overline{N}}$ into a
pronoun if a coreferential $\overline{\overline{N}}$ is higher and to the left of it, and (ii) an
interpretive rule, which specifies that no $\overline{\overline{N}}$ (including a pronoun, which
will be generated directly in the base and not via a transformation) can
refer to a $\overline{\overline{N}}$ lower ar 1 to the right, unless the lower $\overline{\overline{N}}$ is a pronoun.

Under the first view, *Julia said she was here* would be derived from
an initial structure along the lines of *Julia$_i$ said Julia$_i$ was here*, with a
transformation changing the lower *Julia$_i$* to *she* under identity with the
higher *Julia$_i$*. (The index subscripts *i* indicate that reference is to the
same Julia in each instance.) The higher *Julia$_i$* could not be converted
to *she* because the rule requires a coreferential $\overline{\overline{N}}$ higher and to the left.

Under the second view, *Julia said she was here* would be the initial
structure and *she* may or may not be assigned the same index as *Julia;*
no transformations are relevant. If the initial structure were *She said
Julia was here*, the interpretive rule would require *she* and *Julia* to have
different indices. So, while *Julia said she was here* may denote either
one or two people, *She said Julia was here* must denote two people.

At first glance, these two proposals might look like mirror images,
but in fact they have many different empirical consequences and the
second proposal is to be preferred to the first. For example, the grammar with the transformational rule will need some other device to generate the *she* in *She said Julia was here* and in *Julia said she was here*
where *she* refers to somebody other than *Julia*.

To take just one detailed example of an empirical difference between
these two hypotheses, assume that the expletive *there* can be inserted
in front of *AUX be $\overline{\overline{N}}$...* where the $\overline{\overline{N}}$ is indefinite. This yields (2), where
a kid is indefinite, but not (3), because *every kid* is not indefinite.

(2)
There was a kid here.

(3)
*There was every kid here.

Suppose now that (2) happens to have been embedded as a complement to *a kid said* (4a), with identity of reference. Then the first hypothesis, using a pronominalization transformation, would convert this to (4b), an incorrect result (compare the analogous derivation from (5a) to (5b), which gives an acceptable outcome).

(4)
a. a kid$_i$ said there was a kid$_i$ here
b. *a kid$_i$ said there was he$_i$ here

(5)
a. a kid$_i$ said a kid$_i$ was here
b. a kid$_i$ said he$_i$ was here

Under the interpretive hypothesis, where pronouns are base-generated and not introduced by a transformational rule, the initial structures (before the insertion of *there*) would be along the lines of (6). *There* could be inserted into (6a) but not into (6b), because *he* is a definite term. So (4b) will never be generated and no further stipulation is needed.

(6)
a. _____ AUX be a kid here
b. _____ AUX be he here

No doubt this problem for the first of our two hypotheses can be handled in some way (perhaps by allowing pronominalization transformations to change only definite noun phrases, thus not deriving the problematic (4b) from (4a) and adopting a different account for the relation of (5a) to (5b)), but it suffices to show that even if two hypotheses look like mirror images, they may have quite different consequences when embedded in a grammar and interacting with other rules.[2]

In general, the interpretive account, our second hypothesis, seems to be superior to an approach using transformations to deal with referential relations. If the theory of grammar includes an autonomy thesis, depriving transformations of the power to derive (5b) from (5a) under identity of reference, we as analysts and children genetically endowed with this theory will be driven to some sort of interpretive treatment; and that seems to provide the best account of the relevant facts. We'll see how the interpretive account works out in detail in the next section.

Again, the theory distinguishes rule classes and we adopt a modular view of grammar. Under this view, there are no valid intuitions in many cases about whether a given structure should be characterized as ill-formed by the syntactic or semantic rules; this will be a matter of convenience to the grammar (not arbitrary convenience, of course, the formulation of the grammar will have empirical consequences and will make a truth claim). Any such intuitions or hunches that one might have about the appropriateness of ruling, say, *himself left* as ill-formed in the semantic component are a function of one's experience as an analyst and depend in part on where one went to graduate school; these hunches are not part of the primary data for which a theory must be responsible.

Logical Form: Referential Relations

Let us adopt now the model presented earlier, in Chapter 3. The output of the transformational subcomponent is a surface structure, and this constitutes the input and the only input to the rules that derive a logical form. These interpretive rules, as we shall see, specify the scope of quantifiers, relations among noun phrases, and so on. Imagine two rules dealing with referential relations: I will call them Same and Different.

The rule Same assigns to a $\bar{\bar{N}}$ the same index as some other $\bar{\bar{N}}$ that is higher and to the left in the phrase marker.[3] If two items have the same index, then they are intended to refer to the same entity. Elements undergoing the rule Same will be reflexives, reciprocals, and abstract (phonetically empty) items like e in (7c) (e stands for empty $\bar{\bar{N}}$, or what traditional grammarians might call here an "understood subject"). These items are *anaphors* and are distinct from ordinary pronouns, like *him, me,* and *they.* In the surface structures of (7) (details omitted), the rule will associate and coindex the rightmost italicized item with the leftmost, which is also higher in the tree in these examples. Notice that (8) are also possible surface structures, since the anaphors *himself, each other, e,* may be generated under any $\bar{\bar{N}}$ position in the initial phrase marker. However, they will not be coindexed by Same because they do not meet the structural description of the rule, having no $\bar{\bar{N}}$ higher and to the left. Therefore the italicized items in (8) will not be coindexed with another $\bar{\bar{N}}$ and will remain uninterpreted, entailing that the surface structures are classed as defective and that the sentences do not occur. In this way the interpretive rules have a filtering function, eliminating certain surface structures that emerge from the syntactic component but cannot be assigned any interpretation—yet another example of modularity, of two subcomponents interacting to give correct results.

(7)

a. *John* washed *himself.*

b. *The men* washed *each other.*

c. *John* tried *e* to become popular.

(8)

a. **Himself* washed John.

b. **Each other* washed the men.

c. **e* tried John to become popular.

The rule Same applies to particular expressions, the anaphors, which must be indexed by this rule if there is to be a well-formed output. The rule Different, on the other hand, applies to all other nouns and specifies that a $\bar{\bar{N}}$ has a different index from another $\bar{\bar{N}}$ that is higher and to the left. So in (9a) the rule assigns an index to *them* different from what is assigned to *they,* which is higher and to the left. This means that *them* does not refer to the same people as *they.* Similarly in (9b) *me* must have a different index from *I,* but since *I* and *me* by their very nature refer to the same person (the speaker of the sentence), we have a contradiction; therefore the grammar characterizes the sentence as ill-formed. In (9c) the rule assigns different indices to the two *Bills,* correctly indicating the usual way for the sentence to be understood, namely that there were two people involved of the same name. In (10a) the lower *they* may in fact corefer with the higher *they,* and (10b) is well-formed, which suggests that these may be counterexamples to the analysis (we shall see in a moment that they are not).

(9)

a. They shot them.

b. *I washed me.

c. Bill shot Bill.

(10)

a. They voted that they should contribute to the fund.

b. I said that I laughed.

Disregarding possible counterexamples for the moment, a still more dramatic proposal suggests itself if this line proves fruitful. The rules postulated here are all so general that they may feature in all grammars. If so, they could be attributed to the genotype and not to the result of exposure to the world. The child developing English would learn which words undergo Same, that is, which are anaphors; the rest undergo

Different. The necessary experience would be to hear a sentence like *Mommy hurt herself* where it is clear that Mommy is hurt; this suffices to show that *herself* undergoes Same. Hearing *Daddy saw him* in a context where it is evident that Daddy saw somebody other than himself (the only possible meaning of the sentence) shows that *him* does not undergo Same. The only relevant role for experience is to show which words undergo Same. Different applies blindly to everything else. Anything not affected by either of these rules is indexed freely; that is, reference is assigned freely. Only minimal experience is needed to trigger the development of the system, which makes this the kind of explanation that we have sought from the beginning.

Even if this explanation is of the right kind, perhaps it can be improved upon. Let us now return to the two apparent counterexamples to the rule Different (10). The rule requires a $\bar{\bar{N}}$ to have a different index from a $\bar{N}$ higher and to the left. Therefore one might expect the lower *they* in (10a) not to corefer with the higher *they* and (10b) to be ill-formed, but this expectation is false. Compare this to (11a,b), which bear out these expectations.

(11)
a.   They expected them to contribute to the fund.
b. *I expected me to laugh.

To understand the difference between (10) and (11), remember the "escape routes" and the Island Condition of Chapter 4: a rule may involve X and Y where Y is contained in a clause or $\bar{N}$ lower than X, only if Y is in COMP or the subject of a nonfinite clause. In (10) the lower *they* and I do not meet this requirement; *they* and I are neither in COMP nor the subject of an infinitive. They are on islands and Different cannot apply to them. Therefore they are free in reference and *they* may or may not refer to the higher subject in (10a); I may, and by its intrinsic nature must, refer to the higher I in (10b). Remember that any $\bar{\bar{N}}$ not indexed by Same or Different (Same cannot apply here because *them* and *me* are not anaphors) is indexed freely; under the free indexing process *them* may chance to have the same index as *they*, or perhaps a different index. On the other hand, in (11) *them* and *me* are each the subject of an infinitive and therefore can be affected by Different. So it seems that the Island Condition is relevant not only for transformations but also for interpretive rules.

Same is also subject to the Island Condition. In (12a) *each other* can be coindexed with *the men* because it is a subject of an infinitive and therefore not on an island. But (12b) is ill-formed; *each other* is on an island and cannot be coindexed with *the men* and therefore remains uninterpreted, just as in (8).

(12)
a. the men expected [each other to win]
b. *the men expected [each other would win]

Pause for a moment to reflect on the logic of all this. In Chapter 4 transformations were defined as restrictively as possible, and the simplest and most general formulation of a rule of English grammar was reached: Move Category. This was motivated by the fact that anything significantly more complex could not be acquired by children developing English under the boundary conditions that I am assuming. In order to explain how this rule could be acquired by a child, I postulated some putatively universal conditions on rule application. Thus an appropriate explanation for a small class of facts was obtained—appropriate in that it showed how the system could be developed when the child is exposed only to some simple sentences. The principle invoked there, the Island Condition, now turns out to play a more extensive role and therefore the circle of reasoning is extended to embrace a greater range of phenomena. The explanation achieves a greater depth and the research program is suitably productive. It seems that two simple and general interpretive rules can be maintained—Same and Different—which are saved from potential error by precisely the principle invoked earlier.

Since this track looks promising, let us follow it further, considering some more complex cases. Note first that we get the right result in (13), where *they* and *them* may corefer. *Them* is in a lower clause and is not the subject of an infinitive; therefore Different cannot apply to *them* and cannot require that it differs in reference from *they*. Also Same cannot apply for the same reason and because *them* is not an anaphor. The reference of *them* is free; it may or may not corefer with *they* and undergoes the free indexing process.

(13)
they expected [Max to visit them]

Similarly in (14), Different fails to apply to *he* and *him,* which therefore may or may not corefer. Different does, however, apply to the pairs *he-Max* and *Max-him;* therefore, whoever *he* and *him* refer to, neither refers to *Max*—another correct result.

(14)
he expected [Max to visit him]

Consider now *He expected to visit him* and the rule Same reenters the arena. The subject of *visit* is not expressed; it is phonetically null or "understood." The structure is (15a) and *e* is an item that undergoes Same. Same coindexes *e* with a $\bar{\text{N}}$ higher and to the left, here *he*, yielding the partial logical form of (15b). Different will not be able to apply to the pair *he-him*, because *him* is on an island, contained in a subordinate clause but not the subject of an infinitive. Different will apply, however, to the pair *e-him*, requiring *him* to have a different index than the higher *e*, yielding (15c). Since *e* has the same index as *he* and a different index from *him*, *he* and *him* have different indices. Therefore (15a) must be interpreted as referring to two people.

(15)
a. he expected [*e* to visit him]
b. he$_i$ expected [e_i to visit him]
c. he$_i$ expected [e_i to visit him$_j$]

Now for a trickier case. *He persuaded/promised Max to visit him* have the structures of (16), again with an abstract (phonetically empty) subject in the lower clause. But these differ from (15) in that there is a direct object for the higher verb, namely *Max*.

(16)
a. he persuaded Max [*e* to visit him]
b. he promised Max [*e* to visit him]

In both examples, Same would be free to coindex *e* with either *he* or *Max*, since both are $\bar{\bar{\text{N}}}$'s higher and to the left. But in fact *e* is coindexed with Max in (16a), and with *he* in (16b). The verbs differ in that the object of *persuade* and the subject of *promise* "control" the lower subjects; this must be stipulated in the lexical entries of the two verbs. For both structures Different specifies that *e* and *him* do not corefer. Therefore, it follows by transitivity that *him* cannot corefer with *Max* in (16a), nor with *he* in (16b). So, under the later free indexing process, *him* may or may not get the same index as *he* in (16a) and as *Max* in (16b). In neither example does Different apply directly to *he-him*, because, again, *him* is contained in a lower clause and is not the subject of an infinitive—again, good results, on the assumption that the child knows that *persuade* is an object-control verb and *promise* a subject-controller.[4]

I shall use reciprocal expressions to illustrate the Island Condition interacting with the rule Same; parallel facts hold for reflexives.

(17)
a. the men expected [each other to have left]
b. *the men expected [that each other had left]
c. *the men expected [Max to visit each other]
d. the men expected [*e* to visit each other]
e. the men were expected [*e* to visit each other]
f. *the men expected [*e* visited each other]
g. who did the men expect [*e* to visit each other]

In (17a) Same applies successfully, coindexing *each other* with *the men*. In (17b,c) the rule fails to apply because *each other* is on an island, contained in a lower clause, and not the subject of an infinitive; *each other* therefore receives no index and remains uninterpreted, so the sentence is ungrammatical. In (17d,e) *each other* is coindexed with *e,* which in turn is coindexed with *the men*. In (17f) *each other* is again coindexed with *e,* but here *e* remains uninterpreted; it cannot be coindexed with *the men* because it is contained in a lower clause and is not the subject of an infinitive. In (17g) *each other* is coindexed with *e,* which is then coindexed with *who;* if *e* were coindexed with *the men* (as in (17d)), the structure would be ungrammatical because there would be no "gap" in which *who* could be interpreted—analogously to *Who did John see Mary?*

As with Move Category and Different, Same may be formulated as a maximally general rule that is saved from misgeneration by the Island Condition. There is much more to be said about all of this, but it should now be clear that if we insist on taking our fundamental goal seriously and on refusing to enrich the grammars for particular languages beyond a minimal degree, we can achieve a theory of considerable deductive depth. With three very general and perhaps even universal rules and some conditions on rule application, we can account for a significant range of facts and some fairly subtle ones. As noted, English-speaking children have to deduce the items undergoing Same, the fact that *promise* means what it means and is a subject-controlling verb, but much else is established a priori and therefore is not left to the child's ingenuity.

The theory so far makes the right predictions for (18a–c), but (18d) presents a problem. In (18a) *he* is not subject of an infinitive and cannot be marked necessarily different from *Bill;* the reference of *he* is free.

Different applies to *him* in (18b) and to *Bill* in (18c), so in each example there are two people involved. However, in (18d) *he* and *Bill* cannot refer to the same person, but our rule Different does not apply to *Bill* because it is on an island. Therefore another rule must be invoked to get the right result, that *he* and *Bill* cannot corefer; this is the rule which says that a $\bar{\bar{N}}$ cannot refer to a lower $\bar{\bar{N}}$ unless that lower $\bar{\bar{N}}$ is a pronoun. This means some complexity and some redundancy for the hypothesized grammar. Perhaps there is a better way of doing things.

(18)
a. Bill said [that he laughed]
b. Bill wanted [him to laugh]
c. he wanted [Bill to laugh]
d. he said [that Bill laughed]

A second fact: the rule Different applies to the lower *Bill* in (19a), predicting correctly that the two *Bills* must refer to different people. But Different cannot apply to the lower *Bill* in (19b), because it is not the subject of an infinitive. Therefore something else must be invoked to get the right result in this example, which is that there must be two Bills involved. This involves still more complexity, which can perhaps be avoided.

(19)
a. Bill wanted [Bill to laugh]
b. Bill said [that Bill laughed]

In refining our theory I shall try to retain at least as much explanatory depth as we now have, giving up coverage of some facts only if we gain more insight elsewhere. Some recent proposals by Chomsky offer a good deal of improvement; they are sometimes referred to as the "Pisa theory," since they were first outlined at the Scuola Normale Superiore there. The idea is that we reformulate the basic insight of the Island Condition so that the theory defines a containing environment or a *Domain* for any category. The Domain is usually the first $\bar{\bar{N}}$ or $\bar{S}$ that contains it. If the item is the subject of an infinitive or in COMP, then its Domain is not the immediate $\bar{S}$ but the next one up.

The theory also defines three kinds of noun, which have different properties with respect to their Domain: anaphors, pronouns, and lexical nouns. An anaphor must be coindexed with a higher $\bar{\bar{N}}$ within its Domain, a pronoun must not be coindexed with a higher $\bar{\bar{N}}$ in its Domain, and a lexical noun cannot be coindexed with a higher $\bar{\bar{N}}$ in any Domain. Otherwise indexing of noun phrases takes place randomly. That is what there is to the theory. In particular grammars there will be a specification of which items are anaphors and which are pronouns; that is what the child must get from his experience. Now for some illustrations.[5]

First, a simple one-clause structure. The anaphors in (7) can all be coindexed with a higher $\bar{\bar{N}}$ within their Domain, which is the $\bar{\bar{S}}$. In (8) they are not coindexed to a higher $\bar{\bar{N}}$ and the structures are ill-formed. Pronouns cannot be coindexed within their Domain, so *them* cannot have the same index as *they* in (9a), nor *me* the same index as *I* in (9b) (hence ill-formedness in this example). Lexical nouns cannot be co-indexed with a higher $\bar{\bar{N}}$ in any Domain, so the lower *Bill* in (9c) cannot be coindexed with any higher $\bar{\bar{N}}$, and there must be two Bills involved.

Second, two-clause structures. In (10) the Domain for the lower *they* and *I* is the immediate clause, and the pronouns are not coindexed with any other $\bar{\bar{N}}$ within that Domain. *They* may or may not happen to have the same index as the higher *they,* but the higher *they* is not in its Do-main. The same holds for *I* in (10b), but here both *I*'s refer to the speaker and therefore must corefer for an independent reason. An ana-phor in this position (12b) is not well-formed, because it needs to be coindexed with some higher $\bar{\bar{N}}$ within its Domain, here the lower clause. Consider again (18c,d) and (19). In these four examples, *Bill* in the lower clause cannot be coindexed with a higher $\bar{\bar{N}}$ in any Domain, being a lexical noun. In (18c) and (19a) its Domain is the higher clause, and in (18d) and (19b) the lower clause, but in no case can it be co-indexed with any higher $\bar{\bar{N}}$; hence two Bills are involved in each example.

Now to nonfinite embedded clauses. In (11) the Domain for *them* and *me* is not the immediate $\bar{\bar{S}}$ but the next one up. They may not be co-indexed within that Domain, a correct result. The Domain for an ana-phor in this position will also be the next $\bar{\bar{S}}$ up and it must be coindexed within that clause (12a).

Checking through the remaining examples (13)–(17) is left as an ex-ercise for the reader. An item's Domain may also be a larger $\bar{\bar{N}}$. So *them* cannot be coindexed with *their* in (20a) because they are in the same Domain, but either *their* or *them* may be coindexed with a $\bar{\bar{N}}$ outside the Domain, e.g. *the candidates.* So (20a) can have any of the "meanings" of (21).

(20)

a. the candidates discussed [their speeches about them]$_{\bar{\bar{N}}}$
b. the candidates discussed [their speeches about each other]$_{\bar{\bar{N}}}$
c. he saw [Max's picture of him]$_{\bar{\bar{N}}}$
d. Max saw [his picture of him]$_{\bar{\bar{N}}}$

(21)

a. the candidates$_i$ discussed their$_i$ speeches about them$_j$
b. the candidates$_i$ discussed their$_j$ speeches about them$_i$
c. the candidates$_i$ discussed their$_j$ speeches about them$_k$

I leave (20b–d) for the gentle reader's amusement. Notice, though, that in (20d) one possible reading is 'Max$_i$ saw his$_i$ picture of him$_j$': *his* and *him* are not coindexed with anything in their Domain, the $\bar{\bar{N}}$, as is required; but also *Max* is not coindexed with a *higher* $\bar{\bar{N}}$ in any Domain, and therefore the structure is well-formed.

Before we leave coreference relations, it is worth observing that the conditions of the Pisa theory hold for logical form; they do not hold for the way that transformational and interpretive rules may apply. Move Category now applies quite freely and yields many surface structures that are uninterpretable. The residue of movement is an empty $\bar{\bar{N}}$, therefore an anaphor, and must be coindexed to a higher $\bar{\bar{N}}$ within its Domain. So after application of Move Category, we might have the surface structures of (22), where *the men* has moved from the empty position. But only in (22a,d) does the anaphor *e* have *the men* within its Domain (in each example, the square brackets indicate the Domain for the *e*).[6] Because (22b,c) do not meet our requirements, they cannot be interpreted.

(22)

a. [the men$_i$ were believed e_i to have left]
b. *the men$_i$ were believed [Max to have left e_i]
c. *the men$_i$ were believed [e_i left]
d. [the men$_i$ were believed by Bill e_i to like each other]

The structures of (22) involve movement of a $\bar{\bar{N}}$ into subject position. Movement of a *wh* word into COMP is not completely parallel, but it obeys the conditions described thus far. As before, movement is free but the residue of movement is an anaphor and therefore must be coindexed to a higher $\bar{\bar{N}}$ in its Domain.[7] This predicts the relevant facts of (23); these are all possible surface structures, but those with a star do not have a well-formed logical structure.

(23)

a. [who$_i$ did you see e_i]$_{\bar{S}}$

b. I wonder [[who$_i$]$_{COMP}$ e_i saw the crash]$_{\bar{S}}$

c. *what$_j$ do you wonder [[who$_i$]$_{COMP}$ e_i saw e_j]$_{\bar{S}}$

d. [who$_i$ do you think [e_i Bill said [e_i Susan saw e_i]$_{\bar{S}}$]$_{\bar{S}}$]$_{\bar{S}}$

e. *who$_i$ do you believe [the rumors about e_i]$_{\bar{\bar{N}}}$

f. *who$_i$ do you believe the stories [which$_j$ Bill told e_j about e_i]$_{\bar{S}}$

g. *who$_i$ do you believe the rumor [that Bill met e_i]$_{\bar{S}}$

In (23a,b,d) the e's are coindexed in their Domains; this is so in (23d) because *who* moves from its original position as the object of *saw* first to the lowest COMP, then to the next highest COMP, then to the top COMP, leaving an e_i marker each time. The Domain for the lowest e is the lowest $\bar{S}$; the Domain for the other two e's is not their immediate $\bar{S}$ but the next one up, because these e's are in COMP. In (23c) the leftmost e is coindexed within its $\bar{S}$, but the rightmost is not—hence an ill-formed structure. Similarly for (f). In (23e,g) e is not coindexed in its Domain.

If the conditions hold for logical form and not for the functioning of Move Category, then we can explain some subtler facts. Intuitively, in a simple passive expression the logical subject appears in a *by* phrase and the logical object appears as a derived subject. It is reasonable to assume that the object is moved into the subject position by the Move Category rule. So (24a) is derived from the initial (24b). Let us assume that this is correct, in which case presumably (25a) has an analogous derivation.

(24)

a. the city$_i$ was destroyed e_i by the enemy

b. [e]$_{\bar{\bar{N}}}$ was destroyed the city by the enemy

(25)

a. the city$_i$'s destruction e_i by the enemy

b. [[e]$_{\bar{\bar{N}}}$]$_{Spec}$ destruction (of) the city by the enemy

Notice first that Move Category is not designated as an obligatory or as an optional rule, because it is difficult to see how a child could make such a decision without being informed that certain sentences cannot occur. Such data are unavailable to children; therefore any inference based on such data cannot appear in a particular child's grammar. For these examples, the facts are that the rule must apply with passive verbs (**was destroyed the city by the enemy*) and is only optional in a passive nominal (so alongside *the city's destruction* we find *the destruction of the city by the enemy,* where no movement has taken place). The correct results are obtained from the theory developed so far, without the need for further stipulation.

If movement fails to apply in (24b), *e* will not be coindexed to any higher $\overline{\overline{N}}$ in its Domain and the structure will not be interpretable. If movement does occur, the resulting *e* in (24a) will be coindexed with *the city*. The same holds for (25a,b). By the phrase structure (PS) rules (Chapter 4), there must be a $\overline{\overline{N}}$ to the left of *was destroyed* in initial structure (24b), and therefore (24a) is the only possible output. A nominal construction may have an empty $\overline{\overline{N}}$ to its left (25b), in which case the empty $\overline{\overline{N}}$ must be filled by application of a movement rule (25a)— otherwise the empty $\overline{\overline{N}}$ will not be coindexed within its Domain. Nominals, however, do not *have* to have a $\overline{\overline{N}}$ to their left; by the PS rules, a nominal might be preceded instead by an article or demonstrative (a determiner, Det), as in (26). In (26) movement is impossible because there is no empty $\overline{\overline{N}}$ for *the city* to move to.

(26)
[[the]$_{Det}$]$_{Spec}$ destruction (of) the city by the enemy

To be sure, I have given only a brief synopsis of one approach to co-reference relations, not even touching on many problems. But when this kind of distinction simply emerges from a theory, without need for any further stipulation, without the need to attribute anything further to the efforts of the child developing English, one has achieved a productive research paradigm and the desired kind of explanation.

Referential relations of this kind have been at the center of recent research and have proved to be a good probe into properties of the theory of grammar, because in this area we have been able to make fairly clear judgments about what the mature grammar must do and about the kind of experience to which the child has access. Sacrificing much to brevity, I have tried to show how a theory can be steadily refined and have described some of the properties that the emerging theory has.

Logical Form: Scope

The ambiguity of *old men and women* provides a simple illustration of *scope* relations. Under one reading the scope of *old* is *men and women;*

under the other reading the scope is just *men*. Such a semantic distinction reflects a different syntactic (constituent) structure (see Chapter
4).

Linguists and logicians often think of quantifiers in terms of scope
relations. So, a sentence like *Many bankers are rich* is said to mean
'There are many x such that this proposition holds: x is a banker and x
is rich.' More formally:

(27)
Many$_x$ (x is a banker and x is rich).

The proposition is within the scope of the quantifier. Now we can talk
about relative scope in sentences like (28) with two quantifiers, *many*
and *not*. These have the logical forms of (29a,b), respectively. In (29a)
not is within the scope of *many*, but in (29b) *many* is within the scope of
not.

(28)
a. Many bankers are not rich.
b. Not many bankers are rich.

(29)
a. Many$_x$ (x is a banker and x is NOT rich).
b. NOT (many$_x$ (x is a banker and x is rich))

So, (28a) means that for many bankers it is the case that they are not
rich, and (28b) means that it is not the case that many bankers are rich.
Thus (28b) contradicts the proposition *Many bankers are rich*, whereas
(28a) does not (because it is possible that there are many rich bankers
and many poor bankers). (28b), but not (28a), is equivalent to *Few
bankers are rich*.

In general, it seems to be the case that the linear order of quantifiers
in surface structure corresponds to their order in logical form. So,
(30a,b) mean (31a,b), respectively. This may be bewildering, but the
most natural reading is that (30a) means that many bankers do very
little reading and are perhaps semiliterate; (30b) means that there are
not many books that have a large readership among bankers. The two
are different.

(30)
a. Many bankers read few books.
b. Few books are read by many bankers.

(31)
a. Many$_x$ (x is a banker and x reads few books).
b. Few$_x$ (x is a book and many bankers read x).

There is much more to say about the scope of quantifiers, but these examples illustrate the close parallelism between the surface structure order and scope relations in logical form. Whatever the precise formulation of the rules determining the scope of quantifiers, they seem to be sensitive to the properties of surface structure.

Let us now return to the pronominal *one* discussed earlier and consider another situation where syntactic structure is relevant for scope assignment. It was argued earlier that some nice results derive from postulating that *a student of chemistry* has a structure like (32a) and *a student with long hair* a structure like (32b), and not vice versa.[8]

(32)

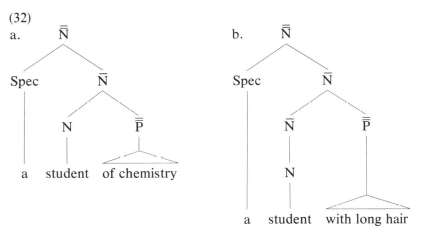

The syntactic structures must be like this, and *a student of chemistry* cannot be assigned a structure like (32b) because of a semantic principle that each N̄ specifies one semantic property. Therefore, to attribute (32a) to John is to attribute one property to him, that he studies chemistry; there is a close semantic relation between the N and the P̄, and *student* cannot be replaced by any random noun (compare the non-occurring **the man/Swede of chemistry*). To attribute (32b) to John is to attribute two properties, that he studies and that he has long hair; the relation between the N̄ and the P̄ is less close and *student* can be replaced fairly freely (*the man/Swede with long hair*). Hence it follows that *John is a student of chemistry*, meaning what it means, cannot be assigned a structure like (32b); conversely, *John is a student with long hair*, meaning what it does, cannot have a structure like (32a).

Again close interaction between syntactic structure and semantic properties can be seen. The initial tree (a specification of constituent structure) provides the right input for the transformational subcomponent that yields a surface structure, which in turn provides the right input for the semantic rules. The analysis of *one* in English predicts a one-to-one correspondence between an expression that can be referred back to by *one* and one that designates a semantic property. So, *a student of chemistry* occurs in a structure like (32a); it therefore designates a single semantic property and *one* cannot refer back only to *student* (33a). *A student with long hair* occurs in a structure like (32b); it therefore designates two properties and you can refer to *student* with *one* (33b).

(33)
a. *The student of chemistry was older than the one of physics.
b. The student with long hair was older than the one with short hair.

Many more predictions emerge. For example, *John is a student from France* designates two properties (John studies and he comes from France) and therefore has a structure like (32b). Therefore it follows that (34a,b) will both be grammatical and have the structures indicated; in each example, *from France* and *with long hair* are to the right of a $\bar{\text{N}}$.

(34)
a. a [[[student]$_{\bar{\text{N}}}$ from France]$_{\bar{\text{N}}}$ with long hair]$_{\bar{\text{N}}}$
b. a [[[student]$_{\bar{\text{N}}}$ with long hair]$_{\bar{\text{N}}}$ from France]$_{\bar{\text{N}}}$

Likewise (35a) is grammatical, but not (35b). Example (35b) is ungrammatical because *of chemistry* must occur as a sister to a N, as in (32a), and not as a sister to a $\bar{\text{N}}$—regardless of whether the $\bar{\text{N}}$ is a simple one like [student]$_{\bar{\text{N}}}$ in (32b) or a complex one like [student from France]$_{\bar{\text{N}}}$ in (35b).

(35)
a. a [[student of chemistry]$_{\bar{\text{N}}}$ from France]$_{\bar{\text{N}}}$
b. *a [[student from France]$_{\bar{\text{N}}}$ of chemistry]$_{\bar{\text{N}}}$

As promised, I have now filled the gap in the earlier account of English *one*. The syntactic constraints postulated in Chapter 4 and the semantic principle that $\bar{\text{N}}$ designates one property limit the range of hypotheses available to the child, to the point that exposure to a few simple sentences will suffice to trigger the correct grammatical rules. The child needs to "learn" that *one* is a pronominal item and that English nouns are followed by their satellites. The rest is given. Since this kind of information is straightforward for the child to deduce when exposed only to a few simple and commonly occurring sentences, the right kind of explanation has been achieved.

In the last two sections I have discussed how logical representations, specifically referential and scope relations, might be put together. In a sense this concerns the "syntax" of logical form. I want to reiterate the point that analysts cannot prescribe an a priori division between phenomena that should be handled by a syntactic rule (as in Chapter 4) and those that must be a function of an interpretive rule (as in this chapter). The appropriateness of any given division is an empirical matter and we shall prefer that division which is compatible with the most explanatory theory. In this framework that means the theory that yields the most plausible account of how children come to master their native languages.

In Chapter 4 and here I have sketched the elements of what seems to be a promising theory. It is reasonable to postulate some abstract principles which determine the form and interpretation of sentences. These principles must be formulated in such a way that they can hold universally and therefore provide a basis for the attainability of any natural language under the boundary conditions assumed throughout this book. No doubt these hypotheses will be revised as we consider more data, particularly more data from other languages. This is normal scientific practice. If we follow the pattern of the natural sciences, for example again genetic experimentation on the fruit fly, we shall hypothesize that the principles restricting the form and functioning of grammars are part of the innate language faculty, which is in turn one component of the mind. These hypotheses are empirical and are open to revision as we consider more data or try to attain theories of better internal structure.

Word Meanings

So far we have been considering meaning at the level of sentence structure. But people also come to know the meanings of words and of even smaller units, as in *un+happy*. Words may refer to objects (*city, book*), events (*destruction, read*), qualities (*sincerity*), relationships (*father, greater*). Other words express concepts like definiteness (*the*), quantity (*many*), time reference (*went*), aspect (*is going*), possibility (*could*), necessity (*must*), negation (*no*). Words may also connote as well as denote: *nigger* may refer to somebody of negroid race, but it also reveals a disparaging attitude. Other words do not correspond to objects or concepts, but have only grammatical meaning: *of* in *the destruction of the city, that* in *the book that I read*. We could continue to classify the kinds of meanings words may convey; several handbooks on semantics do just that.

We could also express various relations among words: some are synonyms (*scared:frightened*); others are opposites (*true:false*); others have more than one meaning (*bank*); others are simply incompatible with each other (*pregnant:toothbrush*); others include, as *sheep* includes *lamb, ram, ewe;* others may express converse relations (*buy: sell, parent:child*); others may have a causative relation, as *kill* does to *die*.

All approaches to semantics recognize that the meanings of words are not unanalyzable wholes. This insight is often made explicit by employing a system of semantic features, sometimes called *componential analysis*. This system represents the meaning of *man, woman, boy, girl, child* as a set of features (36). So, *boy* is human, nonadult, male; *child* is human, nonadult and is unspecified for sex.

(36)

	HUMAN	ADULT	MALE
man	+	+	+
woman	+	+	−
boy	+	−	+
girl	+	−	−
child	+	−	0
person	+	0	0

Such an analysis allows a definition for many words in terms of a few basic, atomic concepts. These concepts may or may not correspond to words in any particular language, as in this example the concepts used (HUMAN, ADULT, MALE) happen to correspond to words in English.

In principle this grid could be extended until it provided sufficient features to distinguish very many words of, say, English. We would then find that for any given language there would be gaps in the grid. While English has words denoting the male, female, and young human, there are no such words for the male, female, or young sparrow or hippopotamus.

This sort of system does give us a way of deriving some of the relations discussed a moment ago. So words referring to qualities might have the feature +ABSTRACT, unlike words referring to objects. In this way, one might define some word classes and some semantic fields: *red, green, blueness,* and *blacken* might share the feature +COLOR; *father, mother, sibling, cousin, daughter* would all share a feature +KINSHIP. The system also gives us a way of deriving some incompatibilities: so, *a pregnant man* can be characterized as bizarre by virtue of assigning *pregnant* the feature −MALE and *man* +MALE. Also, we could deduce some entailments: *Children go to school* entails *Boys go to school* and vice versa because the semantic features of *child* subsume the features of *boy*. Furthermore, we can derive some contradictions; *John is scared of Sam but he's not frightened of him* can be seen to be contradictory if *scared* and *frightened* share the same feature specification, being synonyms. And we can derive some tautologies: *This man is an adult* is tautological if *man* contains all the features of *adult*.

However, componential analysis does not express all semantic relations adequately. One can say that the transitive *break* is +CAUSATIVE and the intransitive is −CAUSATIVE, but this says less than the sample lexical entry (40) in Chapter 4; it does not express the fact that *John broke the pot* entails *The pot broke* — that is, it does not specify what is caused. Also, the *parent-child* relation is not fully expressed in a feature system unless the features are somehow directional.

Although this system provides a way of classifying the meanings of various words and of talking about some of the relations among them, and although the system can no doubt be enriched to provide a more complete taxonomic framework (see Leech 1974), it so far casts no light on the central problem of explaining how children acquire their native languages. Susan Carey (1978) has pointed out that by age six the average child has learned to understand (not to use actively) over 8,000 root words (ignoring inflectional distinctions between, e.g., *think, thinking, thought*). If vocabulary growth does not begin until about eighteen months, this comes to an average of five new words a day. For each word, the child learns its phonological shape, its syntactic category, and the frame in which it can occur, its role in the lexicon and thus its relations to other words, and its meaning. As elsewhere, children's apparent wizardry as word learners can be explained by showing what they bring to the task by virtue of their genetic endowment. As in all aspects of grammar, explanation calls for a universal framework that gives the child the means with which to acquire all the word meanings.

It has often been pointed out that where componential analysis has been carried out, notably with kinship terms, an analyst can provide many equally plausible analyses for the same set of words. The analyst simply juggles the set of basic primitives. Then it is not clear which analysis is to be preferred—the taxonomist's familiar problem of data being compatible with several descriptions. A universal framework is needed to constrain analysts' hypotheses and those of the child learning a vocabulary.

Such restrictions might hold at various levels. One might postulate limits on possible concepts: Bertrand Russell held that languages can designate only objects contiguous in time or space. So, no language has a word referring to exactly three of a horse's legs; no language will have a term *grue* such that one can say *This chair is grue,* meaning blue before 1980 and green afterward. This idea will need to be enriched somewhat to allow for the nameability of Calder mobiles and the like.

At another level, one might formulate a universal, genetically encoded disposition to respond to whatever are biologically and culturally salient properties. In that case, languages will tend to lexicalize those semantic distinctions: e.g., ±SOLID, ±ANIMATE. So, throughout the languages of the world features that are most commonly salient will play the most extensive role in the feature grids. Presumably every language has a word designating a female young human, because the relevant features are highly salient, but very few languages would have a word for a female young sparrow because some of the features distinguishing sparrows from other concepts are much less salient. One would not be surprised to know that Eskimo has several different words for various kinds of snow or that a linguistic community in which sparrows played a significant role had a special word for a young female sparrow. Of course anybody can talk about young female sparrows; what is at stake is whether or not there is an individual word for the concept. In its inventory of words a language incorporates some of the accumulated experience of its speakers.

The notion that languages tend to lexicalize concepts according to their degree of biological and cultural saliency has provoked detailed work on semantic fields like color terminology. It is often impossible to translate color terms word for word from one language to another. Some languages have only two basic color terms, others have three or four, and languages like English have eleven. Also, the boundaries delimiting roughly equivalent terms in different languages often do not match perfectly. So, the Welsh word *glas* covers what English speakers call blue and some parts of the spectrum that we would call green and grey.

Berlin and Kay (1969) claimed that there are eleven physically definable focal areas within the spectrum and that there is a hierarchy among at least six of these focal areas. This hierarchy determines which color words may occur in any given language. If a language has only two basic color terms, the focal areas will be black and white; languages with three terms have words for black, white, and red; languages with four terms have words for black, white, red, and either green or yellow. And so on. Berlin and Kay also claimed that children seem to acquire color terms in an order reflecting the same hierarchy, first black and white, then red, then green or yellow. This shows that speakers are not free to find words for concepts on a random basis. There is an indefinitely large class of concepts which might be lexicalized, but only a narrower range actually occurs. As in syntax, so in the context of word meanings the child's experience radically fails to define fully what meanings words may have.

Studies of this kind are beginning to suggest some universal structure to be imposed on semantic primitives. This will enable us to account for why the meanings of certain words are easier to learn if the meanings of other words are already known. Carey (1978) has advanced this work by showing that there seem to be two stages in the learning of a word by a child: the word is instantaneously assigned to the relevant semantic field and then its exact place in that field is established over a longer period. Under this view children have ready access to semantic fields, which would be defined in terms of the most salient features.

Whatever the limits on nameability may turn out to be, it may be profitable to approach the problem of how children acquire concepts with the same approach to learning that we have adopted in earlier chapters, viewing the child as fixing parameters that are defined by the genetic structure. Thus the semantic dimensions of any concept are innate, waiting to be triggered by the environment. Fodor argues for just such a position in his contribution to Piattelli-Palmarini (1980) and, more fully, in his *Language and Thought*.

The child's hypothesis space is also restricted in that a possible word meets various other, nonsemantic requirements. It belongs to one of the syntactic categories defined by the grammar's PS rules, occurring in one of the possible frames and interacting with the lexical rules (see

Chapter 4). It also meets the phonological specifications of a grammar (Chapter 7) and the requirements of a class of word formation rules that I have not discussed (see Aronoff 1976 and, for a brief but good introduction to word formation rules, Akmajian, Demers, and Harnish 1979: Chapter 7). Together these requirements restrict and guide a child's ability to interpret what he hears around him, and to learn to use words and occasionally to make up new words that he has never heard from anybody else. As in other areas, so with the form and meaning of words: we try to show how hypothesis space is restricted and structured in order to show how children always acquire more than they experience.

The Real World

If it is correct that semantic features provide a means to characterize *a pregnant man* as ungrammatical, then the nonoccurrence of this phrase constitutes part of every speaker's linguistic knowledge. On the other hand we may wonder whether it is correct that a grammar, the characterization of a mature speaker's *linguistic* knowledge, should exclude *a pregnant man*. Perhaps the grammar should be allowed to generate the phrase and its nonoccurrence should be attributed to what people know about the world, particularly that men, toothbrushes, and several other things don't get pregnant.

I have assumed that one can profitably distinguish knowledge of the real world from the linguistic knowledge that one seeks to characterize in a grammar. These two kinds of knowledge will intersect, as illustrated in the diagram (5) in Chapter 3, but drawing such a distinction (an instance of the logic of modularity) will permit us to identify restrictive principles of grammar that make it possible for a child to develop a sufficiently rich linguistic system. After all, speakers can judge whether a sentence is well-formed quite independently of whether it is meaningful. We all know that *Colorless green ideas sleep furiously* is well-formed although meaningless in all but the most unusual circumstances. Compare this to *Green furiously sleep ideas colorless,* which is word salad. If it is correct to make this dichotomy, then we need not be disturbed by the potential problem that arose when *Sincerity broke the milk* emerged as no less grammatical than *Susan broke the pot*. Under this view the bizarreness of the former sentence is a function of speakers' knowledge of the world and is irrelevant for a grammar.

Where precisely the distinction should be placed is an empirical matter and cannot be decided on any a priori ground. It will be placed where it is consistent with the most explanatory solution to our central empirical problem. Some illustrations might suggest something about the correct division.

When *but* links two sentences, a contrast is expressed. This may be a contrast of values or a violation of expectations. The grammar need say nothing more than this and need not stipulate the particular values or expectations that may hold in any given context. Imagine an American mine owner who wanted to employ only sportsmen. He might know that basketball players are usually very tall but he might say *This candidate is a basketball player but he's tall,* meaning that it is good that he is a basketball player but bad that he is tall, because miners need to be short. Somebody hearing the sentence and knowing nothing about basketball might think that the mine owner presupposes that basketball players are normally short (interpreting *but* to express a contrast of expectations).

Similarly, *John is married but he's a priest* might mean something different to a Roman Catholic (for whom there is a violation of expectation) than to somebody looking for a married man with no religious convictions (for whom there is a contrast of values). *Mary is a blond but she's mortal* is difficult for me to make much sense of and comes close to the meaninglessness of *Colorless green ideas . . . ,* but for Quechuan Indians at the time of Cortés it would have been perfectly sensible because they believed that blond women were immortal; the sentence would express a violation of their expectations.

In describing the linguistic knowledge of the mine owner, Catholic, or Quechuan Indian, one does not need to incorporate their various expectations and values. In fact, one would not want to because to do so would make their grammars infinite in size; presumably they can hold an indefinite number of views about the world, although, like language, always falling within genetically given limits. Rather, the grammar will simply say that the conjunction *but* expresses a contrast of values or a violated expectation; whatever those values or expectations might be is a function of one's beliefs about the real world. So, a speaker's use of *but* will reflect those beliefs, but a grammarian need not specify them.

There are many other examples of this sort. Consider the use of heavy (so-called contrastive) stress in (37). This sentence was uttered by somebody whom you have never met or heard of, but you can deduce that the speaker (and Susan) believe that buying somebody a banana is an insult. This deduction can be made on the basis of what you know about your language, particularly about the role of contrastive stress.

(37)
Bill bought Susan a banana and then SHE insulted HIM

As a final illustration, consider the difference between (38a) and (38b). We may infer that the speaker who utters (38a) is probably a flat-earther and is planning to go to Rome; no such inference can be drawn from (38b). The grammar need say nothing about particular beliefs, only that anybody uttering a *because* clause normally believes its content to be true. To go beyond this is to go beyond what can be usefully formalized.

(38)
a. Because the world is flat, I'm going to Rome.
b. If the world is flat, I'm going to Rome.

This is an aspect of grammatical study that has led to some remarkably dogmatic statements: that because use of language is a function partly of knowledge of the world it cannot be excluded from the grammar; that grammatical rules (like those determining the distribution of *but*) must have access to speakers' beliefs about the world. And so on. It is, of course, quite correct that the way people use language reflects their beliefs, but this observation scarcely entails that a theory cannot distinguish the two. As noted, this is another example of the modular approach. Just as there is no a priori basis for an analyst to decide whether a certain phenomenon should be handled by a syntactic or semantic rule (or by a combination), the same holds for the distinction between grammar and real-world knowledge. As elsewhere, the distinction will be drawn wherever it is compatible with the most explanatory theory, as judged by the insight shed on the problem of acquisition.

Presumably real-world knowledge too has some kind of internal structure: certain *kinds* of beliefs can be held and others cannot. Like the sentences of a language, the class of available beliefs is still presumably infinite, but they may have to fit certain kinds of requirements. Some of those requirements may be genetically prescribed. Put differently, given genetic structure, human beings may be equipped not only to attain certain kinds of grammars but also certain inventories of lexicalized concepts and certain systems of belief. That is, perhaps people can think certain kinds of things but not others.

The distinction between linguistic and real-world knowledge relates to another kind of creativity. Linguistic creativity enables speakers to utter an indefinite number of different sentences of indefinite length. This creativity is reflected in the formulation of grammars and correlates with the recursive or "looping" property of PS rules. The creativity of what words may be inserted into indefinitely large and indefinitely numerous trees, what ideas can be expressed and under what circumstances, is a creativity of a different order, relating to questions of free will. This ability is not formalized in grammars, and it is hard to see now how it could be subjected to scientific inquiry.

Grammars impose only grammatical constraints on how words may be combined but an indefinite number of ideas may still be expressed. Some quite bizarre sentences can be uttered and interpreted. Two hundred years ago a sentence like *The horseless carriage took off in a cloud of smoke and rode on a cushion of air* would have hit the high spots of mysticism, but now would be banal or even quaint to somebody operating hovercrafts. No doubt, in a suitably bizarre context or given a rich enough flight of fancy, my old toothbrush could become pregnant. If it could not, we would live in a poorer world. But there are limits: no amount of mysticism or scientific progress will make *Green furiously sleep ideas colorless* banal, and there is no literal interpretation for the grammatically well-formed *Colorless green ideas sleep furiously*.

Notes

1. The autonomy thesis does *not* mean that we should postulate syntactic rules without thinking about meaning or that the grammar says nothing about meaning, although some writers have criticized an autonomy thesis with that sense. Some of the criticisms are well-founded, but it is hard to find anybody actually advocating the position that is being criticized!

2. Dougherty (1969), Wasow (1975), and Lasnik (1976) give reasons to adopt an interpretive account of pronouns, basing their arguments on empirical consequences of just this kind.

3. "Higher and to the left" is an informal and slightly inaccurate version of Reinhart's (1976) "constituent-command": a constituent-commands b if the first branching node over a also dominates b (and where a does not itself dominate b). So in a structure like (i), a constituent-commands b, but not vice versa.

(i)

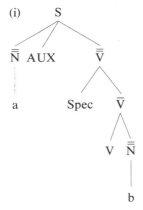

4. In a wide variety of languages, the vast majority of verbs occurring in structures like (16) are object-controllers. Children seem to realize that *promise* does not conform to this norm only at a late age, usually around ten years. For discussion, see Carol Chomsky (1969).

5. I am leaving out many details; for those you must read Chomsky (1981b). I am also using some different terminology and making some changes of substance in order to make the links with earlier theories a little more transparent, given the details that are being omitted.

6. Example (22b) needs further comment. If *e* were coindexed with *Max*, the structure would nonetheless be ill-formed. This is because the subject of a passive verb must be linked to a *e;* there would be no *e* available for *the men* in this example.

7. Here I differ from the account in Chomsky (1981b). I do this not in order to argue for a preferable theory but in order to be able to keep to a simple exposition of the main ideas and to avoid discussing a subtheory of case-assignment.

So far I have spoken of coindexed items as referring to the same entity: so *the candidates* and *their* corefer in (21a). This has been a convenient way of putting things, although it is somewhat odd to speak of an empty noun as "referring." This terminology now becomes a little misleading because an interrogative element like *who* certainly does not refer in any usual sense. Example (23a) presupposes that you saw some person and *who* serves to question the identity of that person. In that sense *who* refers to the person seen. I shall persist with this terminology, despite this cautionary note.

8. As noted in Chapter 4, the initial structure of *student of chemistry* might be [[student]$_N$ [chemistry]$_{\overline{\overline{N}}}$]$_{\overline{N}}$, with *of* being inserted at a later stage of the derivation. This is probably a better analysis, as I assumed in the discussion of *picture of Reagan* in Chapter 4. What is important here is that no $\overline{N}$ exhaustively dominates *student* in *student of chemistry*, whereas the structure of *student with long hair* is that of (32b). The status of *of* is not relevant, so I do not distinguish here between initial and surface structures.

Suggested Reading

By far the most comprehensive work on this kind of syntactic and semantic theory is Chomsky 1981b, the culmination of much work in the 1970s. This is essential reading for anybody intending to work in this area, but Chomsky 1981a provides a digest of some of the main ideas. For a clear, readable analysis of coreference relations of pronouns, see Lasnik 1976.

Outside the area of reference and scope relations, there has not been a great deal of work on questions of meaning from our acquisitional perspective, although, of course, much work from other points of view. Norbert Hornstein's "The study of meaning in natural language" (in Hornstein and Lightfoot 1981) tackles the topic of time reference, showing how to recast some of the work by logicians and construe it in the context of the present perspective on language acquisition.

Chapter 7
Sound

The Physics of Speech

In introductory classes linguists often invite students to compare the two *p* sounds of *paper*. If one holds a small flame in front of one's mouth, it will flicker significantly at the first *p*, but not at the second. English *p*s are pronounced with a puff of air or aspiration at the beginning of a stressed syllable but not elsewhere. There is nothing necessary about this, because French speakers never aspirate their *p*s, but it is a distinction that every English speaker makes to some degree.

The notion of a language lottery is again relevant: a given speaker may have slightly more or less aspiration each time he pronounces a *p* at the beginning of a stressed syllable, and he may tend to aspirate more or less than other speakers. There is even variation among dialect groups, and degree of aspiration on initial *p*'s is one key to knowing where somebody comes from. But there is a cut-off point: with too little aspiration in the right places, with the *p* of *pin* pronounced with no aspiration, the speech begins to sound foreign; listeners understand what is being said but wonder whether the speaker is actually a Frenchman in disguise. This kind of detail can be measured and might constitute part of a phonetic description of a sequence of speech. After all, a grammar provides for any sentence a pairing of sound and meaning; that is, it specifies that a certain string of sound waves correlates with a certain logical form.

The physical process of speaking is a complex matter involving over 100 muscles and an intricate nervous system controlling and synchronizing them. Sentences uttered in real speech are physically continuous and not broken down into convenient separate chunks. The child has to discover the various discrete units. On the face of it, this is not easy considering that the speech sounds are articulated (and therefore processed and understood by hearers) at a very rapid rate. Normal conversation has been calculated to use about 200 syllables per minute, but it can go much faster. The normal conversation rate involves some eight separate speech sounds or *phonemes* per second. So eight times per second an order must be given to the 100 muscles involved in speech, and these orders must be sequenced correctly.

In earlier chapters I tried to distinguish things that it might be useful to formalize and build into linguistic descriptions. Linguists do not write rules specifying the bizarreness of *My toothbrush is pregnant* or the equivalence of *The bottle is half full* and *The bottle is half empty,* or why some speakers adopt one reading of *John kept the car in the garage* more readily than the other. Formulating such rules seems to contribute nothing to the basic empirical problem, to account for how children might acquire their native languages despite the deficiency of their stimulus. That is, at the present state of linguistics, the equivalence of *half full* and *half empty* does not reflect any interesting or even identifiable property of the mental genotype, in a way that, say, knowing the ungrammaticality of **the men persuaded John to visit each other* reflects what speakers know about Domains and anaphors. If the goal of linguistic analysis is to discover such principles, only phenomena whose analysis casts light on the genotype/phenotype distinction need be considered. The same consideration will play a role in determining which aspects of sound we choose to describe.

Difference in aspiration is nonfunctional in English; there is no difference in meaning between the French tourist's [pɨn] and the native's [pʰɨn] (the raised *h* indicates aspiration). The aspirated versus nonaspirated (*pʰ/p*) distinction is of no semantic significance, and it can be predicted exactly where the aspirated form will occur, namely at the beginning of every stressed syllable. The *p/b* distinction, however, is semantically relevant: [pɨn] and [bɨn] mean different things. In another language the facts might be reversed: [pɨn] and [bɨn] might be meaningless variants like English [pɨn]~[pʰɨn], while [pɨn] and [pʰɨn] mean different things. So in Hindi the aspirated [kʰiil] means 'parched grain' and the unaspirated [kiil] means 'nail'. Therefore, it seems reasonable to say that in English my [pʰ] and [p] in *paper* are perceived at some essential level as the same sound (unlike in Hindi), while [p] and [b] are different (unlike in Menomini where the *p:b* distinction is as nonfunctional as *p/pʰ* in English). Similarly, my *p* is perceived as the same as the *p* of a New Yorker, who may use less aspiration. When I have a cold, my initial *p*s are aspirated less than when I am in good shape, but in some sense my *p*s are perceived no differently. Instead of comparing the details of various *p* sounds, perhaps even using elaborate machines to aid and refine the descriptions, it is reasonable to invoke a level of analysis involving only semantically relevant sounds; representations at this level are mapped into phonetically more accurate forms by rules deriving predictable aspects of a person's pronunciation, for example aspiration on an English speaker's initial consonants.[1]

I have spoken of a *p* sound, but a moment's reflection will show that it is not appropriate to regard a *p* sound as an unanalyzed, atomic unit. For Hindi one must distinguish an aspirated and nonaspirated *p*, which are different sounds. So, aspiration is a dimension by which semantically relevant sounds may differ in some languages, although not in others. Voicing and point of articulation are two other such dimensions. So English /p/ and /b/ have the same point of articulation, being pronounced at the lips and being *labial,* unlike /k/ and /g/, which are both pronounced at the back of the mouth. The sounds /p,k/ differ from /b,g/ in that the former involve no vibration of the vocal cords and are *voiceless,* while the latter are *voiced.* These dimensions can be treated as phonological features, similar to the semantic features discussed earlier, and we can regard each segment of sound as a cluster of features. So, the features are the atomic units. Thus English /p/ has the values +LABIAL, −VOICED; /b/ is +LABIAL, +VOICED; /k/ is −LABIAL, −VOICED; and /g/ is −LABIAL, +VOICED. None of these sounds would have features indicating aspiration, because the quality of being aspirated is not needed to distinguish any sound from any other sound in the language. In Hindi aspiration is distinctive and distinguishes /p/ from /pʰ/, both of which are +LABIAL, −VOICED. Given a few more features, one would have a sufficient basis for distinguishing all the relevant sounds of English. A string of speech is then represented as a sequence of such feature sets.

As with semantic features, phonological features can be treated as the universal building blocks on which a particular grammar may draw to establish its particular inventory of sounds. They define the limits to a possible sound segment in human languages in general. After all, the relevant sounds in the languages of the world form only a small subset of all possible sounds; many sounds that human beings can make play no systematic role in any language (like grinding teeth or snapping fingers). The system of phonological features has been studied more intensively and successfully than the system of semantic features defining available concepts. Through a small set of universally available phonological features, the theory of grammar defines a finite set of possible sounds on which a particular language may draw.

The available features limit not only the total inventory of available segments but also the possible combinations. For example, sounds may differ along the phonetic dimensions of lip-rounding, tip of the tongue being turned back, and pharyngealization (being pronounced deep down in the throat) but an analyst may choose to represent all these dimensions in the single feature FLAT. This choice makes an empirical claim and entails that no language may have two sounds contrasting only in terms of these dimensions: so no language may contrast a rounded and a pharyngeal /k/, nor a rounded and a retroflex /t/. Under this hypothesis sounds may be either +FLAT or −FLAT, where +FLAT might entail one of a number of phonetic consequences: lips rounded, tip of the tongue turned back, or pharyngealized.

In addition to a set of phonological features, the theory of grammar also governs the available sequences of segments and the variety of segments that any particular grammar may select. Such laws might predict that if a grammar has one vowel, it will be /a/; if it has two basic vowels, they will be front unrounded and back rounded; segments that are +VOCALIC will always also be +VOICED. And so on.

Some of these implicational laws may turn out to be special cases of more general principles relating to pronouncability, perceptibility, or even memory capacity. So there may be physical properties of the vocal tract or of the ear making certain sounds or sequences of sounds difficult to pronounce or perceive. The fact that most grammars lack a syllable-final [h] may stem from final [h] being less perceptibly distinct than initial [h]. Also a system must presumably provide enough readily perceivable contrasts to distinguish relevant concepts and to do it in a way not exceeding normal memory capacity. For example, limitations on memory capacity would preclude a fanciful language with one vowel and one consonant, and where each word consisted of consonant-vowel syllables such that one syllable meant 'mother', two syllables meant 'father', three 'sincerity', four 'go', five 'eleven', six 'went', and so on. Under this view grammars are the way they are partly because of the structure of our brains, ears, and mouths.

Whether or not some of these generalizations can be derived from other, more general principles, this kind of feature system provides a means of restricting the inventory of sounds and combinations of sounds that may be relevant in any grammar. This is their classificatory role. But perhaps the feature system should be required to meet a higher goal and provide an appropriate basis for phonological rules that map the abstract representations into more fully specified forms.

Phonological Features in a Grammar

Phonological features provide a way of specifying which sounds and combinations of sounds occur in natural languages. But the sound system of a speaker's native language involves much more than an inventory of sound segments, and, as in syntax, speakers know many things that nobody actually taught them and of which they may not be aware consciously. Features play a role in determining the form of much of this knowledge.

One example of untaught knowledge shared by English speakers has already been mentioned: any /p/, /t/, or /k/ at the beginning of a stressed syllable is aspirated. This does not hold for French and many other languages; it is not a universal and not something to be explained directly by the mental genotype or by the structure of the human mouth, ear, or brain. This knowledge can be expressed as a rule relating a basic unaspirated /p/ to a phonetically aspirated one:

(1)
Aspirate a /p, t, or k/ that begins a stressed syllable.

Halle (1978) provides another example of untaught knowledge by citing ten words from various languages: *ptak, thole, hlad, plast, sram, mgla, vlas, flitch, dnom, rtut*. Three of these are actually exotic words of English. Without ever having encountered them before, most English speakers would easily identify them as *thole, plast,* and *flitch*. We all know that the others are not possible words of English, because they contain consonant clusters that do not occur in English. Again, this knowledge could be expressed by writing rules specifying the permitted consonant clusters of the language. Nobody taught us these rules, but they have emerged and represent part of our mature linguistic knowledge.

Morris Halle points out that English speakers know more about these three English words, in particular how to form their plurals if they are nouns. There are three forms that a regular plural suffix may take: words such as *bus, bush, batch, buzz, garage, badge* add /ɨz/; words like *lip, pit, pick, cough, sixth* add /s/; words like *cab, lid, rogue, cove, scythe, cam, can, call, car, tie, gun, blow, tray, sea* add /z/. These plural forms are clearly not learned individually by exposure to the singular and plural of each word of the language. We know that *flitch* must have a plural with /ɨz/, like *batch*. Again we know something in which we were not instructed and of which we are often not conscious. This knowledge might be represented as a rule:

(2)
If a noun ends in /s, z, š, ž, č, ǰ/, the plural is /ɨz/.
If a noun ends in /p, t, k, f, θ/, the plural is /s/.
If a noun ends in anything else, the plural is /z/.

If rules such as (1) and (2) are part of English speakers' mature knowledge, one may wonder whether this is their appropriate form. Instead of listing the individual sounds, one might do a feature analysis. Now it would clearly be no advantage to replace the first line of (2) with the full feature specification for /s/, for /z/, for /š/, and so on. Instead just the minimum number of features might be written that are needed to designate the group of sounds unambiguously. The rule might thus be written as (3), where the lines are ordered: if the noun ends in something that is +SIBILANT (regardless of what the other features may be), the plural will be /ɨz/[2]; if it ends with any *other* voiceless sound, /s/; for all remaining sounds the plural is /z/.

(3)
$$\text{plural} \rightarrow \begin{cases} \text{ɨz if the last segment is [+SIBILANT]} \\ \text{s \ if the last segment is [−VOICED]} \\ \text{z \ elsewhere} \end{cases}$$

There are empirical grounds to suppose that our knowledge has the form of (3) rather than (2). One test involves the plural of a foreign word ending in a sound that does not occur at the end of English nouns. An example is the name *Bach,* which ends in the voiceless, velar fricative /x/. Under (2), the plural would be /baxz/, because /x/ does not occur in the lists of the first two lines. If the rules were (3), a speaker would perform a feature analysis on /x/ and classify it as −SIBILANT, −VOICED and therefore form a plural /baxs/. This is clearly what speakers would say; if Johann Sebastian and one of his brothers were coming for dinner, we might say that the Bachs are coming and use the voiceless sibilant, never the voiced counterpart, never the "Bachz."

Since the correct form of the rule seems to involve features rather than sounds as atomic units, speakers must have the capacity to recognize /x/ as −VOICED, and so on. Children and mature speakers are usually not trained phoneticians, so it is difficult to imagine what would constitute evidence for the recognition of /x/ as −VOICED. This suggests that one might look for some form of a priori knowledge that makes such a recognition possible.

Even if there were no empirical evidence of this kind, for quite different reasons features might still be preferable as the fundamental units of phonology rather than segments like /p, a/. Rule (1) might be recast as (4), where the items undergoing the rule are not listed individually but by their distinctive features (I omit the conditioning environment).

(4)

Aspirate something that is $\begin{bmatrix} -\text{VOICED} \\ -\text{CONTINUANT} \end{bmatrix}$.

This is a fairly straightforward rule of the kind that occurs in many grammars. But suppose that the facts were different and that only /p, t/ (and not /k/) were aspirated in the relevant environment, or, even more extraordinarily, /p, z, e/. If segments are used as the primitives, the rules would be (5) and (6), which are not qualitatively different from (1).

(5)
Aspirate p, t.

(6)
Aspirate p, z, e.

Linguists know that (5) is a fairly strange rule and that (6) is totally impossible. Rules like (6) simply do not occur in grammars of natural languages and therefore should not be available hypotheses for the child, since the space to be searched by children to find the correct grammar of their native language should be restricted as narrowly as possible. Using features as primitives provides a way of making this restriction. In a feature notation the rules would be (5′) and (6′), respectively. Rule (5′) is a slightly more complex rule than (4). Rule (6′) shows (6) in its true light, an extraordinarily complex rule. By virtue of the feature notation, (6′) is qualitatively quite different from (4).

(5′)

Aspirate something that is $\begin{bmatrix} -\text{VOICED} \\ -\text{CONTINUANT} \\ -\text{VELAR} \end{bmatrix}$.

(6')

Aspirate something which is

$$
\begin{bmatrix} -\text{VOICED} \\ -\text{CONTINUANT} \\ +\text{LABIAL} \end{bmatrix} \text{ or } \begin{bmatrix} +\text{VOICED} \\ +\text{SIBILANT} \\ +\text{DENTAL} \end{bmatrix} \text{ or } \begin{bmatrix} +\text{VOCALIC} \\ +\text{FRONT} \\ +\text{MID} \\ -\text{ROUND} \end{bmatrix}.
$$

The languages of the world have many rules affecting /p, t, k/ or /i, e, æ/ or /s, z/ and these therefore constitute *natural classes* of sounds. Conversely, there are no rules affecting /p, z, e/. The feature system gives us a way of characterizing natural classes: the less natural the class, the more complex the feature specification.

Given the discussion so far, the feature system must meet several demands: it must define the class of sounds available for natural languages; it must enable us to write universal implicational statements of the form that if a language has a certain kind of sound it will not have another kind; it must provide a way of defining natural classes for the purpose of defining available rules. One line of research seeks an optimal feature system that will meet these demands as well as possible.

Suppose that a linguist analyzed Hixkaryana and discovered an extremely complex rule, perhaps even as ugly as (6'). This suggests three responses: (1) Revise the feature system such that the rule is no longer complex and one can define the items involved as a natural class; since the feature system is part of the theory of grammar, this will have implications for other languages because one will change the universal definition of a natural class. (2) Hope that the rule is wrong and try to show that with a better analysis the complexity turns out to be unjustified. (3) Perhaps the feature system and the analysis of Hixkaryana are optimal and this really is a complex rule. A complex rule will be less readily attainable by a child, requiring a more elaborate triggering experience for it to emerge in its final form. Therefore the rule might be attained late by children, be subject to dialect variation, or be liable to reanalysis as the language changes over time.

For example, there was a rule in Classical Greek changing /kʷ/ to /t/ under certain circumstances, to /p/ under other, and to /k/ under others. This may look like an odd rule, but analogous rules showed up in the analyses of other languages and the phenomena seemed to be fairly common. Such a rule was one factor suggesting to some researchers a revised feature system.

Phonologists try to find the optimal feature system, assuming that it constitutes part of the genetically prescribed equipment available to children and permitting them to attain grammars under the now familiar conditions of an impoverished stimulus. The feature system does quite a lot of work in restricting the class of grammars and must meet several conditions. As in other domains, we seek the deepest explanation. So, the innate knowledge may consist of a set of features such as VOICED, FLAT, SIBILANT, some implicational rules, and so on. Maybe, as deeper levels of explanation are reached, it will be revealed that these facts reflect more abstract principles and that therefore the innate knowledge is codified in quite a different form. Perhaps one day the explanation will be linked with certain facts about the chemistry of the brain, but that day is almost certainly a long way off and for now generalizations must be pursued at higher levels of abstraction.

Phonological Rules

There is more to phonology than features and linguists can make richer hypotheses about the genotype insofar as it enables us to master the sound system of a language. Under the general form of a grammar (Chapter 3), a set of phonological rules maps a surface structure into a phonetic representation. A phonetic representation is a sequence of symbols of the universal phonetic alphabet, where each symbol is analyzed as a full set of feature values; this is the output of the phonological component. The input is a surface structure, which contains the appropriate information for the phonological rules to yield the correct kind of phonetic matrix.

The syntactic rules generate an infinite set of surface structures, each of which is a labeled bracketing of a string of minimal elements like (7) (several details omitted).

(7)
$[[\text{everyone}]_{\bar{\bar{N}}} \ [[\text{dis-regard-ed}]_V \ [\text{the pen}]_{\bar{\bar{N}}}]_{\bar{V}}]_S$

Each element is a string of segments, and each of these is a set of specified features. So *pen* is the string /p e n/, a shorthand for the distinctive feature matrix (8). This will be provided by the lexical entry, which also gives the syntactic and semantic properties of elements.

(8)

$$\begin{bmatrix} -\text{VOICED} \\ -\text{CONTINUANT} \\ +\text{LABIAL} \end{bmatrix} \begin{bmatrix} +\text{VOCALIC} \\ +\text{FRONT} \\ +\text{MID} \end{bmatrix} \begin{bmatrix} +\text{NASAL} \\ +\text{DENTAL} \end{bmatrix}$$

Lexical entries specify only idiosyncratic properties and not what results from general rules. The general rules mapping these abstract entries into phonetic representations may hold of certain dialects of a language, of all dialects, or universally of all languages. So the entry for *pen* indicates that the first segment is a labial consonant, but the degree of aspiration is not given in the lexical entry and is a function of a general rule of English (4); the fact that /n/ is +CONSONANTAL follows from an English rule that all segments that are +NASAL are also +CONSONANTAL; and the fact that /n/ is +VOICED follows by universal convention from the fact that it is a nasal consonant.

The rules considered so far all elaborate the abstract form by specifying more detail at the phonetic level, such as that the /p/ of *pen* is aspirated and that the plural of *flitch* is /ɨz/. The rules may also modify the abstract form. So a good analysis of English might show that *logic, logicism,* and *logician* all share the same root: /lojɨk/. This root may occur with suffixes like /ɨzm/ or /yɨn/, where *-ism* indicates an abstract noun (as in *dogmatism, agnosticism, atheism*) and *-ian* a practitioner (as in *mathematician, physician*). So the lexical entries would be (9).

(9)
a. lojɨk
b. lojɨk+ɨzm
c. lojɨk+yɨn

Now rules modify the last segment of the root so that it is pronounced as [s] in *logicism* and as [š] in *logician*. Those rules are, of course, English-particular and might be stated informally as in (10), where (10a) says that a voiceless velar or dental sound becomes a sibilant before a high front vowel or glide.

(10)

a. $\begin{Bmatrix} k \\ t \end{Bmatrix} \rightarrow$ s   in front of *i* or *y*

b. $s \begin{Bmatrix} i \\ y \end{Bmatrix} \rightarrow$ š   in front of a vowel

Thus *logician*, [lojišin], would be derived from the lexical entry (9c) by successive application of (10a), yielding [lojis+yin], and then (10b), where the *sy* sequence becomes *š:* [lojišin].

Whether or not a given rule elaborates or modifies a form, all phonological rules must meet certain requirements imposed by the theory of grammar. The logic here is identical to that pursued in the chapters on syntax and semantics: one seeks to narrow the space to be searched by the language acquirer by defining as narrowly as possible the form of phonological rules and the way in which they may function. Various constraints have been proposed: that a rule may change or add only a prescribed number of features, that the environment for a rule may refer only to an immediately adjacent segment or syllable, and so on. These constraints, as in syntax and semantics, gain or lose plausibility according to whether optimal grammars can be postulated in accordance with them. One seeks the most restrictive organizing principles that allow optimal analyses for particular grammars.

For example, phonological rules seem to operate in a cycle, in a manner determined by the surface structure. Such a mode of application is a good candidate for a universal principle of grammatical theory. The output of the syntactic rules is a surface structure, a labeled bracketing like (7). On the first cycle the rules apply to the longest continuous part of the string containing no internal brackets. When the rules have applied, the innermost brackets are erased and the rules operate on a second cycle. And so on, until all the brackets are eliminated.

The cyclic mode of rule application can be illustrated with some rules for stress assignment in English.[3] In phonetic representation segments have one of several degrees of stress, but this is not marked at the level of surface structure. The complex stress contours arise after the application of rules like (11) and (12), which must apply in the order given.

(11)
In nouns, assign primary stress to the leftmost of two primary stressed vowels.

(12)
Otherwise, assign primary stress to the rightmost stress peak.

A vowel is a stress peak if on that cycle there is no vowel more heavily stressed. By convention, when primary stress is assigned to a certain vowel, all other stress levels are reduced by one degree.

Let us take a very simple surface structure (13), where only rule (12) will be relevant.

(13)

[[[John]$_N$]$_{\bar{\bar{N}}}$ [[saw]$_V$ [[Bill]$_N$]$_{\bar{N}}$]$_{\bar{V}}$]$_S$

The rules first apply to the innermost units [John]$_N$, [saw]$_V$, and [Bill]$_N$. Rule (11) is irrelevant because the nouns do not have two vowels, and (12) assigns primary stress to the vowel in each case. The innermost brackets are now erased, yielding (14), where 1 indicates primary stress.

(14)

$$\overset{1}{\text{[John}} \; \overset{1}{\text{[saw}} \; \overset{1}{\text{Bill]}}_{\bar{V}}]_S$$

On the next cycle, the rules apply to $[\overset{1}{\text{saw}} \; \overset{1}{\text{Bill}}]_{\bar{V}}$. Rule (11) is again irrelevant, but (12) assigns primary stress to the vowel of *Bill*, yielding (15) after erasure of the brackets (recall that stress on *saw* is reduced by one degree by convention).

(15)

$$\overset{1}{\text{[John}} \; \overset{2}{\text{saw}} \; \overset{1}{\text{Bill]}}_S$$

On the next cycle, (11) is again irrelevant, but (12) assigns primary stress to *Bill*, weakening the other stresses. The result is (16), which has the phonetic stress contour indicated. So *Bill* is pronounced with slightly more stress than *John*, and *John* with more stress than *saw*.

(16)

$$\overset{2}{\text{John}} \; \overset{3}{\text{saw}} \; \overset{1}{\text{Bill}}$$

Consider now the more complex example of *John's blackboard eraser*, which has a surface structure (17). (I use normal English spelling instead of feature matrices; readers should not be lured by the spelling into forgetting that *board* has one syllable and *erase* two syllables, the second *e* not being pronounced as a vowel.)

(17)

[[[John]$_{\bar{N}}$'s]$_{Spec}$ [[[[black]$_{Adj}$ [board]$_N$]$_N$ [[erase]$_V$ er]$_N$]$_N$]$_{\bar{N}}$]$_{\bar{\bar{N}}}$

On the first cycle, (11) is irrelevant and (12) assigns primary stress to the rightmost vowel of *John*, *black*, *board*, and *erase*. On the second cycle the rules apply to *John's* and *eraser*, but no changes are effected. After the erasure of brackets the result is now (18).

(18)

$$\overset{1}{[\text{John's}}\ \overset{1}{[[[\text{black}}\ \overset{1}{\text{board}]_N}\ \overset{1}{\text{eraser}]_N}]_{\bar N}]_{\bar{\bar N}}$$

The domain for the next cycle is [black board]$_N$. Here (11) is relevant, because the noun has two primary stresses. *Black* receives primary stress and the stress on *board* becomes secondary. After erasure of brackets, the next domain is [black board eraser]$_N$. Again (11) is relevant and assigns primary stress to *black,* weakening the other stresses by one degree. The final cycle of the rule applies to (19), where (11) is irrelevant and (12) assigns primary stress to the rightmost primary vowel, weakening all the others and yielding (20).

(19)

$$\overset{1}{[\text{John's}}\ \overset{1}{\text{black}}\ \overset{3}{\text{board}}\ \overset{2}{\text{eraser}]_{\bar{\bar N}}}$$

(20)

$$\overset{2}{\text{John's}}\ \overset{1}{\text{black}}\ \overset{4}{\text{board}}\ \overset{3}{\text{eraser}}$$

If instead of *blackboard eraser* we had taken *black board* (board that is black), the stress contour would have been quite different. Since *blackboard* is a noun, rule (11) assigned primary stress to *black* and reduced that on *board*. If the constituent structure had been [[black]$_{Adj}$ [board]$_N$]$_{\bar N}$, primary stress would be applied to both *black* and *board* on the innermost cycle (as with *blackboard*), but on the next cycle only (12) would be applicable, yielding primary stress on *board,* because *black board* is a $\bar N$ and not a N in this interpretation (and written in this way). So the phonological rules are influenced by syntactic form, as one would expect if the input to these rules is the output of the syntax. What is more, the phrase structure rules, particularly the distinction between N and $\bar N$, have implications not only for the syntax and semantics but also for the sound system of an English speaker's grammar.

Given the cyclic mode of rule application, one can attribute the simple rules (11) and (12) to the phenotype, part of the mature speaker's knowledge of English. With this equipment speakers will know the proper stress contour for *John's black board, John's blackboard eraser,* and countless other expressions they may never have heard before.

A single illustration can never carry much conviction, but the cyclic principle has been shown to play a role in the phonology of many languages. That is, maximally simple rules can be postulated in particular grammars by invoking this general mode of application.

There is, then, a good deal of evidence that the cyclic principle exists and that the cycle is used in grammars. Under the logic used throughout this book, it does not follow from the mere existence of the cycle that it is learned by children in various speech communities; in fact, it is very difficult to see how it could be deduced by even the most ingenious child. It is more likely that it is available a priori, as part of the genotype. Substantiating such a claim requires not only cross-linguistic studies showing the relevance of the cycle in various grammars, but also an account of how the presence of such a principle in the genotype renders the correct grammar of English attainable by the child under the boundary conditions assumed here: that children have access to an unorganized and fairly random set of utterances, but no systematic information about which sentences, phrases, or words are ill-formed, ambiguous, paraphrases, or other such exotic data.

In the examples of this chapter four levels of stress have been postulated. More complex examples involve still more levels. Trained phoneticians can recognize many distinctions, but probably not all these contours represent a physical reality detectable by the untrained human ear. How then could a child attain such a system without access to a phonetics laboratory, good training, or a carefully organized and "complete" set of facts?

The physical signal distinguishes clearly two degrees of stress and children can hear the difference between *blackboard* and *black board,* the first being ⌐＼, the second ＿／⌐. This is sufficient evidence to trigger the development of rules (11) and (12), assuming a parallel syntactic analysis labeling *blackboard* a N and *black board* a $\bar{\text{N}}$. If children also have the cyclic principle, given as a property of the genotype, they will now be able to perceive the proper stress contour of *John's blackboard eraser* and countless other phrases without further instruction and even if it is not always manifested clearly in the physical signal.

Under this account, the child will correlate the different stress contours of *blackboard* and *black board* with their different syntactic and semantic properties and this will be a sufficient trigger for rules (11) and (12) and thus for a system that will generate appropriate stress contours for an infinite range of expressions. This assumes that a partial syntactic and semantic interpretation of a phrase is a prerequisite to hearing its full phonetic representation. So the structure of language partially determines what is linguistically relevant in the actual sound waves. If the cyclic principle and rules (11) and (12) are available, it can be shown how children might attain the ability to make up the appropriate stress contours for innumerable novel utterances.

As with syntax and semantics, in the domain of sound structure people attain the ability to master a system of rules that is underdetermined by the data normally available to them. Again, this mastery is explained by attributing to the genotype certain properties. These properties may be fairly abstract, like the principle of the cycle holding of phonological rules, or more concerned with the nature of possible sound segments, like the feature system and its associated implicational rules.

The properties of the phonological rules are closely related to those of the syntactic rules, in that the phonological rules, like the semantic rules, exploit the entities defined by the syntactic rules. Therefore, the syntactic rules must be of such a form that there can be simple and attainable phonological and semantic rules. The distinction in Chapter 4 between N and $\bar{\text{N}}$ was needed to define the correct constituent structure for syntactic processes, but those constituents are exploited by other kinds of rules and the N/$\bar{\text{N}}$ distinction facilitates straightforward rules about semantic properties and stress assignment. Changing the hypothesis about the PS rules might have dramatic consequences for the phonological and semantic hypotheses. Again the modular approach pays off in a fairly tight and economical overall system.

In this exposition I have shown how significant explanations might be achieved in the domain of sound similar to those in syntax and semantics. In the history of linguistic research, it is probably true that work on phonology set the model for work in syntax and semantics, rather than vice versa. In fact, phonologists have postulated quite a rich system of universal principles and tested them against a wide variety of the world's languages.

Coffee Break

Once upon a time there was a shipwreck and three men were washed up onto three different desert islands. On each island there was also washed up a can of baked beans, but none of the three men had a can-opener. The problem was how to open the can. One of the men was a physicist, so he used the principles of his discipline, made a fire, heated the can to the point that enough pressure was created for the can to explode: the baked beans splattered all over the island. Another was an engineer. He had saved his slide rule and calculated the optimal point at which to strike the can so that the lid would fly off, and he devised a contraption to catch the contents. This worked fairly well, and he dined on what he caught. The third man was a linguist. He brought to bear on the matter the principles of his discipline and simply assumed that he had a can-opener, that it was available a priori, perhaps even given by the genotype. He dined like a king.

Lest I have given the impression that it is easy to postulate genetic principles, bear in mind that what is attributed to the genotype must meet strict conditions. Wherever a description is underdetermined by the available data, the genotype postulated must provide a means by which the correct grammar of the language may be attained by the child. The theorist cannot simply build in the rules of the grammar to the genotype, because that genotype must also give an account of how the grammar of *any* human language could be attained. This imposes strong requirements, even if the theory is limited to the kind of data discussed in the last four chapters. Stronger demands can be imposed if one also expects the theory of grammar to play a role in explaining how languages may change from generation to generation, how linguistic capacity is represented in the neural circuitry of the human brain, what kinds of deficits arise in the event of brain damage, how speakers analyze and process the sentences that they hear, how they produce sentences in actual speech, how a language may be acquired in stages by young children. In the next two chapters we shall have a change of pace and show how such explanations can be reached, and how data from these domains may cast light on the proper form of grammars and of the genotype.

Notes

1. Representations at the more abstract level are written between slashes /pɨn/; phonetically more accurate forms are written in square brackets [pʰɨn].

2. There is no need to bother here with spelling out the acoustic correlates of +SIBILANT, nor any unfamiliar symbols in (2). Let us just assume that this feature specification will identify the sound segments listed in the first line of (2). For details of one feature system (not the one presupposed here), see Chomsky and Halle 1968:298ff.

3. Here I shall follow the exposition of Chomsky 1967; for a more detailed account, see Chomsky and Halle 1968. I shall be concerned here only with stress contours in phrases and sentences and not with stress contours within words; so I shall not deal with differences between, say, *telégraphy* and *telegráphic,* although the cycle is also relevant for such distinctions.

Suggested Reading

Morris Halle's "Phonology in a generative grammar" (*Word* 18, 1962:54–72; reprinted in J. A. Fodor and J. J. Katz, eds., *The Structure of Language: Readings in the Philosophy of Language,* Englewood Cliffs, N.J.: Prentice-Hall, 1964) provides a good introduction to this approach to phonology. Part I of Stephen Anderson's *The Organization of Phonology* (New York: Academic Press, 1974) gives a good account of the basic concepts of phonological rules and representations. Chomsky and Halle 1968 is the most comprehensive work and is essential reading for anybody working in the area.

For more on the physiology of speech, see Lenneberg 1967, especially Chapter 3. For a clear account of word formation rules, only briefly alluded to here, see Chapter 7 of Akmajian, Demers, Harnish 1979; Aronoff 1976 gives a more detailed treatment. Stephen Anderson's "Why phonology isn't natural" (*Linguistic Inquiry* 12 (no. 4, 1981):493–539) offers a particularly clear account of some areas of debate in phonological theory.

In the late 1970s a novel approach emerged that has already yielded very productive results; this is so-called metrical phonology. There is no genuinely introductory work yet, but M. Liberman and A. S. Prince, "On stress and linguistic rhythm" (*Linguistic Inquiry* 8 (no. 2, 1977):249–336) was the first major paper to develop the approach.

Chapter 8
How Languages Change

The Phenomenon

Anybody who has attended a performance of *Macbeth* or read the King James version of the Bible knows that English has changed over the last 400 years. Shakespeare's sentence structures were not like today's English, although most of them are not difficult to understand. Difficulties do arise, however, if one goes back 200 years more to Chaucer's *Canterbury Tales*, where the language is a good deal less familiar. Going back much further to *Beowulf*, and one may as well be reading a foreign language.

Not only does sentence structure change in the course of time, but so do the meanings of words, their form, and their pronunciation. Consider the first four lines of Shakespeare's Sonnet XI:

As fast as thou shalt wane, so fast thou grow'st
In one of thine, from that which thou departest;
And that fresh blood which youngly thou bestow'st
Thou mayst call thine when thou from youth convertest.

A modern speaker would not use *convert* in the sense of line 4. There are unfamiliar word forms: *shalt, grow'st, thine. Depart* can no longer be used as a transitive verb. Lines 2 and 4 do not rhyme today, but they did rhyme for Shakespeare, who pronounced *convert* as if the *e* were an *a* (as in the modern British pronunciation of *clerk, Derby*). So, more difficulties would arise for a modern audience if actors tried to imitate Shakespeare's pronunciation. Those difficulties would be greater if a time machine enabled us to hear Chaucer reading his own poetry: the vowel of *ripe* would be pronounced like the modern *reap*, and *rout* like modern *root*, and the language might sound about as alien to our ears as Dutch does today.[1]

It is normal, then, that languages change over time in many different ways. Over a large enough time span, the changes may result in the language being quite different from what it once was. So Old English is quite different from Modern English. Italian has descended more or less directly from Latin but the speech of Sophia Loren would be incomprehensible to a revived Cicero.

There is an old explanation for why there are so many languages and dialects in the world and why they are constantly changing—in other words, for why the language lottery exists. It says that people once tried to build a tower high enough to reach heaven, the Tower of Babel. For this act of hubris God punished them, making them speak different languages so that they would no longer be able to understand each other. Whether we believe this or not, it is clear that languages do not differ from each other or change historically in entirely arbitrary ways. Perhaps we can build a better explanation, without being guilty of a new form of hubris.

Linguists study the changes that languages undergo from several points of view. Some workers seek to classify the changes that have affected some language or group of languages over a period of time, recording that such and such a construction or word was introduced or lost from the language at some date or that the pronunciation of some word changed in the midfifteenth century. Others try to make an educated guess about the prehistory of some languages, perhaps tracing them back to a common ancestor, which no longer exists. Others describe modern languages in such a way as to reflect their history as fully as possible. With the biological approach of this book, linguists will be curious to know whether historical changes can be studied in such a way as to cast light on human genetic endowment.

We aim to discover the invariant properties of grammars, where a grammar characterizes the subconscious linguistic knowledge of a mature speaker, and to specify the genetically determined properties that permit children to master their languages. We assume that many properties of the mental genotype are invariant from person to person, whether people living in America or China today or people living in modern or medieval France. Of course, going back far enough in time might reveal significantly different human genotypes, but these are unlikely to be revealed for a tiny period of some 3,000 years, the period for which evidence about language has been found. No records exist to support claims about people's grammars of more than 3,000 years ago. Therefore language change must be viewed as reflecting different grammars, all attained in the usual way on the basis of a more or less common genetic inheritance. Shakespeare's internalized grammar was different from mine because it generated a different set of structures. Historical change can hence be viewed as change in the internal makeup of grammars.

Linguists have tried to write grammars for speakers of Old English, Middle English, Modern English, and the various stages within any one of these categories. Sometimes difficulties arise in formulating a grammar for a dead language because of the lack of native speakers; the available texts may happen not to contain a crucial sentence that the hypothesis claims to be well-formed, and there is nobody to say whether other sentences are ungrammatical, paraphrases, or ambiguous.[2] Indeed, for the vast majority of the world's languages records go back no more than 200 years and therefore it is not possible to write a grammar of a much earlier stage. Despite the limits of the available records, with a good theory of grammar, it is in principle possible for an analyst to formulate and compare at least fragments of grammars of various stages of a language. Sometimes this can suggest things about properties of the genotype.

Although particular grammars may change from one generation to the next, all grammars of the last few thousand years can be assumed to accord with the theory of grammar and with our common genetic inheritance and to be attainable by a child on the basis of exposure only to the usual linguistic environment. Looking at the point where certain changes take place may inform us about the limits to attainable grammars, about when the linguistic environment changes in such a way as to trigger a different kind of grammar. In the next few sections I shall show how this might work out in practice. I shall illustrate with changes affecting the syntactic component, but one can take an analogous approach to phonological and semantic changes.

The Challenge

A good theory of grammar illuminates the nature of historical change but one must be careful not to demand too much. A theory of grammar should not seek to explain all the changes that a language might undergo, because the history of a language is not fully determined by the properties it shows at some arbitrary starting point and by the properties of the mental genotype. Many changes are due to other things, some of which can be regarded as chance or at least nongrammatical factors.

A moment's reflection will show that this must be the case, because a language may split in two and then pursue different courses, diverging more and more. Latin, for example, developed into French, Rumanian, Italian, and several other identifiable languages. Most European and several languages spoken in India descend ultimately from a language called Proto-Indo-European, for which there are no direct records. The parent language is usually supposed to have had an underlying word order of subject-object-verb (SOV); its descendants have quite different orders: Hindi has retained SOV, English has developed SVO, Welsh and Irish have VSO. Given the possibility of divergent development, historical changes cannot be fully determined by the properties of Proto-Indo-European and the (invariant) demands of the theory of grammar, our genetic endowment. The theory of grammar cannot prescribe a universal path for languages to slide along at various rates, acquiring properties in a predestined order; it cannot prophesy which changes a language will undergo in the future, because it cannot predict which chance factors will operate or when.

Nonetheless languages do not change in completely arbitrary ways; many changes recur in one language after another. Despite the role of nongrammatical factors and chance, some changes and the manner in which they arise can be explained and occur as a matter of necessity. The interaction of chance and necessity can be seen in the much studied phenomenon of word order change.

Consider a language changing from SOV to SVO order. English is an example, because the grammar of Old English had a PS rule $\overline{V} \rightarrow \overline{\overline{N}}\ V$, generating object-verb order in the initial phrase marker, and Modern English has $\overline{V} \rightarrow V\ \overline{\overline{N}}$. So the parameter of (12) in Chapter 4 came to be fixed differently. How could this change have taken place?

First, while the sentences of Old English are very different from those of Modern English, differences are much smaller over a shorter time span. In the speech of two adjacent generations, some parents and their children, the difference between the sentences uttered is usually quite small. This is not surprising because the speech of the immediately preceding generation, particularly that of the parents, usually provides a significant part of the linguistic environment that triggers the development of the child's grammar.

For any usual parent and child, the output of their grammars will be quite similar.[3] This follows from the way in which children develop grammars, stimulated by their linguistic environment, and it imposes a tight limit on the class of possible historical changes. For example, no grammar with PS rules generating SOV order could undergo a reanalysis of its PS rules to generate initial SVO structures unless there were already some SVO sentences in the language. This fact about word order changes is explained by the way in which children acquire grammars. A consistently SOV linguistic environment would not trigger a grammar with basic SVO order, that is, with the $\overline{\overline{V}} \rightarrow V \ \overline{\overline{N}}$ PS rule. Therefore an order change from SOV to SVO cannot take place without warning, suddenly and across the board.

A speaker whose grammar has PS rules generating an initial object-verb order may nonetheless utter sentences with verb-object order. In fact, it seems that all underlying SOV grammars "leak," allowing some surface instances of orders other than SOV. This is due to limitations of human processing abilities, to the fact that multiple center-embeddings strain short-term memory capacity. A SOV language incurs the danger of center-embedding with object complements, because the grammar would generate initial structures like (1). Consequently a SOV grammar will have some device eliminating these structures—for reasons of necessity relating to short-term memory capacity. A transformational rule converting SOV to SVO would suffice: (1) would be transformed into the right-branching and harmless (2), where there is no center-embedding.

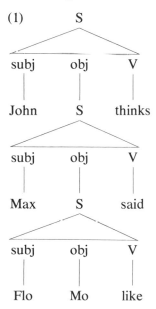

(1)

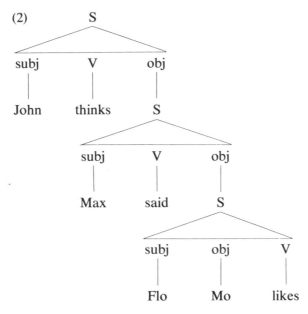

(2)

Many SOV languages have such a rule changing SOV to SVO when the object consists of a sentence. No doubt there are other solutions, so presumably there was nothing necessary about the fact that this particular solution was adopted by Classical Greek, Old English, Dutch, and German.

It is a fact of biological necessity that languages always have devices to draw attention to parts of sentences, and people may speak more expressively by adopting a novel or unusual construction, perhaps a new word order. When they first occur, these novel forms may not be part of the output of a grammar but may be quite irregular, specially learned accretions in the way that formulaic expressions like "Good morning," "Hi," "Wow," are part of my language but quite idiosyncratic and not a function of any general rule.[4] Although there are limits, one cannot forecast which novel forms will be introduced or when; least of all can one forecast which novelties will catch on and be perpetuated. Chance or nongrammatical factors are at work. At a later stage the forms originally introduced as novelties may become "grammaticalized" and have a general, predictable and rule-governed distribution. Grammars at that stage would have a transformation or some other device that has the effect of permitting them to be generated.

Dislocation sentences fall under this rubric: *Mingus, I heard him* and *He played cool, Miles*. These forms, they are still regarded as novel in

English and as having a distinct stylistic force, focusing attention on the noun phrase; they are common in Yorkshire dialects, with British sports commentators and in the speech of many Jewish Americans. However, such expressive forms characteristically become bleached and lose their novelty value as they become commonly used. This can be illustrated with the parallel dislocation sentences in French: *Pierre, je le connais* and *Je le connais, Pierre* were originally stylistically marked alternants of *Je connais Pierre,* but now they have lost much of their special force and have become relatively unremarkable construction types, to the point that in simple, affirmative main clauses they are the norm and the former *Je connais Pierre* is vanishingly rare.

This process is familiar with lexical change, where, to the constant dismay of the purists, adjectives are regularly "devalued" by a kind of linguistic inflation: *excellent* comes to mean merely 'good', *enormous* to mean 'big', and *fantastic, fabulous,* and so on lose their original force. As this happens, so new superlatives must be invented to describe the end point on some scale: hence the currently popular *ginormous, fantabulous.* Similarly metaphors lose value and become standardized through frequent use, requiring a constant effort on the part of speakers to find new forms with the old surprise value.

So in syntax new constructions are introduced, which by their unusual shape have a novelty value and are used for stylistic effect. The special stylistic effect slowly becomes bleached out and the constructions lose their particular force, become incorporated into the normal grammatical processes and thereby require speakers to draw on their creative powers once more to find another new pattern to carry the desired stylistic effect. So sentences such as *Mingus, I heard him* seem to be fairly recent innovations and have a special focusing effect in most dialects; in other dialects, notably those of North Americans with a Yiddish background, the construction has already become bleached of its special effect, like the dislocation sentences of French. This is an important kind of change in syntax.

Again, although languages necessarily have some means for expressiveness, the particular means varies (within limits) from language to language—in accordance with the rules of the language lottery. Given a grammar generating object-verb order, speakers may come to develop a transformation allowing verb-object order in some contexts, perhaps for reasons of focusing.

That transformation will not be structure preserving, since the output (verb-object) is not generated directly by the base rules; therefore it can apply only in root clauses (recall the structure-preservation principle). This is a matter of necessity, dictated by human genetic endowment. It follows that any innovation that is a function of a non-structure-preserving (and nonlocal) transformation enters a language first through main clauses, only later percolating through to affect structures in embedded clauses. The manner of these changes is explained by a theory of grammar with something like the structure-preservation principle.

Numerous examples can be cited of changes progressing in this fashion. The SOV-to-SVO change affected English first in main clauses and later in subordinate clauses. Modern Dutch and German are like early Middle English in having a more recent SVO order in main clauses and an older SOV order elsewhere. Basque now seems to be undergoing a similar change in a similar way. Such changes are entirely consistent with the theory outlined in Chapter 4, unlike, say, a change affecting first subordinate clauses and then spreading to all other clause types. Such a change could not be interpreted in this theory, because it is not possible to have a movement rule that affects only subordinate clauses. The theory therefore explains why changes do not percolate up historically from subordinate clauses to main clauses, whereas the reverse direction is quite common.

Linguists studying change have traditionally noted that main clauses are the most progressive environment; innovations are first introduced there and spread later into other environments. In fact, the structure-preservation principle yields finer predictions than the traditional account. It follows from this theory that rules moving major categories enter the grammar as root transformations, affecting main clauses before subordinates; it does not follow that a morphological change, say, should affect verbs in main clauses before subordinates. In other words, only certain kinds of change will percolate from main to subordinate clauses. This finer prediction seems to be more consistent with the facts.

If the earlier appeal to perceptual modes is correct, all SOV grammars have in them the seeds for a change to underlying SVO order. This is because they typically show SVO surface order when the object consists of a sentence, as noted. The language may also develop a focusing process and perhaps other rules that yield a surface SVO order. If the surface SVO forms proliferate sufficiently, at some point the linguistic environment will trigger in children an *underlying* SVO order as part of the most readily attainable grammar; that is, the PS rules will come to generate verb-object order instead of the earlier object-verb. This kind of change in the PS rules is called a *reanalysis;* it arises as a matter of necessity dictated by the theory of grammar. Given the earlier changes, the linguistic environment has become such that the theory of grammar requires that the best grammar contains a PS rule $\overline{\text{V}} \rightarrow$ V $\overline{\overline{\text{N}}}$. Presumably an underlying SOV grammar with a number of transformational processes yielding surface SVO order was unattainable under these circumstances, being too complex and opaque; a theory of grammar would explain the change if it could specify that this degree of complexity makes the grammar less readily attainable than one with the PS parameter fixed differently.

As an indication that a change has taken place in the PS rules, one would look for a variety of simultaneous changes in the occurring sentences, most notably a significant increase in the occurrences of the innovating order in nonroot, subordinate clauses. There is good evidence that English underwent just such a PS reanalysis in the thirteenth century, whereby SVO became the base-generated word order.

There is also good evidence that this change in PS rules helped to provoke several further changes, such as a change in the meaning of the verb *like*. Sentences like (3) occurred in Middle English.

(3)
The king liked the queen.

Such sentences were construed as object-verb-subject with *like* meaning 'please, cause pleasure for'. So the sentence meant 'The queen pleased the king' and it occurred alongside sentences like *Him liked the queen* and *The king like the pears* (which are manifestly object-verb-subject structures). *Like* and about forty other verbs occurred typically with their object preceding and the subject following them. These structures were generated by a grammar with underlying SOV order. But it can be shown that such an object-verb-subject analysis could not occur in a similar grammar, differing from that of early Middle English only insofar as the PS rules generated a SVO order. Therefore, as the grammars of Middle English speakers became underlying SVO, that is, with a different PS rule, these constructions had to be eliminated—as was dictated by the theory of grammar.

In early Middle English grammars with underlying object-verb order, (3) had an initial structure (4a) and was derived by the movement indicated, a perfectly healthy and honorable movement that would be a credit to anybody's grammar.

(4)

a.

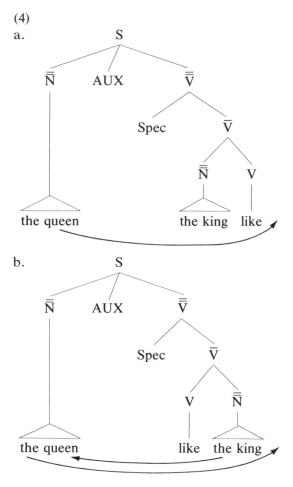

b.

For a person with the newer grammar, with underlying verb-object order, one might imagine that (3) was derived from an initial (4b) by the movements indicated. But such a derivation is illegitimate, violating an invariant condition called the *Trace Erasure Principle,* which says essentially that a noun phrase (*the king* in (4b)) cannot move into a position which has been vacated by another noun phrase (the subject position of (4b)); see Lightfoot 1981 a,b for elaboration. Now if derivation (4b) is not available, how would a child with verb-object PS rules react to hearing a sentence like (3), knowing that it meant something along the lines of 'The queen caused pleasure for the king'? Since such a child could not adopt a derivation like (4b), the only available syntactic analysis would be to treat *the king* as the underlying subject and *the queen* as object; no movement rule would be applicable. If that were the syntactic analysis, it could be squared with the known meaning only by taking *like* to mean 'derive pleasure from', unlike the earlier generation, for whom it meant 'to cause pleasure for'. Given this new analysis, clearly object-verb-subject sentences like *Him liked the queen* and *The king like the pears* would drop out of the language, as in fact happened.

So for the earlier generation with object-verb PS rules, (3) is analyzed as O-V-S, the subject having moved right as in (4a) and *like* meaning 'cause pleasure for'; for the later generation, with verb-object PS rules, (3) is analyzed as S-V-O, *like* meaning 'derive pleasure from'. The two analyses of (3) convey the same "message" and are mutually comprehensible. Communication between generations was never endangered and the meaning change of *like* took place suddenly, not creeping from main to subordinate clauses; speakers at the time were almost certainly unaware that any change was taking place.

The change in meaning of *like* (and the other verbs that used to occur in a O_____S frame) is explained by two things: the change in PS rules and a theory of grammar incorporating some invariant principle along the lines of the Trace Erasure Principle (or the more recent Projection Principle of Chomsky 1981b). This principle prevents a child with verb-object PS rules from analyzing *the king* as an object in (3) and therefore explains why the change in meaning of *like* should occur at the same time as the change in underlying word order.

Seen in this light, it is unremarkable that the Indo-European languages have undergone some parallel changes. If most of the early Indo-European languages were underlying SOV, they also allowed some surface SVO forms as one way of solving some perceptual difficulties. Rightward movement rules also provided a means for focusing and for arranging complex structures in such a way as to avoid "heavy" elements in the middle of a sentence and thereby entailing more processing difficulties. There was nothing necessary about the development of these rightward derivational processes, but they are not surprising. Given enough surface VO forms, the theory of grammar would necessitate a reanalysis of the PS rules. This reanalysis in turn might entail complex and unattainable derivations elsewhere in the grammar, e.g., (4b), thereby contributing to further changes. The form of these subsequent changes could vary, but the new grammar would have to be attainable in the existing linguistic environment; the changes would therefore be constrained significantly. Thus the structure-preservation and trace erasure principles, both imposing necessary and invariant conditions on particular grammars, have helped to shape certain changes in the history of English.

With this view of change, parallel changes affecting several languages independently are not surprising. Change is a function of chance and necessity: it is sometimes a matter of chance (or at least due to nongrammatical factors) that the linguistic environment should change in a particular way, perhaps incorporating a new kind of expression for a focusing effect or an expression borrowed from a neighboring language. It is a matter of biological necessity that the grammar should be readily attainable and allow only the simplest analyses, that surface strings should be processible with minimal perceptual difficulty, and that generations should maintain mutual comprehensibility. Such necessities each force reanalyses at certain points, encourage certain kinds of rules, and restrict the possibilities for change in any given grammar. In this way the partial similarity of developments in French, English, and Lithuanian is explained.

The fact that different languages may undergo parallel changes independently will not surprise a biologist. Evolutionists distinguish two reasons for a certain feature being shared by two or more species: that similarity may be due to common genetic ancestry, being *homologous*. Alternatively, the similarity may be due to a common function but arising independently in each species, being *analogous*. So the wings of birds and insects are analogous features, since they developed independently and the common ancestor did not have wings (see Gould 1978:254ff).

Since the theory of grammar aims to specify what constitutes an attainable grammar, it will shed light on those historical changes where a reanalysis has occurred because part of the old grammar is no longer attainable. Conversely, light will be shed on the proper formulation of the theory of grammar if one can discover the point at which such a reanalysis occurs, the point at which the linguistic environment (the child's trigger experience) has changed in such a way that certain aspects of the old grammar become unattainable. We have seen how a PS rule $\bar{V} \to \bar{\bar{N}}$ V can become unattainable; likewise the old meaning of *like* in Middle English.

Reanalysis

So change is viewed as progressing as a function of chance and necessity, just as Monod (1972) viewed change in genetic structure.

Changes may be necessitated by the theory of grammar; such changes are therefore explained by the theory of grammar. Conversely, noting the point at which abstract reanalyses take place teaches something about the limits to attainable grammars. What should be looked for as evidence of a base reanalysis?

To see what is involved in a base reanalysis, consider the history of the English modals. There are two stages to this story. In Old English *can, could, may, might, must, shall, should, will, would, do, did* behaved exactly like normal verbs; there was no reason to hypothesize a separate modal category. As a result of changes in the grammar during the course of Middle English, these items became a distinct subclass of verbs, distinguished by various properties that need not be elaborated here (for details see Lightfoot 1979). It was now no longer clear that they were verbs. If they were verbs, they had several exceptional features. Put differently, their verbal nature was opaque, harder to figure out, less readily attainable. In the sixteenth century a radical reanalysis took place whereby a new modal category was introduced and some rules were formulated differently. This suggests that the exceptionality or opacity of this area of grammar had reached a critical point beyond which it could not remain attainable by a child. How else could the change be explained? A good theory of grammar should be able to characterize why this degree of exceptionality is unattainable by a child. Here I am concerned not with why this change took place but with the evidence for the reanalysis: a cluster of simultaneous changes all of which follow automatically from the introduction of a new PS rule, AUX → Tense Modal.

The earlier grammar was along the lines of (5), where *can, could*, etc. were instances of V. The later grammar (6) contained a new PS rule and a new category, Modal; perfective and progressive markers were specifiers of $\overline{V}$ at all stages.

(5)
$$S \rightarrow \overline{\overline{N}} \ \text{AUX} \ \overline{\overline{V}}$$
$$\text{AUX} \rightarrow \text{Tense}$$
$$\overline{\overline{V}} \rightarrow \text{Spec} \ \overline{V}$$
$$\overline{V} \rightarrow V \begin{Bmatrix} \overline{\overline{X}} \\ \overline{\overline{S}} \end{Bmatrix}$$
$$\text{Spec} \ \overline{V} \rightarrow \text{Perfective} \ \text{Progressive}$$

(6)
$$S \rightarrow \bar{\bar{N}} \; AUX \; \bar{\bar{V}}$$
$$AUX \rightarrow Tense \; Modal$$
$$\bar{\bar{V}} \rightarrow Spec \; \bar{V}$$
$$\bar{V} \rightarrow V \begin{Bmatrix} \bar{\bar{X}} \\ \bar{S} \end{Bmatrix}$$
$$Spec \; \bar{V} \rightarrow Perfective \; Progressive$$
$$Modal \rightarrow can, \; could, \; may, \; might, \; do, \; \ldots$$

We know that a reanalysis along these lines occurred because several changes that took place together around 1525–1550 all reflect the introduction of the new Modal category. Under the earlier grammar, where *shall, can,* and so on were instances of verbs, they could occur together side by side as in (7a), just like other verbs (compare *I want to begin now*); they could occur with a progressive marker (7b) or a perfective marker (7c); they could occur in infinitival form (7d). In all of these respects *can, may, must,* etc. behaved like normal verbs.

(7)
a. I shall can do it.
b. I am canning do it.
c. I have could do it.
d. I want to can do it.

Grammar (5) generates the sentences of (7). Such sentences occur in the writings of Thomas More and earlier but have not occurred since the sixteenth century, and a grammar like (6) does not generate them: the PS rules of (6) clearly allow only one modal per verb and therefore cannot generate (7a). Under the rules of (6) a modal cannot occur to the right of the aspectual marker *have* or *be,* as in (7b,c), or in an infinitive (because in a nonfinite clause AUX is manifested as *to* instead of Tense and Modal). Sentences like (7) ceased to occur at the same time, which is consistent with saying that people used to have grammars like (5) but came to have grammars like (6).

In a grammar like (5), which assigns *could* and *leave* to the same category, V, transformational rules could not distinguish them. So negatives might be found to the right of the first V, regardless of whether it was *could* or *left* (8), and questions like (9) occurred, where the first verb has been moved to the front of the main clause, again regardless of whether it is *could* or *left*.

(8)

a. John could not leave.

b. John left not.

(9)

a. Could John leave?

b. Left John?

In a grammar distinguishing modals from verbs, such rules would be expected to affect one or other class of items but not both. In fact the (8b) and (9b) forms were replaced with expressions with *do,* which suggests that only modals could receive a negative or be inverted. The change was a consequence of the new modal/verb distinction. I shall return to this in a moment.

These changes occurred simultaneously; they all follow from saying that the later grammar distinguished modal and verbal categories, whereas the earlier grammar did not. The fact that the surface changes were simultaneous suggests that in the grammar there was just one change with various surface manifestations.[5] In general, when such clusters of simultaneous changes occur, it may be possible to explain their simultaneity by attributing them to a single change in the abstract grammar. Conversely, if one has a hunch that there is a major difference between the grammars of, say, Old and Modern English, one looks for a cluster of simultaneous changes that follow from saying that the one grammar was replaced by another, that some parameter of grammar is fixed differently.

Saying that one grammar replaced another idealizes away from variation among individuals or even dialects. *All* speakers of Old English could utter sentences like (7), and *no* speakers could utter them after the time of Thomas More. Somewhere in between these two stages presumably some but not other people uttered them. Analysts depend on the available texts and we can know only the date of the last attested example of some construction type that still survives in the written literature.[6] Of the spoken language at that time we know virtually nothing. Sometimes we can refine our claims, specifying that the sentence died out in one dialect before another, but for the most part analyses must be conducted at a fairly gross level, abstracting away from such details. Grammars are triggered by linguistic environments, so the linguistic environment of Thomas More, when he was a child, triggered quite a different grammar (5) from that triggered in the next generation (6); that is what it means to say that one grammar replaced another. In no case can we specify *exactly* what the linguistic environment was for any individual and compare it with the environment available for that individual's child, who developed quite a different grammar. But then, we cannot do that for an individual child growing up in London today. So if the idealization of a linguistic community is appropriate for the analysis of Modern English (see Chapter 5), it is presumably also appropriate for Old English.

Let us return to the new negative and inversion sentences, which I said were due to the new modal/verb distinction. With the introduction of a category Modal, further changes were required as a matter of necessity, imposed this time by the nature of acquisition. If there were no further changes, the old rules of Negation and Inversion, interacting with the new PS rules, would yield quite different surface patterns, of a kind to strain communication across generations to breaking point. The old rules placed the negative after the first verb and inverted the first verb. If incorporated unchanged into a grammar with the new PS rules, they would give new surface forms like (10) and (11), because *go* is now a verb and *can* is not. These forms are quite different from the existing (10′) and (11′), which are what the child would hear from his parents.

(10)   (10′)
John can go not.   John cannot go.

(11)   (11′)
Go John can?   Can John go?

In other words, if a child developed category rules like those of (6) and was exposed to sentences like (10′) and (11′), the old Negative and Inversion rules would no longer be triggered; such rules would yield (10) and (11), which would grate on parental ears and perhaps create domestic chaos. Rather, a linguistic environment including forms like (10′) and (11′) would trigger new Negative and Inversion rules operating on Modal and not V. The new Negative rule places a negative on the right of the first Modal (instead of the first verb), and the new Inversion rule moves only a Modal; these rules generate (10′) and (11′).

The sixteenth-century child heard (8b) and (9b), but such types were clearly not robust enough to trigger Negative and Inversion rules applying to Modal *and* to V. We know this because in fact such sentences dropped out of English and ceased to occur in the texts. Alongside these forms, the child also heard forms with *do: John did not go, Did John go?* These were consistent both with grammar (5) (with Negative and Inversion applying to V, *did* being a V at this stage) and with grammar (6) (with the rules applying to Modal, *did* now being a Modal); (8b) and (9b) were consistent with grammar (5) and not (6) (assuming for all stages Negative and Inversion rules applying to only one category, either V or Modal). Therefore, as grammar (6) developed, so the *do* forms continued to occur; (8b) and (9b) did not serve to trigger any elaboration in the grammar that might have permitted them to survive alongside the *do* forms, and they dropped out of the language. I have not offered an explanation for this particular reanalysis, but I have used it only to illustrate how to discover when a reanalysis occurs.

Grammatical reanalyses meet strict conditions: they must lead to a grammar fulfilling the restrictive requirements imposed by the theory of grammar; they must constitute the simplest attainable grammar for a child exposed to the new linguistic environment; they must yield an output close to that of the earlier grammars. For any reanalysis, these requirements impose narrow restrictions on the available options.

A grammar is not an object floating smoothly through time and space but a contingent object that arises afresh in each individual. Sometimes one individual's grammar may differ significantly from that of his parents; that constitutes a reanalysis. Assuming that changes over time can inform us about the limits to grammars, the study of diachronic change can show how idiosyncratic properties may be added to a grammar without affecting its internal structure, and what it takes to drive a grammar to reanalysis, with a parameter fixed differently. Examining historical reanalyses allows special insight into what kinds of trigger experiences elicit grammatical reanalyses and what kinds are not robust enough to have that effect. The point at which reanalyses take place sheds light on the load that can be borne by derivational processes; the limits are manifested by the occurrence of the reanalyses; the reanalyses are manifested by the simultaneity of the relevant surface changes. In this way research on historical change informs work on a restrictive theory of grammar and is fully integrated with that general enterprise.

Not only does the mere occurrence of a reanalysis suggest things about the proper shape of the theory of grammar, but it also suggests the particular cluster of properties that the reanalysis encompasses. The theory of grammar includes parameters which are fixed on exposure to relevant experience. Fixing a parameter one particular way, say fixing a PS rule as $\bar{V} \rightarrow V \; \bar{\bar{N}}$, may have elaborate consequences for the form of somebody's knowledge, for the range of possible surface structures. We have seen several examples of this, and research aims to define the parameters as accurately as possible. If in historical change a parameter comes to be fixed differently, the precise definition given by the theory for that parameter will have implications, often far-reaching, for what exactly will change in the surface structures. Examining the cluster of properties encompassed by particular reanalyses often suggests things about how the theory should define its parameters. For example, the changes discussed in this section suggest that the theory should allow grammars to use distinct categories of Verb and Modal; this is something denied by some people who argue that there is, even in the grammar of modern English speakers, no distinct category Modal.

It may be objected that this approach to language history accounts only for some changes and not others. Typically a theory works where it works and usually has no principled basis for not dealing with certain phenomena. In this particular domain one *must* allow a role for chance and nongrammatical factors; historical developments cannot and should not be totally predictable, for the reasons given earlier. Moreover, one cannot know in advance precisely which changes are due to chance factors and which are prompted by the theory of grammar. It is reasonable to suppose that changes involving the *loss* of certain sentence types, like those of (7), must be due to principled factors, because it is hard to imagine why a sentence type could cease to occur for reasons of stylistic force or foreign borrowing. Similarly, the change in the meaning of *like* is more likely to reflect a problem of attainability than a chance innovation for reasons of expressiveness. On the other hand, the gradual introduction of a new dislocation structure (*Mingus, I met him*) can plausibly be attributed to the need for strikingly new forms. But there are no firm guidelines. The theory of grammar used here casts light on historical changes by explaining certain reanalyses; looking at the point at which reanalyses occur may suggest revisions to the theory of grammar. If a given theory explained change x and not change y, then x is a predictable reanalysis and y is due to nongrammatical factors. As in other domains, theories should be evaluated by the explanations that they offer. If a theory aimed only to explain historical changes, there would be a problem of indeterminacy here and there would be no way to choose between theories that explained and attributed to chance different changes. In fact, the theory must meet many more demands, as shown in earlier chapters, and at this stage of research it is hard to imagine having to choose between a variety of theories all of which met the empirical demands that we are making. The problem, rather, is to find one adequate theory.[7]

Evolution of Grammars in the Species

So far I have been talking about language change within the realm of recorded history. Texts of, say, Old English or Classical Greek can be used to formulate plausible grammars, although certain difficulties may arise from the absence of native speaker intuitions.

Just as French, Italian, Rumanian, and Spanish are all descendants of Latin, so other languages, such as Classical Greek and Latin, probably descended from a common ancestor, although there are no surviving texts of that parent language. Some linguists try to penetrate prehistory, making hypotheses about the form of the prehistorical parent language on the basis of what can be observed in the attested daughter languages. A good deal of speculation is involved in this work, but the reconstructed languages have all of the essential properties of modern languages and do not go back further than a few thousand years. For that period an invariant genotype can be assumed, an assumption enabling us to explain historical changes that have taken place within the period for which we have recorded language.

If one wants to give free rein to one's imagination, one might speculate on how language as we know it came to emerge in the species and how the present genotype developed. In the linguistic literature one comes across the bow-wow theory, claiming that human language has evolved from animal cries; the heigh-ho theory, that language emerged from grunts of socialized effort (along the more sophisticated lines of sea chanteys); and the ouch theory, that it all developed from cries of pain. These supposed theories have in common the assumption that there has been a gradual development of an ability to communicate. Needless to say, very little evidence is offered in the context of such proposals and it is difficult to see the relation between, say, cries of pain and human beings' present ability to deal with the scope of quantifiers and the properties of anaphors.

Another idea is that the crucial element in the emergence of language was physiological. It is sometimes claimed that the throat of Neanderthal man was constructed in such a way that it was not possible to articulate a variety of vowel sounds, as would be necessary for human language. It is hard to imagine that the language faculty lay idle and unexploited until the shape of the lower throat happened to change in a certain way, so perhaps Neanderthal man used some other modality, perhaps a form of sign language, until his throat changed shape. This strikes me as a most unlikely history, but, whatever the fossil evidence, such a view would not be helpful for somebody who views language as the product of a mental organ with a rich structure provided by the genotype. Such a person might like to know how that mental organ emerged in the species.

Traditional approaches to this kind of issue have involved ethological analyses comparing observations of the typical behavior of living animals and psychological studies testing and measuring the abilities of various species. These analyses seek to compare living animals in such a way as to hypothesize an evolutionary history, rather as a linguist might hypothesize the prehistory of Greek, Latin and Sanskrit by comparing the internal structure of those languages: the variety of present patterns of behavior are projected backward to likely ancestral patterns. It is in this context that people study the so-called language of chimpanzees, dolphins, or bees. A problem is that although many animals can communicate danger, anger, fear, food sources, and the like, communication is not the same thing as language. Even in the chimpanzee, whose internal world seems to be fairly similar to man's (see Premack and Woodruff 1978), there seems to be very little remotely comparable to the linguistic principles that must be attributed to the human genotype.

It is sometimes claimed that chimpanzees do in fact have a capacity for language and can be trained to use and understand English. There are some fairly wild and quite unsubstantiated claims about what has been achieved with chimpanzees in laboratories (for discussion see Fodor, Bever, and Garrett 1974; Gardner 1980; or Premack and Woodruff 1978). In any case the important question concerns not what an animal *can* learn, but what an animal does in fact learn under natural conditions. It would be an incredible evolutionary accident if chimpanzees had a usable capacity for humanlike language but in fact did not use it except when subject to laboratory training programs. Recall that children are not trained to use language and research into the mental genotype has focused on language and not, let us say, on chess-playing skills, precisely because it is a capacity that develops naturally in each child without instruction (although not, of course, without the stimulus of a trigger experience).

The traditional methods for establishing an evolutionary history are not very helpful for considering the emergence of language, because there is no close analogue of the human language capacity in other species. However, there is a novel approach to the evolution of functions: this is the approach of paleoneurology. If the human mental organ evolved, investigators might be able to identify a physical correlate of the mind that is manifested in fossil records. H. J. Jerison has tried to trace the "index of encephalization," a measure of actual brain size relative to the size of the brain that can be expected for a certain species given a certain body weight and size. It is known that the human being's most distinctive anatomical feature is the central nervous system and that human evolution has been marked above all by progressive increase in cranial capacity. Jerison aimed to establish the brain and body sizes of fossil vertebrates and identified periods where there was a four- and fivefold increase in relative brain size for the average mammal.

Major evolutionary changes may take place without significant advances in relative brain size. Jerison reports that, according to paleoneurological evidence, the advance from fish to amphibian around 350 million years ago took place without an increase in encephalization. This was possible because there were only minor changes in the neurological and behavioral organization of the earliest amphibian as compared to its immediate ancestor among the bony fish.

Although the step from reptiles to mammals required a certain amount of encephalization (approximately a fourfold increase in relative brain size . . .), mammalian encephalization did not progress immediately but remained at a steady level for at least 100 million years. . . . That stability for such a long period of time suggests a successful response to the selection pressures of a stable new ecological niche. Progressive evolution of encephalization within the mammals came late in their history, in the last 50 million years of a time span of about 200 million years. That evolution transformed the archaic mammalian map into the map of living mammals by another four- or fivefold increase in relative brain size for the average mammal. (Jerison 1976:95)

The picture that emerges is that the brain may have increased in relative size in a series of explosions, as one might expect if encephalization (and intelligence) evolved like other traits. One of the early explosions may have been associated with the development of upright posture, which correlated not only with specialization of the foot but with many changes in muscle and bone structure, particularly in the vertebrate column and the position of the skull in relation to it. Man's evolution, as often noted, must have been greatly spurred when he stood erect and his hands became free as he walked and ran.[8] Jerison claims that the hominid brain evolved to its present size in relatively recent times, having been completed only within the last million years, long after the development of erect posture. There is no evidence of a change in encephalization in any other mammals in the past five million years.

The evolution of hearing and smell to supplement vision as a distance sense is sufficient reason for the evolution of an enlarged brain in the earliest mammals. The reason is to be found in the way neural elements are packaged in vertebrate sensory systems. In the visual system many of the circuits are in the retina, which contains an extensive and complex neural network that allows elaborate analysis of visual information. The corresponding neural elements of the auditory and olfactory systems of living vertebrates are in the brain proper. . . .
An auditory system analogous to the visual system would presumably have to have about as much integrative circuitry as there is in the retina. . . . There is no space for this in the middle and inner ears; the obvious place to package the additional material is in the brain itself, and solving the packaging problem would therefore require the enlargement of parts of the brain involved in audition. (Jerison 1976: 98–9)

The optics of the eye and the arrangements of retinal elements enable visual information to be encoded at the retina. No such encoding is possible for sounds and smells, and the introduction of finely tuned hearing and smelling required encephalization as a means to encode this neural information. If the vertebrate brain was first enlarged in this way, as a solution to a packaging problem, then intelligence and language may have evolved as an incidental consequence, just as it is often suggested that our genetically determined capacity to deal with the number system would not have been specifically selected through evolution but arose as a byproduct of something else. The brain now encoded dimensions of time and space and so had the means for dealing with a number system and for creating a world, a basic ingredient for human consciousness, mental imagery, and thus for language. Once language emerged, it brought with it the means for communicated traditions and a new kind of evolution, the cultural evolution described in Chapter 1. At that point the whole emphasis of human development changed.

Whether or not language actually developed out of the sensory-perceptual system, as a side effect of the brain's role in the construction of reality, as Jerison suggests, the brain can be viewed as evolving in a series of explosions and qualitative changes, and not as a gradual development. Presumably something like this happened for most physical features, since evolution typically is a discontinuous process, prizing only fully adaptive innovations. Even if relevant facts are in short supply, it can be speculated that perhaps something similar happened in the evolution of the mental genotype in the species. As with the emergence of the heart or upright posture, so with language. These properties can be said to have emerged rather suddenly and to have been adaptive. Nobody has any idea how this happened with physical or mental organs; there are no principles that allow us to predict that from some organism some particular property must evolve. That is not to say that these developments are inexplicable, but that they are unexplained at the present state of knowledge. From that perspective the evolution of the human heart and mental organs are on a par.

Notes

1. Looking at a written page involves other difficulties because of changing spelling conventions and even different symbols, like ʃ for *s* and þ for *th*.

2. Therefore as analysts we are in roughly the same position as the child developing its grammar, at least in terms of the data we have access to.

3. It does not follow from this that their grammars will be similar, because there is no one-to-one relation between difference of output and difference of internal grammar. Two wildly different grammars might yield fairly similar outputs; conversely two similar-looking grammars might yield wildly different outputs. Imagine, for example, the drastic consequences for the output if one retained all the rules discussed so far in this book but simply changed the initial PS rules from $S \to \bar{\bar{N}}$ AUX $\bar{\bar{V}}$ to $S \to \bar{\bar{V}}$ AUX $\bar{\bar{N}}$.

4. The existence of such forms is one reason why a person's grammar does not define all of the expressions of his or her language, and why there may not be a mechanical device that can generate all these expressions (see Chapter 5). These forms are presumably learned, that is, shaped in direct response to experience, perhaps even in adulthood.

5. So the simultaneity of the changes is explained by their singularity. An alternative analysis would say that the loss of (7a–d), (8b), and (9b) were each due to different factors, to independent changes in the grammar, in which case their simultaneity would be a remarkable accident.

6. For this kind of information about the history of English one relies heavily on handbooks such as the *Oxford English Dictionary* and Visser's monumental *An Historical Syntax of the English Language*.

7. There is a potentially rich source of information about historical reanalyses in studies of what happens when a *pidgin* forms much of the linguistic environment of a child. A pidgin is an artificially simplified language used by colonial traders of different mother tongues. In those circumstances, the pidgin acts as a trigger and sets off in the child the development of a natural grammar in the usual way. The child naturalizes the pidgin, making it into a *creole*. That naturalization process, or creolization, typically involves many reanalyses occur-

ring in quick succession from generation to generation, as a bona fide natural language emerges. It is often difficult to gather reliable data, but there are some interesting studies. For one example, see Sankoff and Laberge 1974.

8. Gould 1978 considers the relation between enlarged brain size and the development of upright posture in an essay called "Posture Maketh the Man." Some anthropologists have held that upright posture was a consequence of increased brain size; others have held that the development of upright posture, freeing the hands for the use of tools and weapons, introduced a new mode of life, which placed a strong, selective premium on intelligence and therefore favored an increased brain size. All agree that the two developments were interdependent and mutually reinforcing.

In the same volume see Gould's "History of the Vertebrate Brain" for some discussion of Jerison's ideas, and "Sizing up Human Intelligence" for some more general discussion of the significance of brain size.

Suggested Reading

Language change is one of my own favorite areas of work, so the reader may turn to Lightfoot 1981 a,b for elaboration of some of the points made here. Lightfoot 1979 examines many examples of historical reanalyses.

Considerably more work has been done on phonological change than on the kinds of syntactic changes discussed in this chapter. In several papers Paul Kiparsky has brought historical phenomena to bear on questions about psychological grammars. His "Historical Linguistics" chapter in J. Lyons, ed. *New Horizons in Linguistics* (Harmondsworth: Penguin, 1970) provides a good introduction to his work.

On the evolution of language, Chapter 6 of Lenneberg 1967 contains several interesting ideas and some good discussion of the significance of some studies of animal communication systems.

Chapter 9
The Growth, Breakdown, and Use of Grammars

Presumably a good representation of what mature speakers have come to know (that is, a good representation of grammars) will help us to understand how young children progress toward this mature knowledge, how linguistic abilities are represented in the brain, and thus how they may suffer in the event of brain damage, and how sentences are analyzed and processed by somebody who hears them. Conversely, just as specific properties of normal adult language reveal aspects of the structure of the language faculty, so too do specific properties of child grammars, specific deficits, and properties of language processing. If phenomena in these areas may be explained by a good theory of grammar, it is not immediately obvious what kinds of explanations to look for.

Work on child grammars, aphasia, and processing is becoming increasingly important, but so far the abstract level of inquiry, as discussed in Chapters 4, 6, and 7, has made a much greater contribution to what is known about grammars and therefore has received correspondingly more attention in this book. I shall not attempt to survey the mass of work that has been done on these topics. As elsewhere, I shall be concerned with how work on child language, aphasia, and language processing can reveal something about the form of grammars. This is tricky and there are special difficulties in making claims about grammars on the basis of these kinds of data. However, it can be done, and there are many potential contributions. I shall show not only what some of the difficulties are but also how they can be circumvented to some extent, giving just some simple illustrations.

Child Grammars

Determining the properties of the genotype that make it possible for children to master their native languages has been referred to as the logical problem of acquisition, which is quite different from the task of describing real-time acquisition, the stages which young children go through before reaching a mature knowledge of their language.

In earlier chapters I have hypothesized several invariant genotypical properties but without mentioning the behavior of young children. This is normal practice among people engaged in this program, but it raises the eyebrows of some commentators and looks paradoxical to them. How can one make claims about the properties that children have at birth without detailed studies on the language of young children?

To put this apparent paradox into perspective, let us reflect again on the kinds of arguments used in this sort of inquiry. For many physical attributes, such as the visual system, biologists characteristically distinguish what is genetically determined from aspects of the organ that are influenced by nutritional, environmental, or even accidental variation. The gradual development of the organ in the growing child rarely plays a significant role in determining essential properties. Similarly for behavioral studies: ethologists often devise ingenious experiments to distinguish learned/unlearned behavior (for nice illustrations see the work of Tinbergen), but only rarely do these experiments relate to observations about the developmental stages that young animals go through. Biologists and ethologists hypothesize genotypical features to account for invariant properties in the mature organism that are underdetermined by the environment. They base their arguments on areas where it can be demonstrated that the stimulus is not rich enough to determine the mature properties, and they devise their experiments accordingly, often depriving a young animal of part of its normal experience or artificially simulating some trigger experience and comparing the results with those of some control group. Similar reasoning is used in the study of the grammar and the mental genotype, but different kinds of experiments must be devised.

For any area of data, whether it concerns the scope of quantifiers, the distribution of the English pronoun *one,* historical change, or developmental stages, the question to be asked is: what can be learned from it. How can the data be exploited in order to illuminate properties of the genotype? At the present stage of research it does not seem that much can be learned from studies of how the grammars of young children develop and change as they grow older. This is not to rule out the possibility of exploiting such data as a matter of principle; perhaps at another stage of research these data will play a larger role. For the moment it is as well to pursue the reasoning of the earlier chapters and to focus attention on claims about the mature state (a steady state emerging before puberty and not changing significantly afterward, perhaps only by the kinds of exceptions discussed in Chapter 8), as if grammars develop instantaneously and without different intermediate stages.

In fact, of course, language does not grow instantaneously, but it does grow rapidly. Parents often observe that their children acquire the ability to put together reasonably complex sentences rather quickly, moving suddenly from isolated words or pairs of words to fairly elaborate structures. Correspondingly, as this explosive growth takes place, linguists and psychologists studying young children find it hard to identify stages with accurate detail because they come and go so quickly.

If grammars emerge quickly but not instantaneously, what kinds of questions might one want to answer about the way in which grammars emerge? One might want to know, for example, whether a child's learning capacity differs at different stages of development. Do certain aspects of the theory of grammar emerge later than others? Is the linguistic environment interpreted differently at different stages? Or are all aspects of the theory available from birth with changes only in other cognitive capacities such as memory or attention span? Does the learning capacity decay in such a way that there are critical periods for attaining various aspects of grammar, as assumed by Monod (1972:128) and many others?[1] Answers to such questions would give us a basis to refine the idealization of instant learning. No substantial answers to these questions exist yet, so it is difficult to exploit possible data about developmental stages.

To illustrate the difficulty, consider the first of these questions: do some aspects of the theory of grammar emerge later than others? We might suppose that the theory defines Domains (Chapter 6), and ask whether this is available at the initial state or emerges only later. Matthei (1981) pursued exactly this question (although couching it in terms of an earlier formulation of the theory), and gave four-and-one-half to six-and-one-half-year-old children sentences like *The pigs said the chickens tickled each other,* interpretation of which crucially involves the notion of a Domain: a mature speaker would interpret *each other* to be co-indexed within its Domain (the lower clause) and to refer to the chickens and not to the pigs. Sixty-five percent of the children studied by Matthei, on the contrary, interpreted *each other* as referring to the pigs, apparently violating the Domain principle. Other children interpreted the sentence as meaning that chickens tickled pigs and vice versa. Matthei concluded that the definition of Domain is not available to children under about five years. But there are several other interpretations. To take just one: under the account developed in Chapter 6, speakers of English have to learn that *each other* is an anaphor with a reciprocal sense; under the theory sketched there nothing more complex is needed than this. Consequently Matthei's children can be interpreted as knowing what a Domain is and that *each other* is a reciprocal but not that it is an anaphor. If it were not an anaphor (therefore coindexed in its Domain), it might be treated like *the other* (a nonanaphor reciprocal) as in *Each got Mary to tickle the other.* Here *the other,* like a pronoun, is coindexed not within its Domain but in the next Domain up. Alternatively, children might interpret *each other* as some kind of adverb, indicating that the two noun phrases had some reciprocal relation: the chickens tickled the pigs and vice versa. This situation is typical in that data can usually be interpreted in many ways. Since one cannot ask children all the questions that one can put to an adult and since children are constantly developing new knowledge, it would be difficult (although perhaps not impossible) to catch children at a stage when it could be demonstrated that they had structures where Domains would be relevant but that they did not "know" what a Domain was. This is what would be needed.[2]

Demonstrating something of this sort would show that the learning capacity differs from stage to stage. It would not follow that the definition of Domain is not genetically prescribed. Genetic prescription entails the development of puberty at around the age of twelve, so there would be nothing surprising about some aspect of the mental genotype being realized around the age of five.

It is quite possible that learning capacity differs from stage to stage, just as it does for motor skills like walking. The idea is that the child cannot benefit from relevant experience until the nervous system has grown or matured in some way. This idea has influenced studies of motor development ever since Carmichael (1926) showed that the emergence of swimming in young frogs depended on the growth of the nervous system. He showed that young frogs paralyzed for the five-day period during which they would normally learn to swim, swam exactly like other frogs when the paralyzing drug wore off.

Carey (1980) surveys some of the follow-up to Carmichael's work, seeking to show that the emergence of motor skills in humans also depends on the growth of the nervous system. The evidence offered in the 1930s and 40s fell into three classes. First, descriptive work established that there were detailed similarities in the sequential stages that all children go through. Second, Carmichael's work inspired some deprivation studies. For instance, one researcher examined the onset of walking in Hopi infants strapped to cradle boards for nine months and found that they started to walk at exactly the same age as Hopi children allowed to move freely. Another study, of the kind that raises ethical questions, had children lying on their backs all day for nine months, sometimes with their hands bound, with no toys and no opportunities to interact with each other. They were not spoken to or smiled at, but nonetheless they had all the usual properties and at the usual times: smiling, cooing, sitting, grasping (see Dennis and Dennis 1935). Third, some experiments trained one member of a pair of identical twins in some skill and compared the results with those of the untrained twin. So at forty-six weeks one twin was trained for ten minutes a day for six weeks to climb stairs. The other twin was kept away from stairs. After six weeks the trained twin performed better, but the untrained twin climbed the stairs spontaneously and mastered the skill more quickly and easily.

Carey notes that this kind of evidence is suggestive but not conclusive. These studies show that a child must be intrinsically ready to make some development; they do not establish that readiness emerges as a result of growth in the nervous system, even though that is a perfectly plausible idea a priori. Carey points to tighter evidence from recent work on neurobiology. Again, there are three familiar kinds of evidence. First, the genetic program prescribes critical periods during which some stimulus fixes some permanent characteristic of the nervous system. This was shown by Hubel and Wiesel (1970) in their work on the stimuli that kittens need in their first few hours of life in order to be able to see normally (see Chapter 3). Second, W. A. Himwich (1976) has argued that the brain matures as a collection of organs, each of which matures at its own rate. At any given time different organs of the brain may be at different stages of development and some organs may mature before others. P. S. Goldman (1972) has claimed that if a particular part of the brain is not sufficiently mature, then there are limits to particular behavioral functions at that stage of development. Third, certain behavior properties emerge at a fixed time and some aspects are more or less independent of any special environmental factors, for example sexual maturity in human beings and the song of the European cuckoo.

It is known, furthermore, that human babies are born with much structural development of the brain still to be completed. Human brains continue to grow at a rapid rate after birth and they grow in spurts. This is quite different from most other species for whom birth comes very late with respect to the structural maturation of the brain; for the guinea pig and most other mammals, the brain at birth does not differ much in structure and size from the adult brain. However, human birth occurs when the brain is only one-quarter of its final size. Stephen Jay Gould discusses this in his "Human Babies as Embryos" (in Gould 1978) and argues that because humans come to have large brains their gestation period must be short and they must be born when the brain is still quite small. This is dictated by the size of the female pelvis and the fact that a child with a fully developed brain would never make it down the birth canal.

All of this suggests strongly that the growth of the neural mechanisms may determine a child's ability to cope with certain aspects of the environment. Carey has done fascinating work on the development of the enormous capacity of human beings to remember and recognize faces. Carey and Diamond (1980) report an experiment where subjects were asked to pick a familiar face from among five high school yearbook photographs; only one of the five came from the subject's own yearbook.

Not only were recognition rates over 90 per cent; they were independent of class size (from 90 to 800) and of time elapsed between graduation and test (from three months to thirty-five years). Thus in a three- or four-year period, and without conscious effort, high school students can make 800 faces familiar as easily as they can make 90 faces familiar. Even more astoundingly, they can recognize those faces years later as well as they can a few months later, indicating that learning new faces does not interfere with the representations of those already in memory. The limits on this enormous but everyday capacity, if any, have not been found.

Much more than a person's identity is read from a face; mood and momentary expression and a host of other properties such as age, health, and character are also read. The social functions served by face perception are considerable, and it is not surprising that adults have developed capacities for extracting from faces the information relevant to these functions. (Carey and Diamond 1980:61)

In effect, a distinct mental organ for face recognition inhabits part of the right hemisphere of the brain. The ability to recognize pictures of faces, as opposed to pictures of houses, cars, and landscapes, is special in that if the picture is inverted, the ability to recognize a face deteriorates much more than with other things like cars and houses; the right hemisphere is crucially involved. A child's ability to recognize upright faces develops in spurts (at ages eight to ten and fourteen to sixteen) with a plateau or even a decline between ten and fourteen years (particular aspects of the skill time the spurts and plateaus slightly differently), whereas recognition of houses, cars, and inverted faces does not show this pattern. Carey and Diamond investigate how our very special ability to recognize faces grows from one stage to another. Experiments suggest that the right hemisphere has no specialized role for young children, comes to have one from nine to ten, loses it between ten and fourteen and regains it from fourteen onward. So children under nine behave similarly to patients with damage to the right hemisphere, particularly to the right posterior cortex. This suggests, but again does not prove, that the improvement in performance at age nine or ten may depend on some growth of the right hemisphere neural mechanisms and that some other development, perhaps something linked to the onset of puberty, temporarily disrupts face encoding abilities in our early teens. Carey and Diamond designed some ingenious experiments in order to cast some light on what the developmental stages are for face recognition and on whether they can be associated with particular changes in the growth of our brains, in the development of our neuroanatomical mechanisms.

Lenneberg (1967) tried to investigate this issue for the linguistic capacity, starting from what is known about the development of the child's nervous system. But it may be more fruitful to work the other way round: to try to gather evidence about behavioral and cognitive development, syphoning off factors that may be due to a changing learning capacity and using that evidence as a means to help refine claims about neural mechanisms, complementing what is known already about neuroanatomical growth in other species. Knowledge about human grammars is already fairly rich and shows every sign of progressing further if the methods sketched in earlier chapters are followed. A lot is known as well about the chemistry of genetic structure, protein synthesis, and cell division. The problem is that work on the growing neuroanatomical mechanisms has provided no principles which refer to neuronal foundations of language acquisition.

Except at a fairly gross level, not many details are known about how human neural mechanisms grow, but if it is the case that a child's learning capacity changes as the neural mechanisms grow and mature, then acquisition of a mother tongue differs radically from learning a second language. If one learns a foreign language as a teenager or adult, one does so when the maturational changes in one's nervous system are complete, or at least advanced far beyond that of an infant.

It may turn out that data about developmental stages will become accessible and interpretable as theories are refined and will show that some aspects of the theory of grammar emerge later than others. Certainly one can imagine experiments bearing on relevant questions. One might monitor and control the linguistic and even nonlinguistic environment of certain children, perhaps withholding certain putatively relevant experience (like certain sentence types) or training children in certain skills. This might affect their eventual knowledge in some predictable way. Such experiments would imitate some ethologists' work on behavior in animals, but they would be difficult or unethical to carry out.[3] Apart from experimental difficulties, it is not clear what could legitimately be concluded from the effects of exposure to an artificial and deliberately distorted linguistic experience. Under normal circumstances there is striking uniformity in the mature state attained despite quite different conditions of upbringing. Principles such as structure dependence seem to hold for all speakers of all languages regardless of differences in their early experience. So, although relevant experiments are imaginable, we have not yet reached the stage where we can point to different aspects of the theory of grammar emerging at different times, such that we can demonstrate that the language-attaining capacity differs at different ages.

Perhaps one reason why so little is to be learned about the genotype from existing studies of child language is that the vast majority of the publications on real-time acquisition concern only the earliest stages, dealing with so-called two-word speech and the like. Utterances at such early stages are irrelevant to most grammatical principles, and it stretches normal usage to refer to this as language.[4] Work is presumably focused on this stage because it is fairly stable, preceding the explosive development that takes place normally between two and three years of age. Although the system is in transition, it is very difficult to figure out exactly or even roughly what the child knows at each stage.[5]

Developmental stages do exist in the emergence of grammars, as Piagetians have found with other cognitive domains, but it is not clear how the learning capacity changes in this domain. Where clear claims can be made, child grammars seem to have the character that linguists would expect, given the kinds of theories available. That is, we do not find examples of "unlinguistic" rules in these grammars. Although child grammars may not now reveal much about how to refine a theory of grammar, linguistic theory can illuminate some of the developmental stages that children go through. This can be illustrated by considering some data on stages in the acquisition of noun phrases and *wh* questions (data from Roeper 1979 and originally Klima and Bellugi 1966). Let us take noun phrases first.

Children seem to acquire noun phrase structures in four identifiable stages. Examples (1) and (2) list some noun phrases occurring in the first two stages.

(1)
car
baby
wa-wa (water)
mama
hands

(2)

a coat	that Adam
a celery	more coffee
a Becky	two socks
a hands	big foot
my mommy	

All children go through the four stages at some point, although the ages may vary. Most children utter the stage 2 forms between one and two years. At stage 3 there is more sophistication.

(3)

mama	my doll	a blue flower
cracker	your cracker	a nice cap
doll		a your horse
(s)poon		that a horse
		that a blue horse
		your blue cap

At stage 4 the mature system emerges, which normally remains more or less constant for the rest of the child's lifetime. But consider (4), some forms that *never* occur in children's speech.

(4)

*blue a flower	*a that blue flower	*flower a
*nice a cup	*blue a that	*house that a
*my a pencil	*that a	
*a that house	*a my	
	*my a	

Recall the parameters for noun phrases developed in Chapter 4. These were hypotheses about how $\bar{\bar{N}}$ structure could vary from grammar to grammar.

At stage 1 these principles are irrelevant, because the child has only one-word structures. Other cognitive capacities are relevant, such as the conceptual system that involves properties and conditions of reference, knowledge and belief about the world, conditions of appropriate use, and so on. These play a role in explaining why *mama* and *cup* are more likely than *photosynthesis* or *grammar* to be among the earliest words in a child's speech.

At stage 2 the child seems to have fixed the first parameter and determined that the order is Spec $\bar{N}$: all specifiers appear at the front of the noun phrase. The occurrence of phrases like *a Becky, a hands* suggests that children cannot distinguish at this stage definite and indefinite articles, and that they do not know that *a* is singular. There is no evidence that the child can distinguish subtypes of specifiers (articles, possessives, numerals, demonstratives), but they all occur one at a time in front of a noun.

By stage 3, children discriminate some kinds of specifiers and establish some more of the relative orders. In fact, the child knows that all specifiers precede adjectives, which in turn precede nouns, and that specifiers are optional, while the noun is obligatory. The stage 3 grammar differs from the mature system in that the child does not yet know that an article may not co-occur with a demonstrative or with a possessive like *your*.[6] This suggests that the child now has the PS rules $\bar{\bar{N}} \rightarrow$ Spec $\bar{N}$, $\bar{N} \rightarrow$ (Adj) N, but that it takes a little longer to determine the status of a demonstrative and whether a form like *your* is a specifier or an adjective. After all, in other languages demonstratives and possessives are often adjectives instead of specifiers.

Noun phrase structure (but not verb phrase structure) has been studied extensively from the viewpoint of acquisitional data. In the various stages identified the child is fixing the parameters left open by the theory of grammar. Children may use some forms that do not occur in adult speech but at no stage do they have a rule contravening the requirements of the theory. The theory helps us to understand the stages.

A similar story emerges when we look at how children master the ability to ask questions. Even at the one-word stage children can assert, inquire, or demand. They know enough about the world for this, and the appropriate pragmatic force is no problem. Acquiring the adult syntax takes longer: the child must master the usual intonation pattern, the presence of a *wh* word (*where, when, what*), and the variation in order (*can we* rather than *we can*).

At the earliest relevant stage children produce questions like (5) (again I follow Roeper's data).

(5)

Fraser water?	Where Ann pencil?
See hole?	Where mama boot?
Sit chair?	Who that?
Ball go?	Where horse go?
I ride train?	What doing?
	Where milk go?

Each sentence has a rising intonation, which children seem to learn before acquiring the adult syntactic patterns. If a *wh* word occurs, it occurs at the front of the sentence with no internal changes. Again, the precise role of principles of the theory would be extremely difficult to demonstrate for such rudimentary linguistic abilities. Children at this stage often do not understand the force of the *wh* word. So, one child responded to *What did you do?* with *head*, which was quite comprehensible in context but did not fit the form of the question. At the next stage *What do you need?* is responded to with *Need some chocolate* and children seem to come to understand the relation between the *wh* word and an empty slot, producing utterances like (6).

(6)

What we think _____?
What the dolly have _____?
What Daddy see _____?
What baby want _____?

At the next identifiable phase, negative questions emerge, marked by a *wh* word and a negative in sentence-initial position. This again suggests that young children employ a strategy of marking sentence types with an appropriate specifier at the front.

(7)
Why not me can't dance?
Why not you see any?
Why not me careful?
Why not you looking right place?

At the next stage questions are introduced by modals in initial position, at first often replicating rather than moving the sentence-internal auxiliary, as in (8). The forms of (8) are soon eliminated in favor of the inversion forms of (9).

(8)	(9)
Can I can come?	Can I come?
Did you $\begin{Bmatrix} \text{did see} \\ \text{saw} \end{Bmatrix}$ it?	Did you see it?
Will we will eat?	Will we eat?

Children now have all the operations needed to form adult questions, but it takes a little more time before they use *wh* words *and* inversion. Meanwhile they produce things like (10).

(10)
Where I should put it?
What you have in your mouth?
Where the other Joe will drive?

All children seem to go through these stages before acquiring the mature form of questions. Consider the kinds of minor deviations in order to see how narrow the range of variation is. One child who was studied went through a phase of using *do/did* as a sentence-initial question marker as in (11). Another child used *was* for the same purpose as in (12).

(11)
Did you were here?
Did you can sing?

(12)
Was this is the boat I saw?
Why was I did break this?
Was you went away?

Another child, when starting to use *wh* words and inversion together, distinguished for a short time between nouns and pronouns, inverting a noun subject (13a) but not a pronoun (13b).

(13)
a. Where is Tom?
   Where is the ball?
   What is Daddy doing?
b. Where you are?
   What it is?
   Why you are here?

The negative system emerges alongside the interrogative system and shows the same properties (see Klima and Bellugi 1966 and Roeper 1979 for discussion). For such areas of grammar where real-time acquisitional data have been studied, we can identify some of the strategies used by children, but no evidence leads us to suppose that at any stage children have rules that do not accord with principles of the theory of grammar or that their genetic equipment is not fully operational. Again, their grammars seem to have the properties that might be expected and data about the intermediate stages do not suggest any refinements in current theories of grammar. Children acquire properties of their mature grammar at different rates. The rates reflect the complexity of the relevant structures, where complexity is a function of several parameters: the length of the structure, the frequency of the words, concepts, and construction types, and, most important, the structure of the theory that leads the child to expect or to be particularly receptive to certain things, while other things may require a more elaborate trigger experience.

I have assumed that for each developmental stage a child knows something about his language. That knowledge can be characterized as a grammar. The grammar of each stage will fall within the limits of the theory of grammar (if it is assumed that all defining principles are available from the initial stage onward), but the grammar of a child at, say, two and one-half may have quite a different structure (within the limits of the theory of grammar) from what obtained three months earlier. I assume, in other words, that a grammar can be restructured radically as the child matures, just as Chapter 8 showed that grammars may be restructured radically in the course of historical development.[7]

To take a simple illustration, consider the acquisition of Dutch word order, characteristically subject-verb-object in main clauses and subject-object-verb in subordinates. If we assume the structure-preservation principle, a Dutch speaker's PS rules generate object-verb order and a transformational rule applies to main clauses yielding the verb-object order; on several grounds this seems to be a good claim about the grammar of mature Dutch speakers. In early stages children control only simple clause structures, mastering embedded structures like relative and complement clauses later on. To characterize the child's knowledge in the earlier stage, one would use PS rules generating verb-object order, the only sequence the child knows. For the later stage, when the child is aware of verb-object and object-verb orders, the PS rules would generate object-verb (necessarily, given the structure-preservation principle). So the grammars for the two stages would have quite different PS rules.[8]

In general, then, children's grammars reveal the kinds of properties that the theory leads us to expect. Some developmental stages can be understood in terms of the child fixing the parameters left open by the theory. However, there are real difficulties for exploiting this kind of data. If we are concerned with refining the Island Condition to the notion of a Domain and then to some further improvement, data from child grammars are likely to be less helpful than analyses of mature grammars of the kind given in earlier chapters.

Language Breakdown

There is a branch of linguistics known as neurolinguistics, whose main concern is to figure out something about the tasks performed by the brain that make it possible for us to use language spontaneously, freely, and effortlessly. What little insight we have on brain functions involving language comes mostly from studies of the different kinds of linguistic deficits which arise after damage to various parts of the brain. The puzzle is to find a way to characterize precisely what kind of deficit, or *aphasia,* may arise. One may also want to identify which of these deficits arises when a particular part of the brain is damaged. Damage to certain parts has no noticeable effect on linguistic capacities, whereas a lesion in another area does have certain consequences. For example, about 70 percent of people who suffer damage to the left hemisphere of the brain experience some kind of aphasia, but only 1 percent of those who suffer a right-hemisphere lesion are similarly affected. Again a good representation of the normal, mature capacity should contribute to characterizing the real nature of certain deficits in pathological cases.

Neurolinguistic studies form one aspect of a much wider concern, relating to the localization of functions in the brain, the extent to which particular parts of the central nervous system govern particular biological functions. So certain functions are guided by the left hemisphere and others by the right hemisphere. Research is designed to make these correlations as precise as possible.

Neurolinguists try to associate grammatical functions with particular parts of the brain by studying what happens when those parts of the brain are inoperative, either as a result of experimental intrusion or damage due to a stroke, car accident, or whatever. So, claims about normal grammatical properties, about the form of particular grammars of mature speakers, may allow us to identify certain aspects of grammars that are defective in an aphasic. We may also be able to correlate particular grammatical deficits with damage to certain parts of the brain. Any investigation must establish what exactly is the linguistic deficit (making a claim about a defective *grammar*) and the precise nature of the neuroanatomical impairment. Both claims involve a fair degree of abstraction; our knowledge of grammars and of brain structures is in many respects tentative.

Consider, for example, patients with lesions cutting through a small area near the motor cortex in the dominant (usually left) hemisphere; this is known as Broca's area, after Paul Broca who reported work in 1861 correlating certain speech deficits with damage to this particular part of the brain. It later turned out that for people with the behavioral symptoms that Broca identified, there was more variation in the size and site of the lesions than Broca had envisaged. In fact, most patients with Broca's aphasia have lesions going way beyond Broca's area. But there is substantial agreement on the behavioral symptoms of Broca's aphasics. The patients typically do not speak fluently, having to exert themselves greatly to utter a few fragmented phrases, but they can communicate with rising and falling intonation, gestures, and so on and hence appear to know what they want to say, even though they have great difficulty producing it. They do not use function words (little words like articles, particles, conjunctions, some prepositions), but they do have major words like nouns and verbs, although not always in the normal form; they often omit tense, plural and comparative markers, and verbs are often nominalized. The speech of Broca's aphasics is telegraphic. This can be labeled *agrammatism*, but what precisely is the grammatical deficit? Is it, for example, a deficit affecting syntactic, phonological, lexical, or morphological capacity, some combination, or none of these things? Indeed, is it a grammatical deficit at all?

It has been suggested that the main problem with Broca's aphasics is not a grammatical impairment but has to do with muscle control, with the physical processes involved in speaking. This suggestion is largely based on the notion that Broca's aphasics comprehend speech like normals. If this account is correct, then Broca's aphasia has nothing to do with the grammar and the study of it is unlikely to reveal anything about the form of normal grammars. In fact, it seems that this account is not correct: the comprehension of these patients is not normal and the deficit seems to reflect an impairment in grammars. Mary-Louise Kean (1981) points out that *The sparrows watched the red ball* is no more a syntactic string than it is a phonological string or a logical structure; it is just a well-formed sentence with a certain syntactic structure, a phonological structure, a logical form, and so on. Similarly for agrammatic strings like *Sparrow watch red ball;* it is not self-evident whether the agrammaticality arises with respect to syntax, phonology, or morphology. This can be determined only on the basis of analysis and therefore on the basis of claims about grammatical theory. One cannot expect to answer or even to ask questions about grammatical deficits without having a reasonably well worked out notion of the grammar, of what is defective.

This is tricky because there is no task of language use that taps only, say, syntactic capacities; all components of linguistic ability are involved in processing some string. Under the modular conception developed here, the mind and the grammar consist of various components interacting in specified ways and may subserve other components. With a system like (14), which subserves some function F, an impairment to C will entail a deviant realization of F. Similarly A and B will appear to be impaired because their contribution to the normal realization of F will be obscured through the deviance of C. And so on.

(14)

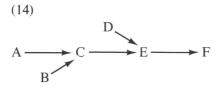

Likewise for the analysis of Broca's aphasia. In the analysis of performance data one needs an analysis of well-formed and ill-formed strings in the context of an explicit theory of grammar. Only with such analyses can blame be assigned for specific instances of ill-formedness. It is clear, for example, that syntactic processing is compromised in Broca's aphasia; the question is whether the syntactic compromise is direct or a by-product of some other impairment.

There has been a lively dispute recently about the precise grammatical deficit of Broca's aphasics, some arguing that it is a syntactic deficit and others that it is a phonological deficit. Kean surveys the debate and convinces me that it is a deficit that can best be characterized in terms of phonological word boundaries. She points out that

what is minimally required of any grammatical analysis of agrammatism is that a systematic account be provided for a substantive partition of the items in a string into the class of items which tend to be retained and the class of items which tend to be unexploited. The central observation on which such an analysis might be based is, perhaps, that those items which tend to be retained are members of the so-called major lexical categories, N, A, V. Noticing this is not, however, sufficient for determining the locus of the ungrammaticality of agrammatic strings. All components of the grammar make reference to syntactic categories, therefore the general observation in no way casts light on the particular aspect of grammatical structure which is relevant to the grammatical characterization of agrammatism. One must inquire as to where the grammar provides for a partition of formatives into nouns, adjectives and verbs, on the one hand, and essentially everything else, on the other. (Kean 1981:189)

Kean argues that for phonological stress to be assigned correctly in a normal grammar there must be a certain convention for assigning boundaries between words. She proposes a convention assigning a marker # to the left and right of each lexical category (N, Adj, V, P, Adv) (for ease of exposition I ignore the further requirement that a # marker should also be placed at the left and right of every category dominating a lexical category). This convention, operating as part of the phonological component, would convert a surface structure (15) into (16).

(15)

$[[[\text{the}]_{Spec}[[[\text{sparrow}]_N \text{ s}]_N]_{\bar{N}}]_{\bar{\bar{N}}}$ $[[\quad]_{Spec} [[[\text{watch}]_V \text{ ed}]_V$
$[[\text{the}]_{Spec} [[\text{red}]_{Adj} [[\text{ball}]_N \text{ s}]_N]_{\bar{N}}]_{\bar{\bar{N}}}]_{\bar{V}}]_{\bar{\bar{V}}}]_S$

(16)

the [#[#sparrow#] s#] [#[#watch#] ed#] the [#red#] [#[#ball#] s]#

This convention (some details omitted) was first proposed for quite different purposes, in order to get the stress rules to work correctly. It is also relevant here and enables us to distinguish properly bracketed strings of the form [# _____ #], where _____ contains no #, (*sparrow, watch, red, ball:* call them *phonological words*) from all others (*the, -s, -ed:* call them *clitics*). The former class includes those items that are retained in agrammatism and the latter class those that are usually omitted: a string like *Sparrow watch red ball* contains no clitics.

Phonological representations like (16) provide a basis for distinguishing items used and unused in agrammatism. So, despite the apparent syntactic poverty of agrammatic language, agrammatism is characterized as an impairment affecting entities defined in phonological structure; those entities, called *clitics*, are not pronounced by speakers with Broca's aphasia. If this impairment can be associated with a lesion in Broca's area, it is reasonable to enrich notions of brain localization by hypothesizing that for normal speakers clitics are represented as such in Broca's area.

What is important from our viewpoint is that a phonological theory involving a convention of the type illustrated allows the distinctions involved in the linguistic capacities of Broca's aphasics; the distinctions are thus explained and add to the plausibility of the phonological theory. If existing theories of grammar allowed no distinction that could characterize the abilities of Broca's aphasics, the agrammatism data would lie among the great unwashed pile of unexplained phenomena and would remain as a puzzle to be solved by a later, more refined theory, or by some other aspect of our makeup, such as muscle control.

After all, grammatical theory characterizes linguistic capacity. If that characterization is appropriate and correct, it must permit an account of that capacity in its normal state and when systematically disrupted. Impairment to linguistic capacity usually reflects the normal capacity minus something.

If Broca's aphasics do not have access to clitics, clitics will be unavailable not only for speech production but also for comprehension. In that case, we need to reevaluate the notion that Broca's aphasics have normal comprehension. Caramazza and Zurif (1976) found that these patients could understand a sentence like *The apple that the boy is eating is red,* where the relations among the major words are constrained by our knowledge of the world: apples but not boys are red; boys eat apples, and not vice versa. A sentence like this can be understood without reliance on the function words and without having to analyze the structure of the sentence in any detailed way. It is therefore not surprising that Broca's aphasics can understand such a sentence. On the other hand, a sentence like *The girl that the boy is chasing is tall* is more difficult. Both girls and boys may be tall, and not only can girls chase boys, but also boys can chase girls. In order to understand such a sentence, one needs to be able to conduct a detailed analysis, identifying the proper role of function words like *the, that,* and *is.* This is beyond the capacity of Broca's aphasics, and they do not understand such sentences in the way that normals do—as one might expect if they do not have access to the clitics.

In short, Broca's aphasics cope well with sentences where their knowledge of the world can get them by. They do very badly when they must rely on a syntactic analysis of the sentence in order to know what it means. Just as they speak in phonological words, omitting clitics, so too do they comprehend only in terms of phonological words, ignoring clitics. Not only is their speech production agrammatic but so too is their comprehension. See Bradley, Garrett, and Zurif 1980 for further discussion and for reports of more experiments supporting the view that Broca's aphasics do not have access to clitics. It seems fair to conclude that Broca's aphasia involves a grammatical impairment and not just a problem with muscle control.

Particular forms of aphasia vary considerably but there are some syndromes, clusters of symptoms, which are fairly well known and well established. Some may be susceptible to this kind of analysis, where one shows that some part of the grammar has been lost or lost access to, but as yet aphasiologists cannot give as clear an analysis for Wernicke's aphasia, conduction aphasia, and so on as they can for Broca's aphasia.

Take Wernicke's aphasia, for example. This is named after Carl Wernicke, who in 1874 described patients with defective understanding of spoken and written language and with lesions outside Broca's area in the left posterior temporal lobe. As with Broca's aphasia, it is damage to part of the left hemisphere that is relevant for grammatical capacities. With Wernicke's aphasics there is a much greater variation of symptoms and the cluster is less well established as an identifiable syndrome; people with different symptoms are grouped together as "Wernicke's aphasics."

Typical patients speak fluently, often very rapidly, but the content ranges from inappropriate to utter nonsense. Kathryn Bayles offers this example:

Examiner: Do you like it here in Kansas City?
Aphasic: Yes, I am.
Examiner: I'd like to have you tell me something about your problem.
Aphasic: Yes, I ugh can't hill all of my way. I can't talk all of the things
I do, and part of the part I can go alright, but I can't tell from the other
people. I usually most of my things. I know what can I talk and know
what they are but I can't always come back even though I know they
should be in, and I know should something eely I should know what I'm
doing . . .
(Akmajian, Demers, and Harnish 1979:chap. 13)

Clearly this is quite a different impairment from that of Broca's
aphasics. So far there has been no success in identifying which aspect
of a grammar is impaired in Wernicke's aphasics, but it has been
speculated that they suffer from a damaged feedback system restricting
their ability to monitor what they are saying.

Despite some success in characterizing Broca's aphasia, neurolinguists are far from a clear view of many aspects of linguistic deficits.
Nor is there greater success in associating lesions in particular areas of
the brain with particular functional disorders. As noted, a fairly wide
range of lesions is found among patients suffering from the best understood deficit, Broca's aphasia. Linguists are nowhere near being able to
show how noun phrases and neurons are related, to link physical properties of neuroanatomy to the entities that feature in descriptions of
knowledge at the more abstract level of grammars.

It does seem that the left hemisphere is usually crucially involved in
linguistic capacity. Damage to it usually has linguistic repercussions,
unlike damage to the right hemisphere. Many other research techniques also point to the crucial role of the left hemisphere. But under
certain circumstances, if the left hemisphere is badly damaged in the
early stages of life, the language functions may be taken over by the
right hemisphere. The right hemisphere is usually crucial for other
skills, such as those involving spatial concepts, certain musical abilities, and face recognition.

It also seems clear that the grammar is not represented uniformly in
the left hemisphere. Damage to a small area does not result in impairment to all linguistic functions. But it is difficult to be much more precise. The location of functions seems to vary from person to person,
and Bever (1980) has argued that it may not be intrinsically or genetically prescribed that the left hemisphere must assume the language

functions; perhaps it usually does so just by virtue of having more computational power. Similarly the clitic sublexicon may usually be stored in Broca's area, but it may equally well be stored elsewhere if necessary. This might be a matter of direct genetic specification or variable within genetically given limits.

To make matters more complicated in the search for the location of functions in the brain, we cannot restrict our attention to linguistic capacities. There seem to be correlations with other functions, like handedness. People who are left-handed, and therefore usually right-hemisphere dominant for their motor functions, tend to recover from aphasia better than right-handers, do not develop such severe aphasias and do not show exactly the same clusters of symptoms as right-handers. To a lesser extent, the same holds for right-handed people with left-handed blood relations. Geschwind (1980) claims that left-handers develop aphasias after a lesion to *either* hemisphere, whereas this is not true in right-handers. This suggests that the left-hander is not the mirror image of the right-hander with respect to the neural organization of language capacities.

The brain is an enormously complex organ. Consider just the fiber tract called the *corpus callosum*, which links the two hemispheres and enables them to communicate with each other via electrical impulses. If each of the 200 million or so nerve fibers making up the corpus callosum has a firing capacity of twenty impulses per second, then four billion impulses can be carried between the two hemispheres per second. The enterprise of understanding how this neuroanatomy works is an enormous one, and progress is inhibited by the available experimental techniques and the fact that there are no comparable animals that can be mutilated in the interest of scientific advance. The problems are magnified by the fact that brains vary significantly from person to person in terms of size and structure, although, as always, within limits. We want to know not only how the brain works but also how the workings of human neuroanatomy are associated with specific behavioral and cognitive functions. The corpus callosum must play some role, but that role may vary from person to person. Sperry (1968) studied a twenty-year-old woman whose entire corpus callosum was missing; she had been obtaining average grades in a city junior college while working twenty hours a week as an office clerk!

A further inhibition stems from the incompleteness of current theories of grammar and other domains. For the moment perhaps something can be learned about grammars by identifying the kinds of aphasias that occur and trying to characterize the precise nature of the impairment, as illustrated with Broca's aphasia. When we have some good idea of the exact impairment, we may be able to help identify the particular neuroanatomical source for the deficit. This in turn may help to establish which aspects of neuroanatomy are involved in which functions for normal speakers with no pathological deficits. Such correlations may turn out to be uniform across the species or to vary within prescribed limits.

At all stages of research we should distinguish between a grammar, which represents what speakers know and can compute at some abstract level, the mechanism that puts that knowledge to use for some function, and the physical hardware of neurons, synapses, patterns of connectivity in which all of this is realized. This is to follow the logic of Marr and Poggio in their work on how human beings see:

The [central nervous system] needs to be understood at four nearly independent levels of description: (1) that at which the nature of a computation is expressed; (2) that at which the algorithms that implement a computation are characterized; (3) that at which an algorithm is committed to particular mechanisms; and (4) that at which the mechanisms are realized in hardware. (Marr and Poggio 1977)

So far in studies of our language capacity, work dealing with the first of these levels, the grammar, has carried much of the weight. The next section deals with the second level.

Language Processing

A grammar characterizes a person's linguistic knowledge, but something else characterizes how that knowledge is actually used when that person utters and hears sentences. So, a theory of linguistic performance consists of a theory of grammar linked with a theory of the computational mechanisms for processing language, both as a speaker and as a hearer.

Not only is a theory of grammar distinct from a theory of processing, but an overall theory of linguistic performance, combining these theories, must be distinguished from other cognitive capacities that are often at play when we use language. Memory capacity certainly interacts with linguistic performance, limiting how much material can be stored at any one moment. Our ability to enjoy a joke is involved when we laugh and say "Wow, that was hilarious." Also, our ability to relate conceptual knowledge to immediate experience plays a role: it enables us to resolve ambiguity readily and, for the most part, unconsciously as we are usually unaware of ambiguity. *Fred broke the ice* is grammatical, processable and, in isolation, ambiguous; but the sentence will be understood unambiguously if uttered beside a frozen pond in wintertime or at a party as the atmosphere becomes more relaxed. With these distinctions in mind, let us consider what is involved in processing language.

Speakers exploit their linguistic knowledge when speaking and when listening (and when writing poems, solving crossword puzzles, or engaging in other sophisticated pursuits involving language). Let us focus here just on what might happen when one hears a sentence; presumably something else happens when one utters a sentence. When exposed to some acoustic signal, a listener unconsciously analyzes that signal into discrete elements (words, units of meaning, and sounds) and assigns the appropriate logical, syntactic, and phonological structure. Perhaps we do more, but this is minimal.

This analytical capacity—call it a *parser*—might work in one of various ways, but some possibilities can be eliminated rather quickly. For example, the possibility can be dismissed that the parser has an indefinitely large memory and can take an indefinite amount of time to analyze a sentence. If the parser did have these properties, it might be a very simple device that searched through random grammatical derivations until finding one that fitted the particular sentence with which it is confronted, assigning an appropriate meaning, syntactic description, and so on. Presumably this is not how things work. Human computational memory capacity is extremely limited and we assign meanings to most sentences instantaneously.

As an alternative, it might be supposed that languages are structured in such a way as to facilitate easy parsing: each element of a sentence might be expected to convey sufficient information for the parser to structure that element and determine how it contributes to the meaning of the sentence as a whole. This also cannot be entirely right because sentences are often structurally or lexically ambiguous and most of these ambiguities cannot be resolved immediately: *drink* may be a noun or verb; *pen* is usually a noun but may refer to various objects. The ambiguity may be resolved by a preceding item (*a drink*), or a following item (*fill the pen with ink*), or only by the situational context. So information needed for resolving an ambiguity about one item or sequence of items may depend on something occurring before, after, or not at all. To this extent languages are not designed for easy parsing.

Consequently much of the research dealing with the parser has concerned the way in which potentially ambiguous sentences are in fact resolved in more or less instantaneous fashion. Why is it that some ambiguities are easier than others? For example, while *the pen* is ambiguous, the sentence *Fill the pen with ink* as a whole is straightforward. But *the horse raced at Ascot* is also ambiguous in that *raced,* in isolation, may be construed as a past tense or a past participle; for some reason *The horse raced at Ascot fell,* where the ambiguity is resolved in favor of the past participle, is less straightforward than the disambiguation of *the pen.*

Dealing with such facts as these, we can hypothesize something about the properties of the parser. This is not an area where we have much firm knowledge, but there are some interesting studies. Frazier (1979) distinguishes three approaches. First, the parser might recognize a potentially ambiguous structure but not analyze it until the subsequent context has been received and analyzed. This approach is implausible because the parser would have to conduct *some* analysis in order to be able to recognize disambiguating information, since this can take a variety of forms. Furthermore, disambiguating information may be very late in coming, entailing a strain on memory limitations, and may not come at all. Second, the parser might compute all the possible analyses and eliminate some as disambiguating information arrives. Again, this makes a great demand on memory capacity, but it will reach the correct analysis. Third, the parser might pick one of the possible analyses and pursue it until the bitter end. This puts minimal strain on memory if the chosen analysis turns out to be correct, but if it turns out to be incorrect the sentence would have to be reprocessed from the beginning. Under this approach one would formulate parsing strategies permitting fast, immediate decisions about which analyses to pursue.

Consider a parsing strategy that interprets *the horse raced . . .* as involving a past tense verb and not a past participle. Such a strategy seems to operate when we hear a sentence like *The horse raced at Ascot fell,* forcing us, when we hear *fell,* to go back and reanalyze *raced* as a past participle. A strategy favoring the past tense analysis of *raced* may be adopted because it is successful more frequently than other strategies or because the chosen analysis is the simplest to compute (both of these reasons appeal to a great deal of experience in the processing of language), or because this strategy is determined, at least in part, by the human constitution. Under the last view grammars are designed in such a way that they can not only be attained by a child under normal conditions, but also so that they can be used when people parse utterances that they hear. We can disregard the possibility that the strategy may be entirely ad hoc and selected arbitrarily, because all English speakers have it.

One's views about the parser will depend on one's views about the grammar, and vice versa. Moreover, there is no a priori division between which phenomena should be accounted for by the grammar and which by the parser. One will develop the overall most successful theory, as always.

The grammar defines various levels of representation: phonetic, phonological, syntactic, and logical representations. If these things are part of our knowledge, they are presumably available to be exploited by the parser. For example, the last section illustrated a convention for assigning word boundaries. This provided a distinction between what were called phonological words (*sparrow, red*) and clitics (*the, -s, -ed*). One can ask how the parser exploits this distinction.

Somebody hearing and processing an utterance must conduct at least a phonological analysis of the acoustic signal, breaking the signal into small segments, identifying lexical items and their category status, and exploiting this kind of information to parse the string. Presumably the clitic/word distinction plays no role in the phonological analysis of the acoustic signal since clitics have no special physical properties making them sound any different from other unstressed syllables. The distinction may play a role in lexical access, because it might conceivably correlate with a distinction in vocabulary types.

Clitics by and large are short (rarely exceeding two syllables), with a high frequency of occurrence and constituting a very limited set numerically (compare the number of articles (*a, the*) and the number of nouns). Now, comprehending an acoustic signal involves some kind of analytical procedure that operates on items in sequence. Clitics may provide distinctive cues to syntactic structure and thereby play a role in parsing. Kean (1981) points out that since clitics are few in number and have limited syntactic distribution, a special access system to a list of clitics would provide the parser with a rapid means of making initial hypotheses as to the constituent structure of the string being processed.

In fact, there is evidence that there is a special access routine for clitics. The rate of access for nouns, verbs, or adjectives is a function of their frequency in the language, but Bradley (1978) has claimed that this is not so for clitics. The matter is still under investigation, but evidence does exist that there may be a special clitic lexicon available to the language user for rapid scanning. This would aid in parsing because the rapid retrieval of clitics makes available a rich basis for parsing: occurrence of *the* would act as a flag for a following noun, *could* for a following verb. Presumably languages are designed so that a very superficial analysis into phrases can be performed by a system with limited memory and a restricted analytical capacity. A further stage of analysis would provide the surface structure and then the logical form. A sublexicon of clitics, if correct, might be extremely useful for the first, superficial analysis into phrases. It is this sublexicon which agrammatic aphasics lose access to, according to Kean.

Assuming all this to be correct, claims about the grammar (relating to stress assignment) converge with claims about the nature of agrammatic aphasia and the processing of sentences. The convention for assigning boundaries plays a role in explaining data from all three domains. Not only does it permit the stress rules to work properly, it also defines a sublexicon that Broca's aphasics lose (or lose access to) and that normal speakers exploit for the easy parsing of sentences. Such a convergence is the hallmark of a successful theory.

There is, of course, much more to be said about the processing of language and the way in which speakers can exploit linguistic knowledge. For example, presumably speakers have strategies that enable them to undo the effects of some transformations, establishing that in *Who do you think that Bill saw?* the word *who* (or *whom*) is understood as the direct object of *saw*. What is important to recognize is the intimate connection between claims about the grammar and claims about the parser. Investigation of the parser will proceed hand in hand with investigation of the grammar.

In practice, this must entail that before investigating how linguistic knowledge is put to use for some function, as for analyzing or parsing an incoming acoustic signal, one will need to have some tentative characterization of what that knowledge consists of. One cannot establish properties of the parser without knowing what kind of thing has to be parsed. Therefore, the proper way to *begin* the study of language is to try to characterize grammars. As we start to understand what grammars look like, so we can start to develop ideas about the parser, which in turn will influence the refinements we make to a theory of grammars. There is no issue of principle here, but this seems to be a reasonable strategy to follow. After some time, it may turn out that different groups of researchers have different grammatical theories, each associated with different parsers. At that stage, one system—a grammar with an associated parser—can be compared with another. Subtheories about how the grammar is put to use for other functions, such as speaking or making up poetry, can also be evaluated by comparing overall models—grammars along with their associated models for parsing, speaking, and writing poems.

In chapters 4, 6, and 7 grammars were considered from two points of view: the capacity to characterize accurately what adults know subconsciously about their native language and their attainability by a child under normal conditions. It is not by mere whim that this focus was adopted; at the current stage of research these two considerations provide the greatest insight on the form that grammars have. In fact, if one reviews the history of the research program, one finds that in the earliest stages, between about 1955 and 1970, the first of these considerations played a dominant role; since then the attainability of grammars has played an increasing role in shaping research questions, emerging clearly in the early 1970s. But grammars must meet other requirements: they must be usable for certain functions. Since utterances can be parsed and understood easily, grammars must be compatible with some plausible theory about our parsing mechanisms. This means that as analysts we shall need to know something about how these parsing mechanisms work. It may be the case that we are now reaching a stage where the theory about grammars can be refined in some way by investigating some of these functions.

It is certainly the case that in recent years there has been a lot of concern with this matter; several papers have appeared with experimental findings directed at this issue. As in any new area of investigation there has been some confusion (for a good review of the issues, see Berwick and Weinberg 1981, 1982).

For example, one new line of thought holds that because sentences must be parsable, the theory of grammars must be structured in such a way as to allow only certain *mathematically* defined classes of languages. Specifically, the theory should allow only phrase structure grammars that generate only so-called context-free languages (we don't need to define 'context-free' for our present purposes). This is because known parsing mechanisms can analyze efficiently *any* language that is context-free; on the other hand, there is no way to guarantee that *all* context-sensitive languages can be parsed as efficiently as the context-free languages. If this line of reasoning were correct, then the kinds of grammars sketched in Chapter 4 would have to be abandoned because they contain transformational rules and are not phrase structure grammars generating only context-free languages.

Berwick and Weinberg (1982) have a perceptive discussion of how to apply mathematical results to the study of grammars and they show that this particular argument, that a plausible grammar must be a phrase structure grammar generating only context-free languages, does not hold water. The essential problem is that an adequate grammar must not only facilitate parsing but also be attainable by a child under the usual conditions; it is hard to see how a context-free phrase structure grammar could meet that fundamental requirement. The second prong of Berwick and Weinberg's refutation is that they sketch an apparently plausible parser of their own (based on the work of Marcus 1980), which can be coupled to the kind of transformational grammar outlined in earlier chapters. They assume the kind of constraints that have been proposed to ensure that a grammar is attainable and show that those same constraints also facilitate efficient parsing.

In this section and elsewhere I have stressed the modularity of the present approach. In the context of language use, this means that the properties of grammars will be investigated alongside the properties of associated parsers, where grammars and parsers are distinct entities. A grammar is a system of rules and processes, which apply in a certain sequence, but this does not describe the successive acts of a parser or a sentence producer. The parser can be viewed as a separate organ with specific properties of its own that permits the grammar to be put to use for a certain function. The brief discussion of clitics illustrates this: the boundary conventions of a grammar allow phonological words to be distinguished from clitics but, if Bradley is right, the parser treats these two classes differently in terms of how they are accessed in actual speech.

Some confusion arises when some researchers do not adopt this kind of modularity but insist instead that the grammar itself offers the means to describe the parsing process, that is, the internal structure of the grammar must be virtually identical to the internal structure of the parsing mechanism used in processing sentences. Under this view the grammar itself would be directly responsible for experimental data about sentence parsing: reaction times, resolution of ambiguities, or memory loads.

One version of this approach might hold that the successive rule applications in a grammar must in fact define the successive states of the parser. This is to assume either that the grammar incorporates the parser, that one mental organ defines what speakers know *and* how they use that knowledge, or that the parser is parasitic on the grammar and has virtually no independent properties of its own. In the early sixties the so-called derivational theory of complexity assumed this view. The notion was that the greater the number of transformations involved in the derivation of some sentence, the more complex the task of the parser. In parsing a sentence there would be at least as many steps as there were transformations; sentences involving many transformations should take longer time and greater energy to be parsed. An attempt was made to interpret a particular set of syntactic rules in this way (roughly the rules assumed in Chomsky 1965), but the attempt failed, as most linguists had expected. From that failure it could legitimately be concluded that *either* the grammatical rules *or* the parser needed to be refined or (most likely) both.

Unfortunately, a common response was that the fault must lie with the kind of grammar being tested. This response would follow on one of two assumptions, neither of which was very plausible. If one did not adopt the modular view and held instead that the grammar itself should account for how sentences are actually parsed, the failure would show that the grammars used in the relevant tests should be rejected. Similarly, if one held the parser constant and assumed that it must have no real internal structure of its own but should reconstruct the same successive steps that the grammar defines, then again it would follow that the grammars used in the tests should be rejected. The first reaction denies the logic of modularity as a methodological a priori, claiming that there can be no parser distinct from the grammar, and the second reaction assumes that the parser *must* have certain properties. We are now beginning to learn something about the properties of parsers, and no doubt this will continue. But the study of parsers is a recent phenomenon with a much thinner basis than the study of grammars. To give up a fairly rich theory of grammars on the basis of speculation about parsers is not a wise move. Some interesting theories about parsers are now beginning to develop but almost nothing was known about them when these experiments were carried out and interpreted in the sixties.

Some tactical advantages accrue from distinguishing a grammar from a parser and from a sentence-producer. If there is a discrepancy between the predictions of the overall theory and some experimentally observed facts, one may hold one's theory of grammar constant and revise one's claims about the parser. Alternatively, it may be more fruitful to revise claims about the grammar, a move that might have empirical consequences for claims about the sentence-producer or some other mental organ that interacts with the grammar. Whatever the revisions made, care must be taken to maintain a grammar that can be shown to be attainable by a child. Again, any grammar must meet various requirements: being attainable and coupled to a plausible parser and a plausible sentence producer. We follow the logic of Marr and Poggio's work on vision and, in Berwick and Weinberg's phrase (1981), modularity of explanation permits a corresponding modularity of scientific investigation.

In contrast, in a system where the grammar, parser, producer, and other components are not distinguished, the analyst cannot exploit them to distinguish what speakers know from how they use that knowledge for some particular function. When facts do not tally with the predictions of a theory, as often happens, the theorist either must reformulate the whole system or must attempt to syphon out those properties that hold irrespective of the particular function for which the system might be used.

What emerges is that it is not appropriate to build directly a theory of language use, anymore than it is appropriate to build a theory of historical change. The central factor is a theory of grammars. Grammars characterize what somebody knows in the linguistic domain; they are attained by children, may differ from one generation to another, are used for parsing incoming acoustic signals and for producing utterances and for many other things. Therefore one may probe into the nature of grammars by investigating the kind of parser or producer that they are coupled with. If the problem is broken down in this way and a modular kind of investigation constructed, a general theory of language will consist of various subtheories. There will be distinct but interrelated mental organs: grammar, parser, producer, and maybe even a crossword puzzle solver and a poetry maker.

Notes

1. For some discussion of these issues, see Chomsky 1975:119–22. Questions like these are posed for other aspects of cognitive development by Piaget and his colleagues. What is known of so-called wolf-children suggests that if children do not interact with other human beings before puberty, they are never able to attain normal grammars. A recent and extensively studied person of this kind is discussed in Curtiss 1977.

2. For more discussion of Matthei's experiment, see White 1981.

3. At least, so I should like to think. In fact some experiments do raise ethical questions, when two-year-old children spend eight hours a day in so-called laboratories being trained to recognize and use words and expressions somewhat earlier than they might otherwise do. Such experiments are sometimes "justified" on the dubious grounds that they help to liberate children from "deprived backgrounds."

4. Chomsky (1975) has suggested that it is about as appropriate to refer to this as "primitive language" as it would be to refer to the first movements of a bird's wings as "primitive flight."

5. The popularity of Piaget's view, that linguistic development must reflect sensorimotor development (this has no empirical support), and the pervasive refusal to entertain properties of the genotype affecting developmental stages may be two other factors impeding work on children's speech. Most people working on real-time acquisition do not use any theory of grammar with much internal structure, often regarding grammatical theory as a separate branch of inquiry.

6. There are other cases where children treat mutually exclusive items as compatible. Forms like *feetses* (with three plural markings), *childrens, wented, camed, drownded* occur in the speech of every child.

7. This is at variance with much of the literature on child grammars, which seems to deny the possibility of restructuring. Writers make a claim about the adult grammar of, say, English, and view the child's development as the piecemeal acquisition of one or another rule (for a clear illustration of this strategy, see Maratsos 1978). I see no merit to this view.

8. If grammars are not restructured in this way in the course of a child's development, it must be claimed that children somehow attain their adult PS rules even at that stage where they utter and comprehend only simple subject-verb-object clauses. This is not impossible but it would be difficult to argue for such a position. The notion that grammars cannot be restructured has no independent empirical support and represents only a priori dogma.

Suggested Reading

Lenneberg (1967) and Marshall (1980) discuss many aspects of the three areas discussed in this chapter. There is an enormous literature on child language, but much of it is rather anecdotal and not much of it addresses deficiency of stimulus problems of the kind that have oriented our discussion here. Lydia White's "The responsibility of grammatical theory to acquisitional data" (in Hornstein and Lightfoot 1981) offers a survey of issues and nonissues.

Kathryn Bayles' chapter in Akmajian, Demers, and Harnish (1979) provides a good brief survey of types of aphasia and some elementary facts about neurophysiology. Kean (1981) clarifies how aphasiological studies can be brought to bear on the acquisitional issue that we are addressing. On language processing Berwick and Weinberg (1981, 1982) survey much of the work and provide the clearest account of where the real questions lie.

Chapter 10
Reflections

Wider Horizons

Throughout this book language has been examined from just one point of view, one addressing the problem of acquisition and asking what children need to be endowed with in order to master their native language. I have looked at areas where the data that children have access to do not suffice to determine what they come to know in maturity, where children acquire more than they experience. I have discussed various properties which must hold independently of linguistic experience for language acquisition to take place under these circumstances, what we have called the circumstances of a deficient stimulus. I also considered facts about how languages change historically, how children master their language in stages, how linguistic deficits arise after brain damage, how speech is processed; it was shown how such facts can be explained and how they can be used to revise, elaborate, and refine hypotheses about what must be in the genotype. Throughout the discussion the acquisition problem has been the focus, and all proposals have been shaped accordingly.

Linguists can now formulate interesting hypotheses, accounting for fairly broad ranges of facts with fairly elegant abstract principles, although it would be foolish to claim that the biological approach to language and the mental genotype presented in this book has reached anything like the maturity of theories about the basic chemistry of genetics. Much remains to be done, but we can show how a child can attain certain elements of grammar by exposure to only an unorganized and haphazard set of utterances; for these elements we have a theory which meets the basic requirements. Given the pace and nature of recent developments, there is every reason to suppose that we shall attain deeper explanations and give a fuller account of how languages are acquired. Perhaps eventually the emergence of language in the child will be viewed as involving no more analytical ingenuity than the growing of hair: under exposure to a random speech community a certain grammar will emerge, just as hair emerges by exposure to certain levels of light, air, and protein.

We study language as a first step to making claims about properties of the mental genotype as a whole, the initial state of the human mind. This is our ultimate goal. It is not easy to formulate a coherent research program with strict empirical demands if we begin by considering, for example, the nature of free will, the ability to solve mathematical problems, or other aspects of cognitive capacity. Instead, we adopt a traditional view among philosophers, that language reflects mental properties fairly directly and provides a particularly clear 'window on the mind'. Thus the study of language is a tool to a larger end, one phase of a bigger enterprise. We focus now on grammars because they seem at this stage of research to give a good handle on this wider problem; they manifest the cognitive capacity most amenable to study.

Research on language offers plausible hypotheses about the initial state of the organism, particularly about its mental properties. If it is organized or 'pre-programmed' in such and such a way, then by exposure to certain kinds of linguistic experience it will develop eventually into a mature state having certain other properties, which enable it to go far beyond that original triggering experience, to embark on and understand novel experiences. This is also true of interpretation of visual space; recent work has shown that this is determined to a significant degree by intrinsic properties of the organism, some of which are activated on exposure to some triggering experience.

One can extend this approach to other domains and speculate that the mind is structured in such a way that people can understand and enjoy certain kinds of music naturally and with minimal experience; to appreciate other kinds of music may require a much more elaborate experience. This is not a new view: Paul Hindemith argued this many years ago and recently Leonard Bernstein has tried to develop something similar (Bernstein 1976; see also the review by Jackendoff 1977). Chapter 9 referred to work showing that people can recognize faces with a facility that they do not have in other domains such as pictures of houses, cars or Greek vases. Other properties of a mature mind, such as mastery of chess, are less spontaneous and require explicit instruction; it is impossible to learn the rules of chess by merely watching a finite set of games.[1]

These are just some of many mental capacities that might be studied, but in order to establish something about the initial state of the organism it seems best to look at those properties that are attained naturally, without systematic instruction and despite a triggering experience that does not fully determine the final ability attained, using arguments from the deficiency of the stimulus. If we obtain rich hypotheses from such a study of language, vision and ethology, we may be able to exploit this and formulate sensible hypotheses about the capacity to enjoy certain forms of music and poetry, to recognize faces, etc.

If we take this larger view, the study of language is just one phase, a tool to obtain better understanding of human intelligence, its initial state and how it can develop by experiencing the world.

More on Alternative Approaches

Retreating to narrower linguistic concerns, note that the biological approach to language is by no means a necessary one. In fact, it has not been adopted by all or even most linguists. It is easy to imagine alternatives that are worthwhile from different viewpoints. But it is a sign of the youth and immaturity of linguistics as a scientific discipline that it is easy to set up alternative approaches in facile fashion, lured by an indiscriminate worship of the false gods of eclecticism and pluralism. Now that we have examined one approach in some detail, we can consider what kinds of alternatives might be available, returning to some considered in Chapter 2.

One might study language with entirely different goals, not being concerned with how grammars are attained by children and not even assigning any psychological interpretation to one's hypotheses. One might be concerned to write a description of a language in such a way as to reflect its history, specifying that, say, *chapter* is a word of English that had the form *chapiter* some centuries ago; this was one of the goals of traditional grammarians such as Jespersen and of dictionaries written on historical principles, such as the Oxford English Dictionary. One might be concerned to describe a language in such a way that it could be readily learned by adults of another speech community, as Poutsma did in writing a grammar of Dutch for the benefit of Indonesian speakers. One might seek to describe a language so as to cast light on the way it may be used in literary texts, in metaphorical usage, perhaps defining the language of poetry as distinct from prose, perhaps showing how a language reflects the culture of its speakers. One might want to build a mathematical algorithm to distinguish the acceptable and unacceptable sentences of some language, correlating their phonetic form with a characterization of their meaning.[2]

It is easy to imagine still other goals to pursue in describing a language. Some of these goals may be more achievable than others and may have greater or lesser implications for other areas of inquiry. What will count as an explanation will differ according to what is taken as the fundamental problem and therefore there is very little point in comparing the success of Jespersen's historical grammar with Poutsma's pedagogical grammar. Theories are not commensurable if they do not share the same goals.

Theories may share the basic goal of accounting for how children acquire their native languages but take different orientations to the problem. The salient facts of language acquisition are impressive—that languages are mastered naturally and in fairly uniform fashion, despite a triple deficiency of data—and analysts look for genotypical properties that allow children to circumvent the deficiency of the stimulus. Somebody else might deny the salience of these facts and argue that children are supplied with data in a more systematic fashion and have a more elaborate trigger. This is not very plausible because it is difficult to argue that data are filtered for children and, even if children were "little linguists" and had access to all the data in the linguistic literature (knowing which sentences do not occur, which are ambiguous or paraphrases, and having comparable data for other languages), one would still want to know why young children arrive at successful grammars so much more readily than professional linguists.

Alternatively, it might be argued that by exposure to the nonlinguistic world of objects and experiences children can deduce organizational principles that in turn form a basis for acquiring language. So it might be argued that children might need to know some principle p in order to master language but that this principle, rather than being genetically encoded, follows in some natural way from what they can deduce about the world and is not genetically encoded; Piaget's sensorimotor constructions are an example of this kind of reasoning. This approach will be convincing to the extent that the analogies between linguistic and nonlinguistic domains are plausible and specific. It imputes less structure to the genotype, but the principles actually provided tend to be too general to account for language acquisition. For example, syntax does involve hierarchical structures just as, say, architecture does, but considerable elaboration would be required to say that the very specific hierarchical principles permitting language acquisition (such as phrase structure templates or Domains) are special cases of general cognitive properties that can be triggered by looking at the structure of a building. Such claims are sometimes made, but the elaboration is never provided. At this stage of research it is appropriate to pursue principles that can be shown to permit language acquisition to take place under the conditions noted, leaving the questions of broader analogies until more is known about the proper form of those linguistic principles and about principles involved in other cognitive domains. This is not to deny the possibility of interesting findings from Piagetian work nor is it to preclude work with that orientation; it is simply to state what seems to be a plausible research strategy for the time being, where one defines one's goals narrowly enough to permit substantive and testable proposals.

Narrowing the range of alternatives to consider only theories seeking an explanation for the acquisition problem and postulating a rich genetic structure, a researcher might still pursue quite different strategies. In this book I have concentrated on English for the purpose of uncovering some areas of grammar where the correct description does not simply follow from the data normally available to the child. I have provided principles showing how some aspects of grammar could be attained and sometimes we have generalized those explanations to account for broader ranges of data. Alternatively, I could have focused on different core data, which would lead to different explanatory principles. In that case, given the similarity of general goal and orientation, there should be enough shared between the different explanations to permit comparison. This in fact happens all the time as linguists abandon, revise, refine, and elaborate their explanatory principles. They compare alternatives, rejecting some and adopting others; alternatives of this kind are essential for any discussion to take place and for any advance to be made.

For core data the researcher might go to quite different languages, to language change, records of aphasic patients, developing children. Again, one cannot be certain about the proper research strategy to follow at any given time. As shown in Chapter 9, some data from language processing were uninterpretable and did not cast light on the proper form of the theory in the early 1960s but may do so now. To date work on phonological features has proved more successful than work on semantic features. Data from grammaticality judgments and scope of quantifiers have so far played an extensive role in amending explanations offered. At a later stage of research different data may play a more important role. As noted earlier, in recent years data about anaphors and reference relations have been a particularly useful probe into the character of the mental genotype. One will always use whatever data are relevant for refining claims; no data are a priori more essential than any other data.

In devoting so much time to English and closely related languages, we follow the research strategy of geneticists who did extremely detailed experiments on fruit flies and then generalized to other species by modifying the principles arrived at via the fruit fly. An alternative strategy might have done a lot of more superficial work on many different species, and similarly linguists might survey a greater range of languages before formulating explanatory principles. One might survey the surface patterns of several languages, applying statistical methods and using the most frequent harmonic correlations as part of the core data. Again, there is no reason not to pursue this line of inquiry, and perhaps it will be successful. But while cross-language studies are needed, careful and detailed analyses are essential. Because languages, like fruit flies, do not come with the correct descriptions assigned, the correct grammar of a language can be hypothesized only through careful analysis and reasoning. Unfortunately, there is a naive tendency in the literature to cite unanalyzed phenomena as refutations of explanatory principles. Stories about curious linguistic properties often make for good cocktail chatter, but stories do not refute a theory. A theory of grammar will be refuted by a grammar of some language that does not conform to its principles; the refutation will be exactly as convincing as the grammar offered.

Yet another alternative approach rejects the goals pursued here and any claims about innateness. Instead, its proponents claim language should be studied "for its own sake," with generalizations formulated wherever they can be found. If a poll were run among professional linguists, that might turn out to be the most popular approach to the subject, and certainly many descriptions offered in the literature pay no attention to explanatory goals. In this view, linguistics is a kind of natural history rather than a scientific study. Since I adopt the view of science outlined in Chapter 5, I shall pass over this approach with no further comment.

Creativity and Political Enlightenment

Linguistic capacity is creative in the sense that any normal speaker can utter and understand an infinite number of novel expressions. Grammars reflect this capacity by incorporating recursive rules. If the grammar of English has PS rules S $\rightarrow$ $\bar{\bar{N}}$ AUX $\bar{V}$ and $\bar{V}$ $\rightarrow$ ...V...S, a speaker can produce a complex sentence of indefinite length and therefore an indefinite number of different sentences.

If such a recursive ability is attained, the acquisition of language cannot be described purely as an imitative exercise, reproducing utterances already heard. This is not to say that imitation plays no role; particular words are learned in part by reproducing what has been heard or read, and similarly for formulaic expressions like *Good morning* and idioms such as *by and large*. But imitation is not the whole story and in many instances quite simple inductive generalizations do not hold. Therefore, an account of language acquisition should not depict children only as good mimics, slaves to their accidental experiences, reproducing only what they have heard and knowing only those things for which there is direct evidence in their experience. Nor should the approach to language development be purely inductive, where the ability eventually attained is just an unrestrained extension of the experience speakers chance to encounter as children.

Constraints on available hypotheses are a source of our creative ability and not a limitation. Given genetic constraints, children can attain a system of knowledge that goes far beyond what they happen to have heard. By exposure to an unorganized set of utterances they attain knowledge about an infinite number of things that they have never experienced: that some sentences can never occur, that other sentences are ambiguous or paraphrases. In this view, our eventual knowledge is triggered by our experience as children, but not molded by it directly; the relation is mediated by the biological constraints that shape our internalized grammars. So the very limits on our capacities, the genetic template, enable us to acquire a rich and complex system of knowledge. Our knowledge is not molded directly by our experience, and it is the constraints, not the absence of limitations, that are the source of our creativity and enable us to go beyond our experience. These same constraints also enable speakers to understand each other, despite different native languages, different accents, oddities of expression, and all the other things that make up the language lottery; the constraints enable us to find our way through all this flux and variation.

Another aspect of our creativity is the ability to speak "appropriately," expressing ideas freely. It seems that by careful reasoning linguists can discover the constraints that enable people to know more than what is contained in their linguistic experience, but no progress has been made in understanding why people express certain ideas at certain times. This is the problem of free will; the ability to speak appropriately is something of a mystery and scientists can offer no principles predicting which ideas will be expressed under what circumstances.

The approach to which this book is devoted is contrary to one traditional view, that the mind contains nothing beyond what the senses convey. Empiricist psychology holds that the form of cognitive capacities is not shaped significantly by genetic factors. Chomsky has commented that

these empiricist views are most plausible where we are most ignorant. The more we learn about some aspect of human cognition, the less reasonable these views seem to be. No one would seriously argue today, for example, that our construction of perceptual space is guided by empiricist maxims. The same, I think, is true of the language faculty, which relates more closely to the essential nature of the human species. I suspect that the empiricist position with regard to higher mental functions will crumble as science advances towards an understanding of cognitive capacity and its relations to physical structures. (Chomsky 1975:126)

Many modern psychologists are firmly committed to empiricist doctrines, that the initial state of the mind is unstructured. This commitment arose for a variety of reasons, partly relating to the lack of firm empirical foundation for earlier speculations on an intrinsic human nature, partly stemming from a reaction against religious ideologies with which the opposing rationalist theories had come to be associated, partly due to the enormous success of Newtonian physics, which was couched in an empiricist epistemology (Hornstein 1979), partly due to the belief that the tabula rasa theory of human nature offers a vision of limitless progress and change. The latter aspect sometimes appeals to social reformers, revolutionaries, and others seeking to put men into a particular mold, and empiricist ideas have derived some credit from what are seen as their social and political associations.

It is true that at some stages rationalist theories, holding that the mind is already structured at birth, have been formulated in speculative and untestable fashion, but the same holds for empiricist theories. There is no intrinsic reason why this should be so for either kind of theory. In the domain of language one can formulate rationalist theories and make testable claims, as shown in the preceding chapters.

Questions of correctness and plausibility are distinct from the social and political implications of a theory. On the issue of plausibility, rationalist theories have much to recommend them when we consider how children attain the cognitive capacity involved in language, whereas empiricist accounts invoke only general learning theories and inductive procedures that offer little hope for explaining how children attain systems that are so much underdetermined by the data available to them.

The issue of social and political implications is more complex. Empiricism was closely associated with classical liberal thinking and so was supposed to be a doctrine of change, progress, and enlightenment when the church was losing its hold on society, capitalism was emerging, and European colonies were beginning to be established in the Far East, the Americas and elsewhere. This association was not a necessary one; empiricism also provided a convenient model within which to state racist and authoritarian views. If human beings in their psychological aspect had no intrinsic nature, they could be defined by the properties imposed on them directly by the environment, such as religion and language. Some people might be judged less than human by virtue of having what others saw as an impoverished language or a superstitious and ill-founded religion. Although there was no necessary connection, articulating such views came easily to empiricist philosophers, who were sometimes professionally involved in setting up and administrating the colonial system (for discussion see Bracken 1973).

After all, if human beings were infinitely malleable, then they were fit subjects for manipulation and control by social engineers and those who had attained greater expertise and claimed a special authority or a superior insight into the best social system for other people. Far from being necessarily the doctrine of progress and enlightenment, empiricism *may* serve as a basis for legitimizing a manipulative authority, whether it is the authority of a colonizing power, a left-wing central committee or a right-wing technical intelligentsia. It has even been argued recently (absurdly, in my view) that a thoroughgoing empiricist must support an unrestricted free-market economy and a political system that outlaws trade unions and does not countenance legislation protecting young children from being exploited in coal mines or any other legislation that might restrict a market economy.

Of course, authoritarian political systems could also be formulated in a rationalist model, perhaps invoking a concept of man's essential nature in order to resist social change and to defend existing privilege. In fact, some form of genetic determinism has often been invoked to defend existing social arrangements as biologically inevitable; so nineteenth-century imperialism, twentieth-century fascism, and modern sexism have been defended on the basis that the victim's plight is biologically inevitable. Under the view adopted throughout this book, the relationship between experience and eventual properties is less direct than an empiricist or a genetic determinist (or a sociobiologist) would assume; the relation is mediated by genotypical structures.[3] A small change in the trigger experience may entail a vast change in the phenotype. This means that a manipulative model of social engineering would require a theory of the mental genotype and thus a theory of how a change in the trigger experience will entail the desired change in the phenotype. No doubt such a theory could be formulated, given sufficient ingenuity and commitment to a manipulative model.

The relevant point is that there is nothing inherent in empiricism that can override its scientific failure and make it necessarily the theory of social freedom; and therefore it has no legitimate appeal on those grounds. The main criterion must be scientific truth. People live with many unpleasant biological requirements, such as the fact that everyone is bound to die. On scientific grounds empiricism has little to recommend it as a basis for explaining the acquisition of language and other cognitive skills that develop naturally and are not only a function of childhood experience.

Rationalists, seeking the laws of the human mind, are not necessarily committed to defending authoritarian regimes or existing privileges; they may be committed to freedom from manipulative control systems.

A libertarian social theory will try to determine these laws [of human nature] and to found upon them a concept of social change and its immediate and distant goals. If, indeed, human nature is governed by Bakunin's "instinct for revolt" or the "species character" on which Marx based his critique of alienated labor, then there must be continual struggle against authoritarian social forms that impose restrictions beyond those set by "the laws of our own nature," as has long been advocated by authentic revolutionary thinkers and activists. (Chomsky 1975:133)

Just as genetically determined mental structures permit the emergence of rich cognitive structures, so a *species character* provides the framework for the growth of a moral consciousness and cultural achievement, going beyond the input, beyond the triggering experience. So human needs and capacities may flourish in a society of a certain form, perhaps one without authoritarian social structures. Such political ideas might be fleshed out and deepened if we apply to them the kind of reasoning that we have pursued here in the domain of language.

Theories about the human mind, empiricist and rationalist, must be judged in terms of the accounts they give of the growth and functioning of our various cognitive capacities. Any alleged political associations they have are very tenuous and loose, and therefore cannot play any role in evaluating them as scientific theories. This book has presented the kinds of explanations that current formulations of rationalist theories can offer for the emergence of linguistic knowledge.

Notes

1. For example, the rule that one can castle only once during any single game would be extremely difficult to deduce from mere observation, as mentioned in Chapter 2. In fact, it would be impossible if one never knew whether games ended by checkmate or resignation.

2. The latter goal differs from ours in that it does not seek a psychological interpretation or an account of how the grammar might be attained by a child; it therefore does not distinguish a theory of grammar and a triggering experience to show how they together determine the form of a particular grammar, nor is there any reason for this approach to concern itself with data from aphasia, language change, etc. This is the approach of Montague grammar. Presumably whenever one arrives at a good description, one can obtain another equally good one by reaxiomatizing the system, since one's axioms will not be subject to any particular empirical requirement.

3. For some good discussion of this distinction see "Biological Potentiality vs. Biological Determinism" and "The Non-science of Human Nature" in Gould 1978.

Suggested Reading

The papers in Baker and McCarthy 1981 and Hornstein and Lightfoot 1981 may be useful for readers who wish to follow up the matters discussed in this book. Lenneberg 1967 discusses several of the biological aspects in great detail; some of Lenneberg's topics receive a more up-to-date treatment in Caplan 1980.

The most helpful thing will be to read the work of Chomsky, on which this book has been based. Chomsky 1975 and 1980 are the best sources for philosophical considerations; Chapter 1 of Chomsky 1965 gives a clear account of the methods to be followed in this line of work; and Chomsky 1981b is the best and most comprehensive discussion of more technical aspects, the substance of current theories of grammar.

References

Akmajian, A., R. Demers, and R. Harnish. 1979. *Linguistics: An Introduction to Language and Communication*. Cambridge, Mass.: MIT Press.

Aronoff, M. 1976. *Word Formation in Generative Grammar*. Linguistic Inquiry Monographs, no. 1. Cambridge, Mass.: MIT Press.

Baker, C. L. 1978. *Introduction to Generative-Transformational Syntax*. Englewood Cliffs, N.J.: Prentice-Hall.

————, and J. McCarthy, eds. 1981. *The Logical Problem of Language Acquisition*. Cambridge, Mass.: MIT Press.

Bateson, W. 1916. Review of *The Mechanisms of Mendelian Heredity* by T. H. Morgan, A. A. Sturtevant, H. J. Muller, and C. B. Bridges. *Science* N.S. XLIV.

Bentley, D., and R. Hoy. 1974. "The neurobiology of cricket song." *Scientific American,* August.

Berlin, B., and P. Kay. 1969. *Basic Color Terms: Their Universality and Evolution*. Berkeley and Los Angeles: University of California Press.

Bernstein, L. 1976. *The Unanswered Question*. Cambridge, Mass.: Harvard University Press.

Berwick, R., and A. Weinberg. 1981. "On the evaluation of grammars as components of models of language use." (to appear in *Cognition*)

————. 1982. "Parsing efficiency, computation complexity, and the evaluation of grammatical theories." *Linguistic Inquiry* 13(2):165–191.

Bever, T. G. 1980. "Broca and Lashley were right: Cerebral dominance is an accident of growth." In Caplan, ed.

Blakemore, C. 1974. "Developmental factors in the formation of feature extracting neurons." In F. O. Schmitt and F. G. Worden, eds., *The Neurosciences: Third Study Program,* Cambridge, Mass.: MIT Press.

Bracken, H. M. 1973. "Essence, accident and race." *Hermathena* 116:81–96.

Bradley, D. C. 1978. "Computational Distinctions of Vocabulary Type." Unpublished PhD dissertation, MIT.

————, M. F. Garrett, and E. B. Zurif. 1980. "Syntactic deficits in Broca's aphasia." In Caplan, ed.

Brannigan, A. 1981. *The Social Basis of Scientific Discoveries*. Cambridge, England: Cambridge University Press.

Broca, P. 1861. "Remarques sur le siège de faculté de langage articulé, suivies d'une observation d'aphémie (perte de parole)." *Bulletin Société d'Anatomie*, 330–57.

Caplan, D. ed. 1980. *Biological Studies of Mental Processes*. Cambridge, Mass.: MIT Press.

Caramazza, A., and E. B. Zurif. 1976. "Dissociation of algorithmic and heuristic processes in language comprehension: Evidence from aphasia." *Brain and Language* 3:572–82.

Carey, S. 1978. "The child as word learner." In Halle et al., eds.

————. 1980. "Maturational factors in human development." In Caplan, ed.

————, and R. Diamond 1980. "Maturational determination of the developing course of face encoding." In Caplan, ed.

Carmichael, L. 1926. "The development of behavior in invertebrates experimentally removed from the influence of external stimulation." *Psychological Review* 37:51–58.

Chomsky, C. 1969. *The Acquisition of Syntax in Children from 5 to 10*. Cambridge, Mass.: MIT Press.

Chomsky, N. 1955. *The Logical Structure of Linguistic Theory*. [New York: Plenum, 1975].

————. 1957. *Syntactic Structures*. The Hague: Mouton.

————. 1964. *Current Issues in Linguistic Theory*. The Hague: Mouton.

————. 1965. *Aspects of the Theory of Syntax*. Cambridge, Mass.: MIT Press.

————. 1967. "The Formal Nature of Language." Appendix to Lenneberg (1967).

————. 1975. *Reflections on Language*. New York: Pantheon.

————. 1977. *Essays on Form and Interpretation*. New York: Elsevier North Holland.

————. 1980. *Rules and Representations*. New York: Columbia University Press.

————. 1981a. "Principles and Parameters in Syntactic Theory." In Hornstein and Lightfoot, eds.

————. 1981b. *Lectures on Government and Binding*. Dordrecht: Foris.

————, and M. Halle. 1968. *The Sound Pattern of English*. New York: Harper & Row.

Clark, H. H., and E. V. Clark. 1977. *Psychology and Language: An Introduction to Psycholinguistics*. New York: Harcourt Brace Jovanovich.

Curtiss, S. 1977. *Genie: A Psycholinguistic Study of a Modern-day "Wild Child"*. New York: Academic Press.

Dawkins, R. 1976. *The Selfish Gene*. Oxford: Oxford University Press.

Dennis, W., and M. Dennis. 1935. "The effect of restricted practice upon the reading, sitting and standing of two infants." *Journal of Genetic Psychology* 47:17–32.

Dobzhansky, T. 1970. *Genetics of the Evolutionary Process*. New York: Columbia University Press.

Dougherty, R. 1969. "An interpretive theory of pronominal reference." *Foundations of Language* 5:488–519.

Einstein, A. 1919. "Induktion und Deduktion in der Physik." *Berliner Tageblatt,* 25 December.

Emonds, J. 1976. *A Transformational Approach to English Syntax: Root, Structure-Preserving and Local Transformations*. New York: Academic Press.

Fodor, J. A. 1975. *The Language of Thought*. New York: Crowell.

————, T. G. Bever, and M. F. Garrett. 1974. *The Psychology of Language: An Introduction to Psycholinguistics and Generative Grammar*. New York: McGraw-Hill.

Frazier, L. 1979. "On Comprehending Sentences: Syntactic Parsing Strategies." Unpublished PhD dissertation, University of Massachusetts, Amherst.

Gardner, M. 1980. "Monkey business." *New York Review of Books,* 20 March.

Geschwind, N. 1980. "Some comments on the neurology of language." In Caplan, ed.

Gesell, A. 1947. "The ontogenesis of infant behavior." In L. Carmichael, ed. *Manual of Child Psychology,* New York: Wiley.

Goldman, P. S. 1972. "Developmental determinants of cortical plasticity." *Acta Neurobiologiae Experimentalis* 32:495–511.

Gould, S. J. 1978. *Ever since Darwin: Reflections in Natural History*. London: Deutsch.

Gregory, R. 1970. *The Intelligent Eye*. London: Weidenfeld and Nicolson.

Halle, M. 1978. "Knowledge unlearned and untaught: What speakers know about the sounds of their language." In Halle et al., eds.

————, J. W. Bresnan, and G. Miller, eds. 1978. *Linguistic Theory and Psychological Reality*. Cambridge, Mass.: MIT Press.

Harré, R. 1972. *The Philosophies of Science*. Oxford: Oxford University Press.

Harris, Z. 1957. "Co-occurrence and transformation in linguistic structure." *Language* 33, no. 2:283–340.

———. 1965. "Transformational theory." *Language* 41, no. 2:363–401.

Himwich, W. A. 1976. "Developmental neurobiology." In R. G. Grenell and S. Galay, eds., *Biological Foundations of Psychiatry*, New York: Raven.

Holton, G. 1973. *Thematic Origins of Scientific Thought: Kepler to Einstein*. Cambridge, Mass.: Harvard University Press.

———. 1978. *The Scientific Imagination*. Cambridge, England: Cambridge University Press.

Hornstein, N. R. 1979. "Philosophical Issues from Linguistics." Unpublished PhD dissertation, Harvard University.

———, and D. W. Lightfoot, eds. 1981. *Explanation in Linguistics*. London: Longman.

Hubel, D. H. 1978. "Vision and the brain." *Bulletin of the American Academy of Arts and Sciences* 31, no. 7:28.

———, and T. N. Wiesel. 1962. "Receptive fields, binocular interaction and functional architecture in the cat's visual cortex." *Journal of Physiology* 160:106–154.

———. 1968. "Receptive fields and functional architecture of monkey striate cortex." *Journal of Physiology* 195:215–43.

———. 1970. "The period of susceptibility to the physiological effects of unilateral eye closure in kittens." *Journal of Physiology* 206:419–34.

Inhelder, B., H. Sinclair, and M. Bovet. 1974. *Learning and the Development of Cognition*. Cambridge, Mass.: Harvard University Press.

Jackendoff, R. 1977. Review of Leonard Bernstein *The Unanswered Question* (1976). *Language* 53, no. 4:883–94.

Jacob, F. 1978. "Darwinism reconsidered." *Atlas*, January (translated from *Le Monde*, 6–8 September, 1977).

Jenkins, L. 1979. "The genetics of language." *Linguistics and Philosophy* 3:105–19.

Jerison, H. J. 1976. "Paleoneurology and the evolution of mind." *Scientific American* 234, no. 1:90–101.

Kean, M.-L. 1975. "The Theory of Markedness in Generative Grammar." Unpublished PhD dissertation, MIT.

———. 1981. "Explanation in neurolinguistics." In Hornstein and Lightfoot, eds.

Klima, E., and U. Bellugi. 1966. "Syntactic regularities in the speech of children." In J. Lyons and R. Wales, eds., *Psycholinguistic Papers,* Edinburgh: Edinburgh University Press.

Koyré, A. 1957. *From the Closed World to the Infinite Universe.* Baltimore: Johns Hopkins University Press.

Lakatos, I. 1970. "Falsification and the Methodology of Scientific Research Programmes." In I. Lakatos and A. Musgrave, eds., *Criticism and the Growth of Knowledge,* Cambridge, England: Cambridge University Press.

Lasnik, H. 1976. "Remarks on coreference." *Linguistic Analysis* 2:1–22.

——. 1981. "Learnability, restrictiveness and the evaluation metric." In Baker and McCarthy, eds.

Laudan, L. 1977. *Progress and Its Problems: Towards a Theory of Scientific Growth.* Berkeley and Los Angeles: University of California Press.

Leech, G. 1974. *Semantics.* London: Penguin.

Lenneberg, E. 1967. *Biological Foundations of Language.* New York: John Wiley.

Lightfoot, D. W. 1979. *Principles of Diachronic Syntax.* Cambridge, England: Cambridge University Press.

——. 1980. "Trace theory and explanation." In E. Moravcsik and J. Wirth, eds. *Current Approaches to Syntax.* Syntax and Semantics vol. 13. New York: Academic Press.

——. 1981a. "The history of NP movement." In Baker and McCarthy, eds.

——. 1981b. "Explaining syntactic change." In Hornstein and Lightfoot, eds.

Luria, S. 1973. *Life: The Unfinished Experiment.* New York: Scribner.

Maratsos, M. 1978. "New models in linguistics and language acquisition." In Halle et al., eds.

Marcus, M. 1980. *A Theory of Syntactic Recognition for Natural Language.* Cambridge, Mass.: MIT Press.

Marr, D., and T. Poggio. 1977. "From understanding computation to understanding neural circuitry." *Neuroscience Research Program Bulletin* 153:470–488.

Marshall, J. 1980. "On the biology of language acquisition." In Caplan, ed.

Matthei, E. 1981. "Children's interpretation of sentences containing reciprocals." In S. L. Tavakolian, ed., *Language Acquisition and Linguistic Theory,* Cambridge, Mass.: MIT Press.

Matthews, R. J. 1979. "Are the grammatical sentences of a language a recursive set?" *Synthèse* 40:209–24.

McGraw, M. B. 1947. "Maturation of behavior." In L. Carmichael, ed. *Manual of Child Psychology,* New York: Wiley.

McNeill, D. 1966. "Developmental psycholinguistics." In F. Smith and G. A. Miller, eds., *The Genesis of Language: A Psycholinguistic Approach,* Cambridge, Mass.: MIT Press.

Monod, J. 1972. *Chance and Necessity.* London: Collins.

Morgan, T. H. 1935. "The relation of genetics to physiology and medicine." *Scientific Monthly,* July.

Newport, E. C.; H. Gleitman; and L. R. Gleitman. 1977. "Mother, I'd Rather Do It Myself: Some Effects and Non-effects of Maternal Speech Style." In Snow and Ferguson, eds.

Olby, R. C. 1966. *Origins of Mendelism.* New York: Schocken Books.

Peirce, C. S. 1966. *The Collected Papers of C. S. Peirce,* edited by C. Hartshorne, P. Weiss and A. Birks. Cambridge, Mass.: Harvard University Press.

Piaget, J. 1970. *Structuralism.* New York: Basic Books.

Piattellini-Palmarini, M., ed. 1980. *Language and Learning: The Debate between Jean Piaget and Noam Chomsky.* London: Routledge and Kegan Paul.

Popper, K. 1959. *The Logic of Scientific Discovery.* London: Hutchinson.

———. 1963. *Conjectures and Refutations.* London: Routledge and Kegan Paul.

Premack, D., and G. Woodruff. 1978. "Chimpanzee problem-solving: a test for comprehension." *Science* (3 November) 202:532–35.

Putnam, H. 1961. "Some issues in the theory of grammar." In R. Jakobson, ed., *The Structure of Language and Its Mathematical Aspect,* Providence, R.I.: American Mathematical Society.

Reinhart, T. 1976. The Syntactic Domain of Anaphora. Unpublished PhD dissertation, MIT.

van Riemsdijk, H. C. 1979. "Marking conventions for syntax." Paper presented at GLOW colloquium, Pisa: Scuola Normale Superiore.

Roeper, T. 1979. "Children's Syntax." Mimeo, University of Massachusetts, Amherst.

Rothwell, N. V. 1976. *Understanding Genetics.* Baltimore: Williams and Wilkins.

Sankoff, G., and S. Laberge. 1974. "On the acquisition of native speakers by a language." In D. DeCamp and I. F. Hancock, eds., *Pidgins and Creoles: Current Trends and Prospects,* Washington, D.C.: Georgetown University Press.

Snow, C., and G. Ferguson, eds. 1977. *Talking to Children: Language Input and Acquisition.* Cambridge, England: Cambridge University Press.

Sperry, R. 1968. "Plasticity of neural maturation." *Developmental Biology Supplement* 2:306–27.

Tinbergen, N. 1969. *The Study of Instinct.* Oxford: Oxford University Press.

Wasow, T. 1975. "Anaphoric pronouns and bound variables." *Language* 51, no. 2:368–83.

———. 1977. "Transformations and the lexicon." In P. W. Culicover, T. Wasow, and A. Akmajian, eds. *Formal Syntax.* New York: Academic Press.

Weinberg, S. 1976. "The forces of nature." *Bulletin of the American Academy of Arts and Sciences* 29, no. 4:28–9.

Wexler, K., and P. W. Culicover. 1980. *Formal Principles of Language Acquisition.* Cambridge, Mass.: MIT Press.

White, L. 1981. "The responsibility of grammatical theory to acquisitional data." In Hornstein and Lightfoot, eds.

Index

Abstraction, 5, 29, 49n, 89, 91, 93–95, 138, 171, 185, 192
Abstract structures, 60, 109, 139
Acquisition
 instantaneous, 173
 logical problem of, 172
 real time, 172–184, 201n
 second language, 178
Agrammatism, 185–189
Akmajian, A., 124, 146, 190, 201
Ambiguity, 17, 34, 44–45, 57, 60, 69, 115, 194–195
Anaphors, 105–115, 131, 174
Anderson, S., 146
Animal communication, 9, 13, 166
Aphasia, 184–192
Aronoff, M., 124, 146
Aspiration, 130, 134, 136
Autonomy thesis, 102–104, 127n

Baker, C. L., 51, 83
Barrett, P. H., 14n
Bar theory, 59–66
Basque, 154
Bateson, W., 94
Bayles, K., 189–190
Bellugi, U., 179, 183
Bentley, D., 94
Berlin, B., 123
Bernstein, L., 203
Berwick, R., 197–198, 200–201
Bever, T. G., 58–59, 166, 190
Bird song, 9, 13
Blakemore, C., 47
Bracken, H. M., 210
Bradley, D. C., 189, 195, 198
Brain
 bats, 10
 damage, 171, 184–192
 electric fish, 10

functioning, 28, 93, 184–192
localization, 10, 177, 184–192
maturation, 175–178
size, 9–10, 167–168, 170n
structure, 12–13
Brannigan, A., 86
Broca's aphasia, 185–192
Brown, R., 19

Caramazza, A., 188–189
Carey, S., 121, 123, 175–177
Carmichael, L., 174–175
Case assignment, 65, 81, 128n
Causative verbs, 79–81, 121
Center embedding, 43, 92, 151–152
Changeux, J.-P., 47
Children's language, 171–184
Chimpanzees, 9, 166
Chomsky, C., 128n
Chomsky, N., 22–23, 31, 33, 35, 38–39, 48, 50, 65, 83, 92–93, 111, 128–129, 145n, 146, 157, 199–201, 209, 211–212
Click experiments, 58–59
Clitics, 188–189, 195–196, 198
Coindexing, 105–115
Color terms, 122–123
Communicative function, 31–32
Complementizer (COMP), 73–75, 107, 113
Componential analysis, 120–122
Conceptual knowledge, 42–46, 53–54, 124–127
Constituent-command, 127–128n
Control, 109, 128
Corpus callosum, 191
Correction of children's speech, 19, 75
Creativity, 17, 127, 208–209
Creole languages, 169–170n
Crick, F., 4, 8
Culicover, P., 20, 35, 100n